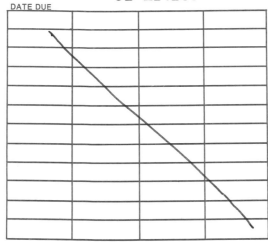

ST ANTONY'S COLLEGE, OXFORD

PUBLICATIONS

NO. 3

GERMAN DEMOCRACY AND THE TRIUMPH OF HITLER

St Antony's College concentrates on research in modern history and social studies, with centres or groups specializing in Europe, Russia, Africa, the Middle East, the Far East and Latin America. This new series is an expansion of *St Antony's Papers*, twenty-two volumes of which have appeared since 1956. It is designed to present a selection of the work produced under the auspices of the College, and it will include full-length books and monographs as well as collections of shorter pieces.

GERMAN DEMOCRACY AND THE TRIUMPH OF HITLER

ESSAYS IN RECENT GERMAN HISTORY

EDITED BY

ANTHONY NICHOLLS
St. Antony's College, Oxford

AND

ERICH MATTHIAS
Mannheim University

LONDON

GEORGE ALLEN AND UNWIN LTD

RUSKIN HOUSE   MUSEUM STREET

FIRST PUBLISHED IN 1971

© *George Allen & Unwin Ltd, 1971*

ISBN 0 04 943016 5

PRINTED IN GREAT BRITAIN
in 12 on 13 pt Fournier type
BY T. & A. CONSTABLE
EDINBURGH

CONTENTS

INTRODUCTION

The editors of this volume would like to point out that it is in no way intended as a general history of Germany between the wars. The essays it contains are designed to provoke discussion and draw the reader's attention to some aspects of recent German history on which light has been thrown by scholarly research. The essays can conveniently be divided into three groups. The first group of five essays is concerned with the establishment of the Weimar Republic, the social and political problems which faced it and the manner in which Germany's political leadership confronted these problems. The three essays in the second group are devoted to the origin and development of National Socialism during the Republican era and the political ideas which motivated its leaders. The last three essays are chiefly concerned with the period of Nazi dictatorship itself. They throw light on the impact of National Socialism on German society and investigate some of the forces inside and outside Germany which maintained some form of opposition to Hitler.

Although in many of the essays the authors have made reference to important archival materials, the purpose of this volume is not so much to provide definite answers to specific questions as to put forward arguments and draw some general conclusions. For this reason the presentation of the essays varies according to the nature of the subject under discussion. Where appropriate, and especially if the documentary basis of the essay is likely to be unfamiliar to the reader, a complete set of references is attached to the text. In other essays numerous footnotes would be unhelpful and even burdensome, and in these cases references have been reduced to a minimum. The editors hope that the essays have been presented in such a way as to make them of value to all who are interested in the problems of recent German history, whether they can be students of the period or not.

Nearly all the essays printed in this volume were originally presented as seminar papers at St Antony's College, Oxford, or the University of Mannheim. They bear witness to the fruitful co-operation which has developed between the two institutions.

St Antony's College, aided by generous financial help from the Volkswagen Foundation of West Germany, has been able to invite university teachers and students from the Federal Republic to lecture and study in Oxford, and seminars on problems of recent German history are regularly held there.

Among the distinguished German guests whom the College has been privileged to welcome to Oxford was Professor Erich Matthias of the University of Mannheim. In the summer of 1967 Professor Matthias and Anthony Nicholls organized a colloquium on the history of the Weimar Republic in which a number of scholars from the University of Mannheim also participated. Some of the papers delivered to this group form the core of the present volume. The editors would like to thank all those – from Oxford, Mannheim and elsewhere – who took part in the discussions; they greatly assisted in the final formulation of the essays. Although it would not be practicable to mention all the participants, we should particularly like to thank Dr A. J. Ryder of Lampeter College and Mr P. C. Hauswedell of Cornell University. An especial word of thanks is also due to Dr V. R. Berghahn, of East Anglia and Mannheim universities, for his patient work in translating several of the German contributions.

Finally, the editors would like to express their gratitude to the Volkswagen Foundation of West Germany, without whose financial assistance this example of Anglo-German collaboration would not have been possible.

ABBREVIATIONS USED IN THE TEXT

ADGB *Allgemeiner Deutscher Gewerkschaftsbund* = General Federation of German Trade Unions.

AFL American Federation of Labour.

BDM *Bund Deutscher Mädel* = League of German Women (Nazi women's organization).

BVP *Bayerische Volkspartei* = Bavarian People's Party.

DDP *Deutsche Demokratische Partei* = German Democratic Party.

DNVP *Deutschnationale Volkspartei* = German National People's Party.

DSP *Deutsche Sozialistische Partei* = German Socialist Party.

DVP *Deutsche Volkspartei* = German People's Party.

GLD German Labour Delegation.

ISK *Internationaler Sozialistischer Kampfbund* = Militant Socialist International.

KPD *Kommunistische Partei Deutschlands* = German Communist Party.

NSDAP *Nationalsozialistische Deutsche Arbeiterpartei* = National Socialist German Workers' Party (Nazis).

NS before other titles denotes a Nazi organization.

OSS Office of Strategic Services.

SA Storm troopers or brownshirts.

SAP *Sozialistische Arbeiterpartei* = Socialist Workers' Party.

SDF Social Democratic Federation.

Sopade Social Democratic Executive Committee.

SPD *Sozialdemokratische Partei Deutschlands* = German Social Democratic Party.

USPD *Unabhängige Sozialdemokratische Partei Deutschlands* = Independent German Social Democratic Party.

CHAPTER 1

THE INFLUENCE OF THE VERSAILLES TREATY ON THE INTERNAL DEVELOPMENT OF THE WEIMAR REPUBLIC

ERICH MATTHIAS

About twelve years ago, a history of the foreign relations of Weimar Germany was published by Ludwig Zimmermann,[1] in which he came to the conclusion that a timely revision of the Versailles Treaty would probably have saved the German Republic from ruin and thus preserved peace.

This scholarly judgment by a contemporary historian who was trying hard to consider all the evidence seems to confirm the popular explanation which is also offered by the survivors of the Weimar Republic when they try to account for the rise of Hitler and for Germany's march into the catastrophe of the Second World War. One good example of this view was presented by Otto Braun, for many years Prussian Minister-President and perhaps the foremost democratic statesman of his time. He wrote in his memoirs, published in exile and entitled *From Weimar to Hitler*,[2] that it would have been better for the world and cheaper for Germany's creditors if they had cancelled the reparations payments while there was still time. According to Braun, an Allied declaration to this effect would 'have preserved

---

[1] Ludwig Zimmermann, *Deutsche Aussenpolitik in der Ära der Weimarer Republik* (Göttingen, 1958), p. 474

[2] Otto Braun, *Von Weimar zu Hitler*, second ed. (New York, 1940), p. 5

the pacifist-democratic regime of Weimar and would have saved the world from the dynamic expansionism of a dictatorship'.

It was at Versailles – so he continued – that 'the axe was put to the very roots of the Republic and that the poisonous seeds of a new German nationalism were sown'. If someone were to ask him why Hitler's dictatorship overwhelmed Germany, all he could answer would be: 'Versailles and Moscow'.

This formula owes its persuasiveness to its simplicity. It underlines the unstable foreign political position of the Weimar Republic between the victorious Western Allies on the one hand and revolutionary Russia on the other. And it explains the course of events on the domestic scene, which was characterized by a continuous narrowing of the democratic centre of the party system as well as by the radicalization and polarization of political forces on the Right and on the Left. This formula, moreover, has the virtue of immediately exonerating all the political parties which were responsible for the establishment of the Republic and which became its principal supporters. It explains the collapse of the Weimar constitution by referring exclusively to external factors which interfered with political life inside the country.

Unfortunately, however, the weakening of the democratic wing of the working-class movement and the lack of initiative displayed by it cannot be blamed – or at least certainly not exclusively – on its left-wing competitors and on the dependence of the Communists on orders from Moscow. Nor is it possible to explain the revival of nationalism during the early post-war years and the later rise of National Socialism solely in terms of the attitude of the Western Allies. The formula 'Versailles and Moscow' must be considered too crude, even if one takes into account the interdependence of radicalization on the Right and on the Left in Germany, during the period 1919-33.

Generally speaking, any attempt to give a monocausal interpretation of the fate of the Republic is bound to fail when put to any serious test. And indeed all such attempts, even those which are presented in a scholarly guise, turn out to have a political intention and a political tendency, even if sometimes a subconscious one.

If we are to understand what happened in Germany we must start from the premise that the erosion and the ultimate doom of the Republic were due to the interaction of a variety of factors. It is certainly wrong to shift the main responsibility for the events of the 1920s and 1930s from Germany to the international scene.

According to a view which has become more widespread in recent writings on the Weimar Republic, it was neither the attitude of the Western Allies and the economic consequences of the defeat nor the sudden sweep of the Great Depression which were of decisive importance to the disintegration of democracy in Germany. No doubt these factors had considerable material and psychological repercussions. But the actual reason why the German Republic, unlike other European Nations and the United States, was unable to cope with the difficulties of the slump and ultimately collapsed under their burden is to be found in the peculiar internal structure of Germany itself.

When seeking explanations for Republican failure we must direct our attention above all to the domestic situation in the Republic. This means that we must consider the party system, its representatives in the parliaments and governments, on the one hand; and on the other, the forces wielding political influence – e.g. interest and pressure groups, such as the unions, the bureaucracy, or the churches.

What is important in this context is that our analysis should not be confined exclusively to the final years of the Republic. Rather we shall have to bring out the significance of the above-mentioned factors for the *permanent* structural crisis of the German state. For the Republic did not only have to bear the consequences of the defeat but also – and quite independently of this – it had to shoulder a burdensome heritage. In fact, it never succeeded in assimilating its own military and bureaucratic foundations; nor could it ever remove the serious conflicts and tensions between its social and its political structure – tensions which had already burdened Imperial Germany to the point where they had become intolerable.

However, it is naturally impossible to deal in isolation with the political attitudes prevalent in the Weimar Republic – attitudes which were themselves the expression of a wide-ranging social and economic continuity between pre- and post-revolutionary Germany. Such attitudes have to be considered alongside, and not in isolation from, the foreign pressures put on Germany as the result of her defeat.

It is not possible here to present a comprehensive evaluation of the Versailles Treaty. Suffice it to say, therefore, that today German historiography is oriented towards a more sober and less prejudiced assessment than was the case during the inter-war period, when national feeling ran high. Certainly, the Treaty of Versailles did not fulfil the highest aim which it proclaimed, namely to effect 'a just settlement of the Great War', and, to create a basis 'on which the nations of Europe can live together in peace and equality'. None the less, a balanced judgment of the Treaty must also take into account the unprecedented difficulties inherent in the task of creating a truly world-wide peace settlement.

This task was bound to exceed the capabilities of the victors even if they had made fewer mistakes and had fallen victim to fewer illusions than in fact they actually did. It should be added that the issue at stake was not just the liquidation of the war but also the problem which loomed over the entire negotiations, namely the containment of the world revolution which seemed to have begun in Russia.

Under these circumstances it is also not surprising that the discussion about the historical relevance of the Peace Treaty for Germany has not yet come near to producing a definite answer. Nevertheless, there can be little doubt that the conditions imposed at Versailles were an extremely heavy burden on the Republic.

However, if we want to assess the actual weight of this burden, we must differentiate carefully between the material consequences of the Treaty and its psychological repercussions. Nobody would raise serious objections today to the argument that the psychological burdens were more decisive for the fate of the Republic than the material ones. The territorial losses were sizeable, and the economic and financial clauses of the Treaty severe enough to unite everybody, irrespective of party affiliation, against

Versailles, although the Reich, contrary to what the Germans thought, had by no means lost its viability. German public opinion remained united on this point throughout the Weimar period, and all parties were unanimous in their belief that a basic revision of the Treaty of Versailles was a necessary pre-condition for the normalization of relations with Germany's neighbours.

Bearing this in mind, it is all the more remarkable that the polemics which emerged from controversy over the Treaty were directed not so much against external foes – i.e. against the Western Allies – as they were turned against political opponents at home. This internal dispute – which never subsided as long as the Republic existed – cannot be simply explained in terms of differences of opinion over the so-called policy of 'fulfilment' which, if one accepts the views put forward by its protagonists, was nothing but the only realistic and successful means of revising the Treaty.

The heated debate over this policy seems all the more fantastic because, despite all the raging against the *Schmachparagaph* and the 'war guilt lie', none of the parliamentary opponents of an acceptance of the Peace Treaty was prepared to assume responsibility for a rejection of the Treaty during the decisive hours in June 1919. Yet when it came to a vote on foreign affairs in the *Reichstag* these elements never felt any inhibitions about demonstrating their 'patriotic orientation'. Indeed, they made extensive use of it, always disregarding the fact that they had once been forced to certify formally the national reliability of those who had put their signature to the Treaty, and to acknowledge their patriotic motives.

The campaign of the German National People's Party (DNVP or Nationalists), against the Dawes Plan in 1924 was waged along very similar lines. For in spite of all its demagogy, the DNVP was not prepared to risk the failure of this particular agreement. The attitude of the forty-eight Nationalist deputies during the third reading of the *Reichsbahn* laws is a case in point, as without their affirmative vote the Dawes Plan would have collapsed.

Five years later, in 1929, Hitler and Hugenberg – who, on

this occasion, presented themselves as allies for the first time – launched their campaign against the Young Plan, and with it they opened the final struggle of the so-called National Opposition against the Republic. Not even the early evacuation of the Rhineland, which was connected with this renewed revision of the reparations question, prevented them from making uninhibited use of anti-Young slogans in the 1930 elections. The National Socialists, especially, demonstrated untiring zeal in coining new catchwords. They spoke of the 'Young Chancellor', the 'Young government', 'Young taxes', 'Young victims', 'Young slavery', 'Young crisis', 'Young misery', and so forth.

But it was not only the DNVP which imitated them. The Communists also made ample use of this vote-catching issue, although the Nazis succeeded in outdoing both parties when exploiting it as a central theme. Impressed by this agitation, Chancellor Brüning pointed out to the Reich Cabinet that the National Socialists had focussed their attention above all on foreign policy. And yet, however indisputable this statement may be, it merely scratched the surface of the problem.

For in fact, at this particular juncture the leaders of the Hitler movement were not really concerned with foreign policy at all. Rather they were looking for an opportunity of defaming the internal enemy, and in the Young Plan they saw an ideal issue for killing two birds – the ruling parties and the oppositional Social Democrats – with one stone. An agitation of this kind, for obvious reasons, could comfortably disregard the international power constellation. The immediate chances of a forceful policy of revision were of no interest to them. What mattered at this point was to redirect nationalist resentments and foreign political arguments towards the domestic scene, i.e. against the Republic.

In doing this, the Nazis employed the same method of persuasion which all factions of the so-called 'National Opposition' had been using ever since 1919. What becomes transparent in this method is an attitude which has been called introverted nationalism. Its basic feature can be reduced to a relatively simple pattern. According to this sort of nationalist argument, the Treaty of Versailles and its consequences are not to be seen as the direct result of the defeat of 1918. Instead, the reality of this defeat as such is denied altogether and is eliminated through a process of psychological suppression. The vehicle for this argument, which is indispensable, is the legend of the 'stab-in-the-back' which offers 'proof' that the defeat of 1918 was in fact no defeat at all; that the army, undefeated on the battlefield, collapsed owing to treachery at home.

In this fashion, the causal connection between the defeat and the Peace Treaty became interrupted. The Revolution of 1918 appeared not as the consequence but rather as the cause of the defeat, so that nationalist energies could now be concentrated against the representatives of the Republic who had inherited the fruits of this revolution. They were portrayed as the accomplices of the Allies and as the beneficiaries of the defeat for which they were said to be responsible – in exactly the same way as they were supposedly responsible for the harsh terms of the Peace Treaty.

A pamphlet by Oswald Spengler, entitled *The Reconstruction of the Reich*, which appeared in 1924, at the time of the Dawes Plan debates, is a particularly illustrative example of this sort of argument.[1]

'Victory', says Spengler at the beginning, 'was denied to us in the greatest of all wars. Thanks to our energy, our industry and our organizational talent we had had an economic prosperity which few nations had seen or even had the potential to achieve. We fought and suffered for four years as probably no nation has suffered before. But the defeat revealed to us a baseness which is without precedent in History.'

For Spengler, therefore, the decisive front of the First World War did not lie between Germany and her opponents, but ran straight through the nation itself. And on the basis of this statement he comes to the conclusion that what is important is 'finally to draw a line between the German people and the perpetrators and beneficiaries of the collapse'. The way in which Spengler phrases this is not without interest. For, in his view, the German people have nothing in common with the 'baseness'

[1] Oswald Spengler, *Neubau des deutschen Reiches* (Munich, 1924)

(*Erbärmlichkeit*) of the internal enemy. It is the latter who lacks patriotism in the sense of the 'National Opposition', and is therefore not to be counted as belonging to the nation.

Where, then, are these sinister elements, the 'perpetrators and beneficiaries of the collapse', who do not deserve to be called German, to be found? Where in fact should this dividing line be drawn? Spengler's answer is plain and simple: 'Weimar'. In the Weimar Republic, so he believes, 'a dictatorship of the party bosses was erected in smiling comfort over the corpses of two million heroes who died in vain, over a nation which withered away in misery and torture of the soul'. To Spengler this was the dictatorship of that same 'most narrow-minded and filthiest of all interest groups' which since the Peace Resolution of 1917 'had undermined our position and committed every possible kind of treason'.

In October 1918, then, these 'heroes' of 1917 – who, in Spengler's eyes, acted in complete agreement with 'Northcliffe, Trotsky, and even Clemenceau' – had finally reached their goal. But their calculations threatened to fail. When the November Revolution broke out – so Spengler continues – they scuttled into hiding. Yet, when they saw 'the Spartacists dividing the prey among themselves', they emerged with a 'sudden zeal'. And it was 'the fear of losing their share of the prey' which induced them, 'sitting on princely velvet chairs and in the pubs of Weimar, to sell off the German Republic', a republic which, as Spengler writes in disgust, is a 'limited company' but not a 'constitutional state' (*eine Firma, aber keine Staatsform*).

In another passage of his pamphlet, Spengler speaks of the 'exploitation of Germany by the trade union of her liberators who are in their own pay'. The terms 'limited company' and 'trade union' thus are synonyms, and epitomize an unheroic, selfish attitude which, for Spengler, is typical of the representatives of the bourgeois democrats as well as of the democratic working-class movement. He visualizes 'the open mouths and avaricious eyes of thousands of party and trade union functionaries, of party journalists, their cousins, and business associates', all of whom demand their share.

This 'glorious activity' inside Germany preconditioned, as Spengler tells us, some sort of an arrangement with the Western Allies which was beneficial to both parties. It was for this reason that the Republicans had invented the policy of fulfilment (*Erfüllungspolitik*) which was being used 'to throw to the enemy one piece of Germany after another'.

The supporters of *Erfüllungspolitik*, Spengler went on, did not even shy away 'from turning Germany into a reparations colony', a 'European India', merely in order to receive recognition as the legitimate executive organs of the Allies and thereby gain a power position which was 'independent of any domestic crisis'.

And this is what Spengler had in mind when he referred to the Dawes Plan as 'the latest act of a party clique whose right wing now completes what its left wing began at Versailles; namely to sell off the entire nation into slavery after disarming it psychologically through five years of bad government, and after deceiving it about its real predicament through noisy party politics'.

The brand of nationalism which we have before us here does not preach a crusade against France, which had just dealt another blow to Germany by occupying the Ruhr; the crusade which Spengler advocates is directed against the party machinations, *Parteiklüngel*, which he believes to be the root of all evil.

The above passages from Spengler's pamphlet can be fitted without the slightest difficulty into the primitive world of ideas of the National Socialists, although Spengler, who considered himself a 'Prussian' socialist, was, to be sure, not a supporter of Hitler. In fact, he always kept aloof from Hitler's movement and rejected its racial anti-semitism with uncompromising rigidity. Statesmanship, Spengler said, 'does not depend on the length of the skull but rather on what is in it'.

Nevertheless, for our purposes the points on which Spengler differed from the Nazis are not important. It is also not necessary to discuss his position in detail or to subject it to a critical historical analysis. The reason why he has been quoted extensively is that the basic outlines of his train of thought reappear in the arguments of the so-called 'National Opposition', whether it was committed to a particular party or not and no matter what view its adherents took of Hitler.

Hitler himself, however, did succeed in achieving the greatest refinement in this method of reasoning. Even on the day of the French occupation of the Ruhr in January 1923 – at a moment, that is, when the German nation was united as it had never been since August 1914–he declared that the cry should be 'down with the traitors to the Fatherland' rather than 'down with France'.

Under the conditions of 1923, when all political forces, including the Communists, began to unite in the 'passive resistance' movement, Hitler's slogan was bound to be unsuccessful. But it is just this bad timing that shows how unwaveringly he stuck to his introverted nationalism and its rationalizations, which, with the failure of passive resistance and the mounting domestic crisis, quickly regained their attractiveness. There was, it is true, another lull after 1924, during the period of stabilization. But by the time of the Great Depression this sort of agitation had again become very popular.

By explaining all domestic difficulties with reference to the external weakness of the Reich, and by putting the blame for this on the alleged traitors and internal enemies – i.e. all forces which resisted the aspirations of the Nazis – Hitler's propaganda deliberately nourished the illusion that a victory of his party at home was all that was needed to wipe out the defeat of 1918, to tear up the Treaty of Versailles, and to re-establish Germany's former position in the world.

Seen from the point of view of this somewhat illogical logic which identified domestic successes with victories abroad, it followed that the Nazi victory celebrations in 1933 looked like victory by the German army in the Great War won, somewhat belatedly, by the triumph of Hitler's brown-shirted battalions. This was so despite the fact that it was obviously rather early to speak of successes in Hitler's foreign policy. Under the pressure of the international reaction to the 'National Revolution', the new government was forced to profess its peaceful intentions, and Hitler's *Reichstag* speech of May 17, 1933 made it appear that he wanted to continue the much-denigrated foreign policy of the

Weimar Republic. Yet, if there was any continuity, it was at best a continuity of the façade. No matter how emphatically Hitler stressed his love of peace, the justified suspicion with which the world viewed his seizure of power drove Germany into isolation. It was understandable that the former representatives of the Weimar Republic were prone to juxtapose this result of Nazi foreign policy with their own successes before 1933. Thus Friedrich Stampfer, the former editor of *Der Vorwärts*, in his history of the Weimar period rejected as a fabrication of Nazi propaganda the allegation that Hitler had saved the honour of Germany.[1]

When the NSDAP took over in 1933, so Stampfer summarized the foreign policy of the Weimar Republic, 'Germany was again a great power and had a seat in the League of Nations. Her status of equality was recognized, basically also in the military field. Reparations had been cancelled. The Rhineland had been evacuated – five years earlier than provided by the Treaty.'

We do not want to deny the essential truth of these statements. And yet the leaders of the Republic succumbed to a dangerous illusion when hoping that the successes of the policy of revision would act as a counter-force to the attacks of the nationalists on the Republic and would result in a consolidation of the domestic situation. Brüning, especially, much more so than Stresemann, abandoned himself to this particular hope. In fact, as a study by Wolfgang Helbig[2] has shown, it dominated his thinking.

Brüning's policy of 'bringing order into public finances at any cost' cannot be understood and becomes increasingly incomprehensible as we follow the course of the economic crisis, unless we give full weight to his attitude towards reparations policy. Economists who have criticized him have frequently overlooked

[1] Friedrich Stampfer, *Die vierzehn Jahre der ersten deutschen Republik* (Prague, 1936), p. 613
[2] Wolfgang Helbig, *Die Reparationen in der Ära Brüning* (Berlin, 1962). A different position has recently been taken by Hennig Köhler in his article 'Arbeitsbeschaffung, Siedlung und Reparationen in der Schlussphase der Regierung Brüning' in *Vierteljahrshefte für Zeitgeschichte*, 17 (1969), p. 27ff

the fact that he did not approach his fiscal and economic policies exclusively from an economic point of view. Brüning himself spoke explicitly of 'a deflationary policy which had been forced upon us and which we did not want'.

His 1930-2 austerity programme was to be the basis of the most loyal fulfilment of the Young Plan and at the same time of a policy of revision which, in his view, offered the only chance of success. More precisely, his fiscal and economic measures were, as the official organ of Brüning's Centre Party wrote in 1932, not an end in themselves, but subordinate to the great foreign political goal of freeing Germany from the payment of reparations and of re-establishing her position in the world.

Brüning deliberately accepted the domestic consequences of this policy, which contributed heavily to a sharpening of the economic crisis inside Germany and to the growth of unemployment. For in the final analysis he believed that this was the most effective way of drawing the world's attention to Germany's plight and of convincing the Allies that it was imperative to revise the Peace Treaty.

In his tenacious fight against reparations – in which he used as his sharpest weapon complete compliance with the terms of international agreements – Brüning constantly appealed to the German nation to bear with him regardless of all sacrifices until his foreign goals had been reached – in this he acted very much like Bethmann-Hollweg, whose policy resembles that of Brüning in more than one respect.

With the proclamation of the Hoover Moratorium, Brüning's foreign policy was able to win an initial success. Its fruits, however, were enjoyed after his fall by the authoritarian governments of Papen and Schleicher as the result of the Lausanne Conference at which reparations were cancelled, and the Geneva Disarmament Conference in the autumn of 1932 which approved in principle Germany's claim for military equality. It must be asked whether the price paid for these achievements may not have been too high. Perhaps the best way of characterizing them is to say that the operation was carried out successfully, but that meanwhile the patient had died under the hands of the surgeon.

This verdict cannot be mitigated by the argument that success merely came too late, or by pointing out that Brüning fell from power just before reaching his goal and that the task was taken over by less scrupulous men. If it was Brüning's rigorous financial and economic policies which contributed heavily to the rise of Nazism – as was demonstrated in the 1932 elections – it is obviously difficult to put most of the blame for this on the regulations in the Young Plan.

The truth is that the Chancellor and the leadership of the German army dangerously underestimated Hitler. On the one hand, Brüning thought the existence of an impatient and radical 'National Opposition' to be useful in advancing his foreign policy objectives, and on the other, he rashly assumed that the satisfaction of national aspirations would be the best weapon against the rising wave of nationalism. In short, Brüning completely failed to see that it was not patriotic indignation that made the masses turn to Hitler. Arthur Rosenberg is quite right in pointing out that, as late as 1929, the 'National Opposition' was unable to rally the masses in a protest movement against the Young Plan and that, conversely, the evacuation of the Rhineland in the summer of 1930 did not cause a wave of enthusiasm.[1]

'What mobilized the masses ever since 1930, young and old, shopkeepers as well as the educated people', says Rosenberg, 'was economic misery; starvation and unemployment.' Brüning's policy therefore operated on the nationalist symptoms of the disease. But it left the real cause of the crisis – which became more dangerous from day to day – without treatment.

This is also evidenced by the fact that – in spite of the rigidity of his crisis-mongering austerity programme – he tried to ease internal tensions from time to time by making concessions to the nationalists, such as the *Tributaufruf* of June 6, 1931, or the idea of an Austro-German customs union. Clearly such concessions were not likely to further his foreign political aims.

In fact the dangerous rise of Hitler's movement in these years was due primarily to the success with which it combined social

[1] Arthur Rosenberg, *Geschichte der deutschen Republik* (Karlsbad, 1935), p. 221

energies originating from extremely divergent sources; it succeeded in identifying personal misery with the state of the nation and in pinpointing the same cause for both.

Taking everything together, it was a very complicated sociopsychological process which was characterized by the manipulation of these divergent energies with the aid of a nationalistic ideology on the one hand, and by the introversion of 'secondary nationalism', as it might be called, on the other.

Certainly the overwhelming majority of those who followed the lure of National Socialism did not want another war, although there was no doubt in Hitler's mind that victory at home was to be used to create a platform for aggression abroad. What was of decisive importance for the development of this process was that at that moment structural changes in the social stratification of the population which had been caused by the inflation of the early 1920s suddenly took their effect. This inflation, resulting to a large extent from the way in which Germany had financed her war effort, had naturally not been deliberately brought about by German industrialists. Nevertheless a good number of them had viewed it as a blessing in disguise and made uninhibited use of the opportunities it presented.

The result of this irresponsible attitude of industry was the expropriation of many middle-class elements. And the structural weakening and proletarianization of these elements, which by tradition had been the supporters of the state, destroyed the basis of the bourgeois parties of the centre and led ultimately to a situation in which this reservoir of voters drained off to the NSDAP.

The consequences of the inflation created the social conditions which led to the radicalization of the middle classes by Hitler. By stating that neither in its origin nor in its course was this inflation the inevitable result of the Treaty of Versailles, we have again reached the starting-point of this essay – the question how far the victors of the First World War can be made responsible for the collapse of the Weimar Republic.

It is possible to reproach the Allies for having pursued a policy which was in many respects unwise, and of having neglected, against their own interest, to support the democratic German Republic effectively. But they can surely not be made responsible for developments inside Germany.

The reasons why the Weimar Republic showed so little coherence and ultimately collapsed are too complex to be expounded in a short essay. It would be quite justified, for example, to ask whether the Constitution of October 1918, which was introduced to save the monarchy but was never given a chance of proving its worth, would have offered a better vehicle for an effective democratization of the country than the Constitution of 1919. Yet quite apart from the fact that such a constitutional monarchy would have been forced to bear the same mark of defeat as the Weimar Republic, the November Revolution did not, of course, simply cut down the possibilities open to constitutional politicians; it also created new ones. It has been quite rightly observed that at first the Republic did not suffer from a lack of support by the masses. 'If anything Klemens von Klemperer pointed out[1], 'it was threatened by the variety of its support.' And indeed, wide circles of the bourgeoisie – among them many who were later to be prominent representatives of the 'National Opposition' and the so-called Conservative Revolution – at first accepted the November Revolution and expected it to bring some radical innovations. They even took it for granted that some sort of socialist society would be established.

If the Revolution failed to create a firm basis of legitimacy, the reason for this is not simply to be found in the difficult foreign political situation. It must be sought also in the fact that the early governments of the Republic, starting from the Cabinet of People's Deputies, showed a striking lack of leadership. It is difficult to estimate just how good the chances of an effective national integration under a new political and social order would have been. But there is little doubt that the governments of the transitional period failed to make use of the potential in their hands. Among other things, they neglected to prepare the nation adequately for the coming peace, whose harshness ought

[1] Klemens von Klemperer, *Germany's New Conservatism, Its History and Dilemma in the Twentieth Century* (Princeton 1957), p. 72

not to have been so surprising to any realistic observer of the situation.

This failure, especially, made it difficult to state clearly and squarely from the very beginning that only a republic supported by democratic forces would be in a position to conduct a policy which met the difficult situation and which was in line with the interests of the nation. In the absence of such clear statements it became possible for the enemies of the Republic to mobilize the forces of nationalism for their own purposes.

Thus the Republic inherited perhaps the strongest internal burden of the Bismarckian Reich, namely the division of the nation into a so-called patriotic faction and another which was denied this attribute. The fanaticism of the domestic political struggle up to 1923 and after 1929 can to some extent be explained in this way.

It is the intention of this paper to show that the consequences of the Treaty of Versailles should be neither underestimated nor overestimated, and that in any event they did not seal the fate of democracy in Germany. On the other hand, it is also impossible to put the blame for the collapse of the Republic primarily on the shoulders of its irreconcilable internal opponents, i.e. the Nazis and the rest of the 'National Opposition' and of the Communists.

Even if their share of responsibility is considerable, the more important question which remains is how far the representatives of the Republic themselves – and last but not least the outspokenly democratic forces – must bear some of the responsibility. The most important lesson which the Weimar Republic can teach us is the realization that a democracy cannot evade responsibility for its own fate.

CHAPTER 2

GERMAN LIBERALISM AND THE FOUNDATION OF THE WEIMAR REPUBLIC: A MISSED OPPORTUNITY?

LOTHAR ALBERTIN

On November 7, 1918 the Independent Social Democrats, ignoring a police ban, celebrated the anniversary of the Russian Revolution with a big rally in Berlin. Did this mean that the incipient German Revolution would be communist in character? Certainly, the nightmare of Bolshevism appeared everywhere. As early as November 8th, the influential left-wing liberal *Frankfurter Zeitung* had implored the proletariat to remember that the concept of the working class was, according to Lassalle, the concept of mankind in its entirety and not that of one class, and the 'future of freedom' would also be desired by the best representatives of the bourgeoisie.[1] The middle classes, however, seemed paralysed. Though they had long before lost their political and social cohesion, they found, in this ephemeral though historically intense moment, common ground in the fear that they might be pushed aside politically, deprived of their material possessions and intellectual pre-eminence.

It was, therefore, a great surprise when the supposed revolution turned out to be something quite unexpected and unprecedented in history. For in its essence this revolution was non-violent and disciplined. The revolutionary movement showed itself a model of self-control. As one of the National Liberal papers admitted as

[1] *Frankfurter Zeitung*, November 8, 1918, A

early as November 10th: 'It would be a mistake to call the government of workers' and soldiers' councils Bolshevist. Private property has not been touched, violence has been avoided as far as possible and honest efforts have been made to maintain order and discipline.'[1] The left-wing liberal Mayor of Kassel, Erich Koch, who later became Reich Minister of the Interior, declared on November 12th in the Kassel City Council: 'There is probably no other people which would start a revolution one afternoon and resume work the following morning.'[2]

With its initial fears turning out to be unfounded, the temporary unity of the bourgeoisie began to disintegrate. Koch was among those who actively rejected the traumatic apprehension that liberalism might be overtaken by historical developments before it had had a chance to complete its own emancipation within the Reich. The shock over their exclusion from politics produced among the National Liberals and other recently politicized groups of the bourgeoisie a new urge to reflect on their situation and revive their own political parties. The DDP (German Democratic Party) and the DVP (German People's Party) embodied two versions of the same objective, i.e. that German liberals should make their own historically necessary contribution to the reconstruction of Germany and to its return to an active foreign policy. Both parties made early attempts in this direction: the DDP entered the so-called Weimar Coalition in January 1919 and the two parties together entered the bourgeois minority cabinet in 1920.[3] The first of these initiatives was potentially the most important political step taken by post-war German liberals.

How did the first stirrings of the revival of liberalism manifest themselves? As Friedrich Naumann wrote on November 14th: 'There is an incredibly large number of people in Germany

[1] *Tägliche Rundschau*, November 10, 1918

[2] *Nachlass Koch*, No. 15, Bundesarchiv, Koblenz

[3] A comparative structural analysis of both parties will be published by the author of this article in 1971. By the same author: 'Die Verantwortung der liberalen Parteien für das Scheitern der Grossen Koalition im Herbst 1921. Ökonomische und ideologische Einflüsse auf die Funktionsfähigkeit der parteienstaatlichen Demokratie', *Historische Zeitschrift*, Heft 205/3, 1967, pp. 556-627

discussing the future of the nation.'[1] And Naumann's old political associate, the suffragette Gertrud Bäumer, observed that decline and revival went side by side.[2] At a mass rally of the two traditional liberal parties, the National Liberals and the Progressives, Falk, a National Liberal Town Councillor from Cologne, coined the slogan: 'The old system has collapsed, the Emperor has left the country; new programmes, new ways, new men are needed.'[3]

These new men emerged spontaneously inside and outside their old parties. Their aims went far beyond any ordinary political revival. As early as November 6, 1918, Alfred Weber, the well-known sociologist, had written in the *Berliner Tageblatt*: 'The debate will revolve around the basic question of our present social order.'[4] At a rally of the members of the Progressive *Volksverein* of Frankfurt, the Deputy Mayor, Luppe, gained thunderous applause when only a few days after the Revolution, he proclaimed his support for a 'democratic and *social* Republic.'[5] Under his leadership the *Verein* issued a declaration which contained a programme of national demands including the socialisation of certain branches of industry and drastic levies on war profits.[6] When the *Frankfurter Zeitung* called upon the bourgeoisie and the farmers to turn the 'class revolution' of the workers' and soldiers' councils into a general one, the paper condensed its domestic political aims into the formula that a 'people's party' – *Volkspartei* – comprising all strata of society, should strive for a new social and economic order which transcended the mere establishment of a political democracy.[7]

The Frankfurt proclamation, which served as a model in several other cities, included foreign political aspirations typical of a vanquished nation, i.e. general disarmament, self-determination and equal membership of the League of Nations. There was ample

[1] *Die Hilfe*, November 21, 1918, p. 554
[2] Ibid., November 14, 1918, p. 539
[3] *Kölnische Zeitung*, November 18, 1918, M
[4] *Berliner Tageblatt*, November 6, 1918, M
[5] *Nachlass Luppe*, No. 9, Bundesarchiv, Koblenz
[6] *Frankfurter Zeitung*, November 15, 1918, 2.M
[7] Ibid., November 16, 1918, A

room for high hopes that democracy would be the peace-giving principle in a new international order during this period, which Troeltsch called the 'fairy-land of armistice'.[1] During the war, liberal pacifists had worked to bring about peace. But they had done so without attempting to mobilize the masses because they feared internal political repercussions. Now it looked – for the first time in German history – as if the restless spirit underlying their schemes for a new international order, and inherent in their pedagogical ideas on international understanding might merge with the fundamental desire for peace which prevailed among the masses.

These innumerable spontaneous local and regional outbursts culminated in Berlin on November 16th with a proclamation announcing the foundation of a 'powerful democratic party for a united Reich'.[2] The initiators of this proclamation had gathered around the chief editor of the *Berliner Tageblatt*, Theodor Wolff, and Alfred Weber. They included journalists and scholars – among them Hugo Preuss, the Rector of the Berlin School of Economics, and Albert Einstein, the physicist. There were also industrialists, merchants, trade union leaders and spokesmen of the civil service, as well as a few politicians from the old liberal parties of the fallen empire. The party which they founded, the German Democratic Party (DDP), seemed to mark a new and more hopeful departure for German liberalism.

The Berlin proclamation made no bones about the belief that Germany had reached a historical turning point which affected the political parties, the old system of government and its traditional social order. 'All this', it proclaimed, 'is irretrievably lost. Nobody will succeed in reviving it again.'[3] If one tries to analyse the political implications of this proclamation against the background of similar statements, it will become clear that the events of November 9th were perceived as being the beginning of a more advanced level of intellectual and social freedom which extended

[1] Ernst Troeltsch, *Spektator-Briefe*, edited by H. Baron (Tübingen, 1924), p. 51
[2] This proclamation is printed in *Zehn Jahre deutsche Republik*, edited by A. Erkelenz (Berlin, 1928), pp. 25-6   [3] Ibid.

beyond the original aims of the revolutionary movement—which was fundamentally a peace movement. It was in this sense that the democratic forces of the bourgeoisie – which avoided the label 'liberal' for the time being – wanted to extend the achievements of the revolution. As a result, they moved nearer to the political attitudes of the socialist working classes, and thus gained the opportunity to develop a political profile of their own. It seemed as if the famous question which had dogged the liberal movement, namely that of its attitude towards the Social Democrats, would find a positive solution at last, in that both forces were struggling for a fundamentally new political and social order.

Nevertheless, an analysis of these democratic proclamations raises the critical question of whether they contained anything other than verbal enthusiasm which lacked really strong support. Alternatively, it may be asked if an analysis of the social background of those who entered the DDP confirms that its proclamations had a real chance of being put into practice.

During the first weeks after the Revolution the DDP gained a greater number of new members. They swelled the traditional following of the left-wing liberals, which came from the intelligentsia and from the skilled workers organized in the Hirsch-Duncker trade union movement. The party attracted some of the old urban bourgeoisie – artisans and small merchants who before the war had voted for conservative parties – and gained a foothold in the traditional strongholds of liberalism in the agricultural areas of Northwest Germany, especially among the landowners with small or medium-sized farms. Above all it gained large numbers of white-collar workers, including members of the lower and middle-grade civil service, as well as teachers. These social groups had grown rapidly in the preceding years as a result of the structural changes in administration and industry.

In 1925 this latter group of employees who did not hold an executive position comprised 5·3 million people, i.e. 16·5 per cent of all those in employment.[1] Such people had been politically neglected by the pre-war liberals, and only the socially reformist wing of the Progressive Party had offered them a political home.

[1] *Statistik des Deutschen Reiches*, Vol. 408, p. 139

The Handbook of that party, published in 1911, had stipulated that 'the centre of power should be based on those masses' who 'were trying to improve their political and social position'.[1] This was a policy which once again became very topical with the outbreak of the November Revolution. Under these circumstances the white-collar employees, alarmed by the wage increases of the unionized industrial workers, rushed to join the DDP and demanded, together with the working classes, the socialization of industry and the democratization of the administration.

These demands were also put forward by the civil servants' organization. At the end of December the membership of those associations which made up the *Deutscher Beamtenbund* had risen to over a million. Its leading functionaries belonged to the ruling committees of the DDP. Many members of the DDP's delegation to the first national congress of the workers' and soldiers' councils in December 1918 also came from this and similar professional groups.

It did not seem unlikely that the party would attract large contingents of this multi-million army of politically mobilized voters and other still dormant forces. Together with the socialist working classes and the strong labour wing of the Centre Party it might shift the political balance in Germany in favour of a new 'democratic middle-class society'.

In the course of the negotiations to bring about a merger between the founders of the DDP and the old liberal parties this hopeful dynamism was deflected by a number of different pressures. But in order to gain a better understanding of this development it is necessary to analyse the decisions which had been taken in the meantime by the bureaucracy, the army, and industry. In his proclamation of November 9th, addressed to the civil service throughout the country, Friedrich Ebert, the new Reich Chancellor, admitted quite openly that it would be difficult for many civil servants to work under the new regime.[2] Although the Social Democrats did not say it in so many words they agreed that civil

[1] M. Wenck, *Handbuch für liberale Politik*, 1911, p. 12
[2] This proclamation is printed in Heilfron (ed.), *Die deutsche National-versammlung im Jahre 1919/20*, 7 vols (Berlin, 1920), Vol. 1, pp. 103-4

servants faced a conflict between their loyalties and their duties. When Ebert asked civil servants to hold out until 'the hour for their replacement has come'[1] this was bound to strengthen the silent determination of those who wished to stay in office merely in order to prepare the way for a return to pre-revolutionary times. Similarly, Ebert's words were bound to push many of those who had not yet made up their minds into a position of guarded neutrality. Reference to 'law and order' was used as a means of effecting a smooth transition to the new regime by democratically oriented civil servants, who were to be found mainly in the local authorities. However, conservative elements in the bureaucracy declared this slogan to be an end in itself. They thus prepared for the revival of the notion that the state existed above the parties and that its affairs were conducted by a civil service which was devoted to the ideal of expert knowledge and guided by the traditional ethos of neutrality. In short, the Council of People's Deputies did nothing to democratize the civil service.

The army reinforced this conservatism. The official receptions which were arranged to greet the allegedly unvanquished army were designed to strengthen respect for law and order among the population and the troops. Certainly it made many a burgher's heart beat faster when he saw his famous *Jäger* Division enter Cologne still with sufficient discipline to manage the goose-step.[2] The citizens reinforced their faith in law and order by watching these disciplined army contingents. However absurd this feeling may seem from a political point of view, it did have the effect that the troops – who were welcomed with black-white-and-red colours in the streets – were also greeted as the guardians of internal order and stability. And soon, as is well known, they were to be employed in this role. Moreover, Ebert's alliance with the High Command not only prejudiced the subsequent reorganization of the *Reichswehr* but also increased the influence of counter-revolutionary ideologies inside the officer corps.

Finally industry soon secured a sphere of political influence for itself by founding the *Zentrale Arbeitsgemeinschaft der industriellen*

[1] Ibid.
[2] *Kölnische Zeitung*, November 23, 1918 and December 12, 1918

und gewerblichen Arbeitgeber – und Arbeitnehmerverbände (Central Working Association of Employers' and Employees' Associations in Trade and Industry). In this organization the trade unions were conceded considerable powers, such as the unlimited right of collective bargaining, recognition as legal representatives of the workers and the introduction of the eight-hour day.

What did the employers gain in return? While the socialists publicly demanded socialization, the trade union leader Legien confidentially informed Stinnes, the industrialist, that the trade union leadership would not abandon its socialist ideals, but would not try to put them into practice.[1] The Council of People's Deputies officially confirmed the agreement between industry and trade unions. But the settlement they welcomed, because it relieved them of embarrassing pressure, contained the germ which helped to weaken their predominant power position. For it was this sort of *raison d'économie* which – by promoting the idea of a socio-economic compromise between capital and labour – shifted the financial burdens of industry on to the shoulders of the consumer.

So far, these socially conservative elements which prevailed in the civil service, the army, and industry lacked a political force of their own. They limited themselves to the preservation of the *status quo*. Even the spontaneous change of policy by the employers was, above all, conceived as an *ad hoc* measure of self-protection, rather than the pursuit of long-range goals. There was nothing inevitable about the way in which industry and the bureaucracy in Germany managed to preserve a great deal of their pre-revolutionary character. Economic pressures alone cannot be held responsible for this development; political factors–such as the emergence of the DVP and the weakness of the socially reformist wing within the Democratic Party itself – were far more important.

Since the Socialist Council of People's Deputies used its wide powers with the greatest self-restraint and thus helped to retard the revolutionary movement, the democratic forces in the bourgeoisie felt themselves deserted and betrayed. Soon the composition of the DDP leadership and the programmatic priorities which it pursued began to change. With the election of January 1919

[1] R. 13 I/115, Bundesarchiv, Koblenz

about to begin, the party's founders became dependent on the traditional party machines. The old functionaries and leaders in the central office and the local organizations regained their former influence. At the same time the negotiations to effect a merger with the National Liberals strengthened nationalistic and anti-socialist tendencies in the DDP's national executive. Alfred Weber resigned. Tactical considerations also facilitated polemics against pacifism. In some circles this even went so far as to lead to internal concessions to anti-semitic feeling. The competition of the DVP, founded by Gustav Stresemann – who had been barred from a leading position in the DDP because of his close association with Ludendorff – acted as a further stimulant. The DVP represented the right-wing tradition in German liberalism.

Thus it was that within a few weeks of its foundation a marked change in the policy of the DDP had become apparent. There was one fact that not only the mass of DDP supporters but also its leading members did not realise, and this was the financial dependence of the party on industry. This problem was as old as the question of universal suffrage. Before the war the industrialists had justified their attempts to influence the decisions of the bourgeois parties with the laconic argument, 'industry does not have voters of its own'. After the Revolution Carl Friedrich von Siemens had founded the 'Curatorium for the Reconstruction of the German Economy'[1] in order to remedy this lack. The Curatorium could deploy large sums of money and developed greater political efficiency than any other similar pressure group. It was founded in Berlin, where it became most active and where the metal, textile, and electrical industries provided most of the financial support.

When at the end of December 1918, industrialists, bankers, and merchants met in the Berlin Chamber of Commerce to sign up for their first contributions to the fund, one of the participants, showing commercial realism, called the Curatorium the 'Central Office for the purchasing of political advantages for the benefit of industry'.[2] It was for this reason that all non-socialist

[1] *Kuratorium für den Wiederaufbau des deutschen Wirtschaftslebens*
[2] Schubert to C. F. v. Siemens, December 28, 1918, *Siemens-Archiv*, Munich

parties benefited from these funds. The Curatorium informed itself about the election propaganda and about candidates who would be favourably disposed towards industry. These were supported with cash. The DDP received the largest sum as it appeared to have the best chance of becoming a powerful *Sammlungspartei* (rallying party) which would penetrate the electorate close to those strata of society wooed by the Social Democrats. If the Democrats and the middle-class parties succeeded in preventing the National Assembly from having a socialist majority, the nightmare of socialization might be removed at the parliamentary level. The leadership of the party met the industrialists half-way in so far as it advised its local organizations against putting up joint candidates together with the SPD. However, not all of these organizations complied with this.

The money from industry imposed heavy obligations on the DDP. In order to win votes and new members and to combine them in a powerful and dynamic people's party, the leadership did not hesitate to make ample use of financial contributions from outside. But the commitments by which it was bound prevented it from retaining these newly won supporters. In other words, the money of the industrialists facilitated the DDP success at the polls, but made its consolidation more difficult afterwards. The party got entangled in the insoluble contradiction between the need to secure its financial base and its desire for political independence.

The factional strife in the party which followed the elections showed, however, that an alternative did exist. It was the decidedly democratic and social-reformist wing, consisting mainly of white-collar employees and civil servants, which tried to turn the DDP into a democratic mass party whose organization, activity, and financial needs would be supported by a broad membership.[1] This wing, however, could not surmount the traditional individualism of the so-called educated classes who had nothing but contempt for the necessities of day-to-day organizational routine.

When the National Assembly opened, the development of the

[1] See, e.g. the minutes of the managing committee (*Parteiausschuss*), December 12, 1919, R. 45 III/10, Bundesarchiv, Koblenz

party was still uncertain. At the polls it had gained 5·6 million out of 30 million votes: i.e. 18·5 per cent (Stresemann's more conservative DVP only won 4.4 per cent of the poll). It was the third strongest party, ranking behind the Majority Social Democrats and the Centre Party. Its voters, who came from socially divergent groups, differed over the hopes which they pinned on the alliance with the Social Democrats. There were those who saw in this alliance the guarantee for the construction of a strong democracy, and others who considered it a protection of the social *status quo* against the danger of a radicalization from the Left. Although, among the seventy-four deputies, the decidedly democratic groups were under-represented, decision-making in the party remained nevertheless dependent on the overall constellation of power inside the Weimar coalition. This was because of the flexibility which existed over a variety of questions.

The National Assembly was confronted with two great tasks, that of making a constitution and that of concluding peace. The DDP was prominent in tackling the first task, because it contained distinguished constitutional experts. As far as the second task was concerned, it claimed a leading position from the beginning. Objectively its best opportunity lay in activating the impulses responsible for its own foundation within the framework of the Weimar coalition. The coalition itself seemed powerful enough, since it commanded a two-thirds majority in the *Reichstag*.

On February 8, 1919 Hugo Preuss, in his capacity as State Secretary of the Interior, declared that the National Assembly was the only 'bearer of the sovereignty of the people'.[1] He did not make further mention of the task of the Assembly to 'secure the results of the Resolution' as his party colleague, the lawyer Anschütz, had done only a few days earlier.[2] Rather, the National Assembly was to be strictly separated from those bodies which, like the workers' and soldiers' councils, derived their functions and aims from a mandate gained through revolution.

The first parliament of the Republic, which fulfilled the double function of law and constitution-making, exercised more powers

[1] Heilfron (ed.), *Die deutsche Nationalversammlung*, Vol. 1, p. 28
[2] *Deutsche Juristenzeitung*, February 1, 1919, column 113

than any of its successors. On the other hand, it did not grant any rights of immediate influence to the people – which had been defined by Preuss as being the primary organ of the state – for almost eighteen months. This meant that post-war energies had a chance of realizing themselves in a legal fashion only in as much as they had become vocal at the elections.

These facts corresponded to a remarkable preoccupation with the need to strengthen the executive which marked the first decisions of the National Assembly. On the day prior to the first plenary session one DDP deputy declared frankly that 'the most important thing was to have a disciplined army'.[1] This was how many others looked at the priorities facing Germany. Even many Social Democrats wished to form a government as quickly as possible in order to put a resolute end to internal unrest. The laws concerning the preliminary Reich executive power (February 10, 1919) and the formation of a provisional Reichswehr (March 6, 1919) were ratified with extreme haste.

In the same way the constitutional construction of the governmental system displayed a tendency to favour a strong executive. This soon became clear when the new constitution continued the tradition of the constitution of October 1918, which had been drawn up on the basis of war experiences in order to fulfil certain tasks: namely to conclude an armistice or if necessary to resume the war effort. If one follows the statements made by the Democrats, the role of Parliament was mainly to support the government rather than to control or guide it. Parliament was to help in the selection and training of leaders and to give the liberal ideal of the individual personality, acting with a representative mandate, a new and belated lease of life. And possibly it could even serve as a platform for new concepts as had been sketched out in Max Weber's typology of a plebiscitarian 'Führer' democracy. Under these circumstances it was not surprising that the position of the Reich President was interpreted in an authoritarian fashion.

It is significant that political parties were not directly mentioned in the Weimar Constitution, which refrained from connecting

[1] DDP delegation meeting, February 5, 1919, *Nachlass Petersen*, Stadt-und Staatsarchiv, Hamburg

40

state institutions permanently with their social basis. Most serious of all were the deficiencies in that part of the constitution which referred to the social function of the state and at the core of which lay the problem of socialization. Although the material preconditions for socialization were almost untested, and theoretical views on its nature and limits differed widely, after the revolution it became the key symbol of general social liberation of the workers from material and personal dependence.

The dictatorial powers of the People's Deputies, the expectations of the workers and employees, and the favourable disposition, or at least the caution, of the bourgeoisie offered the best possible conditions for socialization. And yet the Council of People's Deputies treated the question of socialization in a dilatory fashion by transferring it to a commission. When the mining workers went on strike, Friedrich Naumann, on whom the social-liberal wing of the DDP had put great hopes, merely shrank back from the nightmare of socialist radicalization. He appealed to those members of the faction who opposed him by saying: 'Of course we want to maintain capitalist enterprise'.[1]

When, in March 1919, the Majority Socialists, under massive pressure from extra-parliamentary workers' groups, tabled a motion to socialize industry and also considered it unavoidable that provision be made for economic councils in the constitution, the DDP made it its task to water these proposals down. The spokesman of the party declared that the law on socialization and the socialization of the mining industry should be considered, not as first steps towards a general social reorganization, but as maximum concessions. Thus, the protagonists of private enterprise had become dominant in the party. They justified their attitude with the old liberal arguments in support of an economic system which, although it had long become a hollow shell, maintained that private initiative and unfettered competition guaranteed the optimal conditions for individual freedom and distribution of goods.

As a result, the party lost its left-wing support, which deserted to the Social Democrats, without being able to stop simultaneous

[1] Ibid., February 10, 1919

41

losses to the right-wing parties which recklessly made even more far-reaching promises to the propertied classes. These losses, from which the DDP never recovered, set in as early as spring 1919.

Consideration of this domestic dilemma of the DDP makes it necessary to turn to the motives and prospects underlying its activities in the field of foreign policy. The party's chances of building up its support under German post-war conditions were small if its activity in foreign affairs was to be used as a means of maintaining its domestic position.

This hypothesis can best be verified by looking at the attitude of the DDP towards the Allied peace conditions. Since the Social Democrats lacked the expertise and trained personnel to take the lead in making foreign policy, the public and diplomatic preparation for the Versailles peace conference became largely the domain of the DDP and the groups close to it. After all, were not the liberals – thanks to their historical tradition – qualified as guardians of the national needs? And were not their leading personalities – historians and international lawyers – mandated and even obliged to give a historical dimension to the renewed conduct of post-war foreign policy? The result was a publicly proclaimed conglomerate of aspirations in which pacifist-democratic views mingled with nationalist and power-political traditions. National pride, which had been shaken as a result of an unexpected defeat and Allied reproaches, tried to console itself with the argument that Germany, having tragically lost its former power position, was called upon to fulfil new tasks of international leadership. The country was looking for new perspectives to satisfy its traditional longing for prestige, and this was to be achieved with the aid of democratically phrased projects for the international protection of labour or the League of Nations.

The DDP and the entire coalition government did nothing to rectify public illusions about the prospects of a 'soft' peace. When, therefore, on May 7, 1919, the Allies handed over the peace conditions, disappointment and bitterness were all the greater. Nevertheless, the government submitted to the parliamentary peace-making committee the proposal to postpone the question of whether to accept or reject the conditions in order to obtain a few modifications by means of negotiations. However, when on May 12th the National Assembly initiated a public wave of protest at a rally in the University of Berlin, Scheidemann, the Prime Minister, declared expressly that the peace treaty was unacceptable. The DDP members of the cabinet had urged him only an hour beforehand to put this passage into his manuscript.[1] This meant that the DDP was trying to assume the leading part in the national protest movement. The Allies, however, made hardly any concessions. The attempt at a united front disintegrated and on June 19th the Scheidemann cabinet resigned. The DDP refused to enter a new government. Worried about its image and under pressure from some of its deputies, the party added further conditions to the so-called points of honour at which the government was baulking – the war-guilt clause and the extradition of alleged war-criminals. Re-entry into the coalition was to be barred at all costs.

But what might have been the alternative? In the last days prior to the expiry of the ultimatum intelligence reports left little doubt that military resistance would be 'madness', as Noske put it, and that the morale of the population had collapsed.[2] Nevertheless, the DDP deputies continued their resistance even though in their hearts they hoped that a majority could be found to sign the peace. When this majority appeared on June 22nd, it included seven Democrats.

The result, however, was immediately put into question when Clemenceau refused to budge on the points of honour. Thus the future of German foreign policy depended on the position which the parties would take on this question. A majority of about a hundred votes had been mustered in favour of accepting the material conditions of the treaty. The only question left was whether or not the 'national humiliation', which had been magnified by party politics, should be accepted. It appeared as if Hegel's statement had been confirmed that 'a nation can entrust its infinity

---

[1] Theodor Heuss, *Friedrich Naumann: Der Mann, das Werk, die Zeit* (Stuttgart, Tübingen, 1946), p. 490

[2] Meeting of the Peace Committee of the National Assembly, June 21, 1919, *Nachlass C. Haussmann*, No. 59, Haupt-und Staatsarchiv, Stuttgart

and its honour to any of its component parts'.[1] This was the absurd position into which German foreign policy had been manœuvred, and the Democrats had played a decisive part in attaining it. There was no alternative left to the middle-class groups which had rejected the peace. They were grateful when the crisis was solved at the last minute by turning it into a legal question and when the parliamentary consent which had been given on the previous day was extended to the unconditional adoption of the peace. The bourgeois groups had gladly accepted the proposal of the Centre Party confirming that the signatories of the treaty had been guided by nothing but 'patriotic motives'.

The DDP had demanded and had received a leading position in questions of foreign policy. When it failed in this policy, the party abdicated its governmental responsibility. Its retreat marked an attempt to evade the domestic political burden of Weimar coalition in order to gather new energies. As part of the so-called 'National Opposition' the DDP might gain a more favourable position if the chance arose for a renewed share of power. The retreat of the DDP from the responsibilities of power reflected a crisis in the whole Weimar system. It was a crisis which called into question the nature of the decision-making process in the Republic, as well as the style of politics, the quality of public leadership and the relationship between parliamentary institutions and those mass elements in Germany which had been roused to political consciousness for the first time by the events of the revolution.

In many ways the National Assembly had disappointed those who had hoped for a new order in Germany. There had been no fundamental changes in the federal structure of the country, in its administration, its armed services or its educational system. Above all, social reforms had been inadequate and democratic institutions had not been effectively strengthened. It was in precisely these fields that the DDP might have been expected to act as a bridge between the Social Democrats and the bourgeoisie. Instead the party fell back on a defence of the traditional capitalist order. The Democrats came to adopt an old-style liberalism which –

[1] Hegel, *Rechtsphilosophie*, para. 334

either from ignorance or self-interest – ignored the realities of social change and declared it possible to surmount the social problems of the nation by nationalist agitation over issues of foreign policy.

In addition, the reputation of the parliamentary system suffered because, contrary to the expectations of liberal ideologists, it did not uncover hitherto untapped resources of potential leadership. On the contrary, the Republic's political leaders aroused disappointment by the purely tactical manner in which they approached the burden of political responsibility. After the débâcle of the Peace Treaty prominent personalities wished to stay in the background and allowed second-rate men to move to the fore. Those who engaged actively in politics did so with the comment that they were thereby sacrificing themselves to the party and the Fatherland. To this was added the unfortunate fact that the personal stand taken by a *Reichstag* deputy on the peace treaty issue was taken for a long time as a criterion of his 'national reliability'. Politicians tended to veil the lack of any real alternative to a policy of surrender by laying down a smokescreen of patriotic moralizing. This promoted a kind of *attentism* which consoled itself by hoping for a better future and left to others the unpopular work of leadership in a defeated country.

The first Weimar parliament was also incapable of harnessing the energy and idealism among the German masses which had been generated at the end of the war. 'Direct democracy' was feared as a rival and not enlisted as an ally. Although the National Assembly had been elected in haste and under somewhat unnatural conditions, the Assembly guarded its rights suspiciously against pressure from extra-parliamentary forces of a radical kind even when, as was the case with the workers' councils, they possessed a mandate from important under-privileged sections of the population, and even when it was clear that they posed no real threat of a 'Bolshevik' character. Whenever it did go some way to meet left-wing demands, as in the case of socialization or the Economic Councils, the Assembly did not regard these as first steps towards a more comprehensive reform programme, but simply as concessions to mass pressure. It was not realized that, if the democratic impulses emanating from politically inexperienced people were not effectively harnessed by the new Republic, other, and more sinister, elements might profit by them.

This deep-rooted liberal scepticism about the political mobilization of the masses, together with a more general lack of imagination, were important factors in the dismal development of German politics after the First World War, a development which saw a mass electorate, roused to political action by the experience of defeat and social upheaval, being allowed to fall under the sway of right-wing radicalism.

CHAPTER 3

GERMAN SOCIAL DEMOCRACY IN THE WEIMAR REPUBLIC

ERICH MATTHIAS

When the German Revolution broke out in November 1918, Lenin and his friends thought that it was an event of world-historical importance. They hoped that it would turn the Russian revolutionary wave into a universal one. Yet with the benefit of hindsight, the German Revolution merely seems to possess a provincial character when compared with what happened in Russia in 1917. It would lead too far to discuss in detail why Lenin's hopes rested on false assumptions, both with regard to the German working-class movement and to the socio-political situation in Germany. But it is precisely against the background of the Bolshevik Revolution that we can see how modestly the German Social Democrats used their powers in the revolutionary period of transition during the winter of 1918-19.

Thus few people today would argue that the November Revolution amounted to a Social Democratic seizure of power in Germany, whereas we feel no inhibitions when talking of the Bolshevik seizure of power in 1917 or of the National Socialist seizure of power in 1933. Of course, it would be foolish to equate Bolshevism with National Socialism, but there seems to be at least one common element in both if one compares the energy with which Hitler and Lenin strove for power and the recklessness with which they defended it.

The German Social Democrats, on the other hand – and this

is true of the Independent Social Democrats (USPD)[1] as well as of the Majority Social Democrats (SPD)[1] under Ebert and Scheidemann – were not properly prepared to assume power. Nevertheless, the apparatus of power which fell into their hands as a result of the military breakdown of the empire was far more impressive than that available to the Bolsheviks after their successful *coup d'état* in Petrograd. Similarly, *Hitler's* nomination as the Reich Chancellor on January 30, 1933, did not apparently provide him with the wide powers available to Ebert in November 1918.

Nevertheless, in spite of their much more unfavourable starting positions, both the Bolsheviks and the National Socialists realized their claims for undivided rule with surprising speed, whereas the Social Democratic People's Deputies of 1918 used their dictatorial powers by and large only in order to bridge, more or less efficiently, the period between the outbreak of the revolution and the creation of a new constitution by the National Assembly.

Even those who do not reproach the Social Democrats for having rejected political terror and the idea of a 'dictatorship of the proletariat', can hardly be satisfied with the argument that the moderation of the Socialists was a commendable example of democratic self-denial. Even if one assumes that there was no chance of creating a socialist regime in 1918 it is still necessary to ask why the SPD leadership failed even to establish a stable democracy in Germany. Did Germany's Social Democratic leaders miss a genuine opportunity to give the young Republic a firm foundation for a democratic future?

The thesis that the Republic was inevitably doomed because of the failures of the revolutionary period is doubtless untenable. Nevertheless, the chronic political instability of the Weimar Republic and its recurrent structural crises cannot be explained unless we take into account the full significance of the fundamental decisions which were taken during the early months of its existence.

If we wish to question the extent to which possibilities existed during the period of transition which were not exploited by the

[1] The USPD split from the SPD in 1917, demanding more vigorous resistance to the war and to the Imperial regime.

revolutionary government there are two further problems which must also be taken into account. Firstly, there is the question of the split in the German working-class movement which had appeared during the war and continued after it. It is necessary to estimate the importance of this split in weakening Social Democratic influence in the Weimar period and thus damaging the parliamentary system. Secondly, we must investigate the role of the SPD as the Republic's 'state party' – the binding force in the whole new system.

This essay will concentrate on these three key problems. It will not attempt to provide a detailed description of the SPD's fortunes from 1919 to 1933, nor will it deal with ideological struggles within the party. It would, however, be useful to bear in mind the size of the political potential which the socialist movement represented in the Weimar Republic.

The best way to do this is to look at the results of the *Reichstag* elections in which – due to the electoral system and the traditional party structure – no party ever gained an absolute majority.

The Social Democrats achieved their greatest success during the elections for the National Assembly in January 1919. It was in these elections that the two Social Democratic parties gained a total of 45·5 per cent of the votes, of which by far the largest portion, 37·9 per cent, fell to the Majority Socialists – the SPD. The Independents (USPD), on the other hand, had to be content with some 7·5 per cent.

This meant a rise in the total socialist share of the poll of over 10 per cent as compared with the last pre-war elections in 1912, although it must be admitted that these figures have but a limited value because of the new post-war electoral system and the introduction of the woman's franchise. The latter, however, tended to work against the Social Democrats.

The elections of 1920, a few months after the Kapp *Putsch*, resulted in a reduction of the total share of the vote falling to socialist parties of about 4 per cent (=41·6 per cent). The Communist Party, founded on New Year's Day 1919 and not yet represented at the polls during that year, played the role of an insignificant sect in 1920 (gaining 2 per cent of the total vote). It was the Independents who benefited from the process of radicalization which had set in ever since the beginning of 1919. They gained a total of 18 per cent, thus almost approaching the share of the Majority Socialists with 21·6 per cent.

The election of May 1924 – the results of which were still influenced by the political and economic crisis of 1923 – was fought by only two socialist parties, the reunified SPD and the Communists – the latter having gained a mass basis after the Independents had split towards the end of 1920.

In 1924 the Social Democrat vote sank to 20·5 per cent while that of the Communists reached 12·6 per cent. This meant that the overall socialist share of the poll had been reduced to about one-third (33·1 per cent), and there was only an insignificant rise during the elections of December 1924 (to 35 per cent). The gradual decline of radicalism was expressed by the fact that the Social Democrats had broadened their basis (to about 26 per cent) at the cost of the Communists (9 per cent). It might have been expected that this process towards moderation would have continued in the years of economic stability from 1924 to 1928. But in fact the Communists as well as the SPD gained ground in that period. Thus the SPD won an impressive victory during the 1928 elections, scoring almost 30 per cent (29·8 per cent) while the Communist share amounted to a little over 10 per cent (10·6 per cent). Taken together, the left wing parties succeeded in attracting as much as 40·4 per cent of the voters.

The elections of 1930 and 1932 were overshadowed by the Great Depression. It was then that the Social Democratic percentage of the poll dropped time after time. During the September elections of 1930, when the Nazis had their first big success, it was down to 24·5 per cent. Two years later, in July 1932, it dropped to a little over 21 per cent (21·6 per cent) and reached a new low in November at 20·4 per cent. The Communists, on the other hand, succeeded in increasing their share, scoring 13·1 per cent in 1930, 14·6 per cent in July 1932 and 16·8 per cent in November 1932.

What is even more remarkable is that the total share of the

socialist parties (including the Communists) hardly showed a change during these three years, and always fluctuated around the 37 per cent mark (1930: 37·6 per cent; 1932 (July): 36·2 per cent; 1932 (November): 37·2 per cent). The total number of votes cast for the two competing left-wing parties ran between 13·2 and 13·3 millions – a figure which is a mere half-million less than the number of votes cast for Social Democracy in the 1919 National Assembly elections.

In summary one can say that the overall potential of the socialist parties remained surprisingly constant throughout the years of crisis. As late as July 1932 it was about equal to the share of the National Socialists (36·2 per cent : 37·4 per cent). And during the November elections of that year it surpassed the National Socialists, who were suffering a set-back, by a considerable margin (37·2 per cent : 31·1 per cent).

Even the Social Democratic share of the vote, if taken separately, held up remarkably well, despite the shift towards the extreme Left. The firmness and loyalty of the SPD's membership is even more impressive. If the latest obtainable figures are correct, the Social Democratic party continued to have more than a million members during the second half of 1932. This meant that the number of organized Social Democrats had dropped by only 65,000 since January 1, 1931 – and this in spite of the newly founded Socialist Workers' Party (SAP) and the much more dangerous attraction exerted on the desperate unemployed by the Communists. This membership figure of over a million was actually about 35,000 more than that of the year 1928. Statistically, at least, Social Democracy remained an impressive force. Why then, did this force exert so little influence on the fate of German democracy?

The collapse of the German Empire effected a change in the distribution of political power. But it became apparent soon after the revolutionary period of transition that the distribution of social power had been left more or less untouched. This explains why Weimar democracy never succeeded in integrating its own bureaucratic and military infrastructure. Such a development would not have been possible without large-scale interference with the social and economic structure, and it was precisely such interference from which the Social Democrat People's Deputies shrank.

Many historians have since argued that, in view of Germany's diplomatic and economic difficulties, the Social Democrats did not have any other choice unless they wanted the Reich to fall into the hands of Bolshevism. Karl Dietrich Erdmann, for example, arguing along these lines, wrote that the freedom of choice for the Social Democrat revolutionary government had been reduced to a 'clear-cut either-or', namely to the alternative between 'social revolution by combining with those forces which were aiming at a dictatorship of the proletariat' or a 'parliamentary republic by combining with conservative elements such as the old officer corps'.[1]

This formula, which really implies that the men in charge had no choice but to act as they did, complies with the standard version put forward by leading Social Democrats in their memoirs. Thus as early as February 1919 Eduard David declared before the National Assembly that it was the merit of Friedrich Ebert and the leading Majority Socialists 'that the German Revolution did not follow the pattern of the Russian one, that it did not lead, as in Russia, to bloodshed and chaos, to the complete dissolution of law and order, to the disintegration of all political and economic life'.

This statement certainly seems very impressive. And yet its validity was called into question by the results of the elections for the National Assembly. For it was in these elections that the dominant position of the Majority SPD within the socialist camp became clearly apparent – in spite of the process of radicalization which had set in since the end of 1918. The extreme Left was supported only by an insignificant minority. The fear of Bolshevism among the Majority Social Democrats and some of the Independents was therefore the result, not of the actual distribution of forces but of a psychosis which was at least partly created by the impact of events in Russia. This explains, among

[1] Karl Dietrich Erdmann, 'Die Geschichte der Weimar Republik als Problem der Wissenschaft', *Vierteljahrshefte für Zeitgeschichte*, 3 (1955), p. 1f

other things, the grotesque misjudgment of the spontaneous appearance of soviets in Germany and the hysterical assessment of the disturbances in Berlin in January 1919, which went down in history books under the misleading name of the 'Spartacist rising'. The author hopes it has become sufficiently clear that, unlike Erdmann and others, he holds the view that the question of the genuine possibility of a 'third way' – neither Bolshevik nor Conservative – cannot simply be dismissed. It is certainly remarkable to what extent the revolutionary government of People's Deputies disposed over a broad basis of confidence which went far beyond the circle of its socialist following.

Under these circumstances we cannot therefore discard as sheer fantasy the idea that the broad centre of the moderate social-democratic working class might have become the nucleus and social linchpin of a democratic process of national integration.

It is undeniable that the lost war, the revolutionary mood of the masses, the international situation and the desperate state of the economy confronted the Social Democratic leaders with an unusually difficult, if not even insoluble, task. However, many measures which could have fostered the young democratic system were never taken. This happened not so much because there was no chance of putting them into effect as because the People's Deputies refrained from any actively progressive policy and because they did not know what to do with the democratic forces which surged spontaneously towards them and seemed to be prepared to follow their lead. What is decisive for a historical assessment of this period is that the leading Social Democrats took as criteria for their actions the ideas and experiences of the pre-war socialist movement, even though the political frame of reference had changed completely since 1914. In fact, it was the petrified pre-war conceptions of the Social Democrats that limited the mobility of the revolutionary government far more than the much-cited 'external conditions'.

These arguments suggest that in trying to assess the effect that the split in the working class had on its subsequent development, we cannot simply accept the argument which Otto Braun advanced in his memoirs.[1] He wrote that, if someone asked him how it had been possible for Hitler to come to power, his answer would be: 'Versailles and Moscow'. This is obviously a neat and simple formula. It characterizes the unstable international position of the Weimar Republic and offers an explanation for the contraction of the middle-of-the-road political forces as a result of a polarization and radicalization of German political life. Moreover, this formula is convenient because, by attributing the failure of the democratic system to factors which affected Germany from the outside, it exonerates completely those parties which had founded and largely supported the Weimar Republic.

But just as it is impossible to explain the revival of nationalism in the Weimar Republic and the ultimate rise of National Socialism exclusively with reference to the attitude of the Western Allies, so it cannot be argued that the weakening and the at least partial failure of the democratic wing of the socialist movement was exclusively due to Communist competitors and their dependence on orders from Moscow.

It has been said earlier that the influence of 'Moscow' and of the Communists was negligible during the revolutionary period. Only disillusionment with the policy of the Social Democratic revolutionary government led to a process of radicalization at the beginning of 1919 which at first reinforced the Independent Social Democrats and the influence of its left wing. It was this wing which gave the Communists their mass basis after the disintegration of the USPD.

It is advisable, therefore, not to confuse cause and effect when one tries to pass judgment on the split in the German labour movement. This is true of the entire Weimar period – last but not least of the final years of crisis. For the growing attractiveness of the Communists at this time cannot be understood without reference to the uninspiring character of Social Democratic policy.

If one tries to put the attitude of the Social Democrats towards the Weimar Republic into a nutshell the most precise definition seems to be that the SPD was the 'state party of the Republic'.

[1] Otto Braun, *Von Weimar zu Hitler*, second ed. (New York, 1940), p. 5. See above, p. 13

This formula was first used by *Vorwärts* in December 1924. Later on its editor, Friedrich Stampfer, writing in exile, characteristically made it the central theme of his history of the Weimar Republic, in which he sought to explain and justify the policies of the Social Democrats in the Weimar period.[1] Even a scholar as critical as Sigmund Neumann based his structural analysis of the German party system of 1932 on the assumption that the SPD was 'no doubt *the* party whose basis has changed most decisively as a result of the November revolution'.[2]

A party, he continued, which before 1914 had been excluded from political responsibility had now become 'a responsible and decisive force' in the Republic. Its 'central position' was evidenced by the fact that the history of its post-war development 'mirrors the most important stages in the development of Republican politics in those years, and the position of all other parties could be understood by examining their attitude towards the SPD.'

Indeed there is a good deal of evidence that the fate of the SPD was more closely tied to that of the Republic than was the case with any other party. This remains true even in spite of the fact that it was not represented in most Reich governments after 1920. After the breakdown of Stresemann's Grand Coalition in the autumn of 1923 it shared power only once – as a result of the 1928 election victory which led to the renewal of the Grand Coalition under the Social Democratic Chancellor Hermann Müller.

It is possible to agree with Stampfer when he emphasizes time and again that no other party made as many sacrifices in support of the Republic as the SPD, and when he claims for his party that it remained the strongest and most determined force upholding parliamentary democracy in Germany right to the bitter end. Moreover it was the *only* Weimar party which never wavered in its clear and uncompromising opposition to National Socialism.

And yet the policy of the SPD during the Weimar period does

[1] Friedrich Stampfer, *Die 14 Jahre der ersten deutschen Republik* (Prague, 1936)

[2] Sigmund Neumann, *Die politischen Parteien in Deutschland* (Berlin, 1932), p. 23. See also new edition, 1965, p. 28

not offer the dramatic material for a heroic tragedy. In fact, nothing would be more dangerous than to view the National Socialist victory of 1933 as a 'natural catastrophe' which descended on the Social Democrats and for which they cannot be made reponsible. It is difficult to avoid the impression of continuous failure which characterizes the policy of the SPD from the fall of the Müller government up to Hitler's seizure of power. This impression remains, even if one fully recognizes the willingness to make sacrifices which the SPD displayed during the period in which it tolerated the Brüning government.

It is impossible to overlook the staggering lack of constructive initiative and tactical elasticity which caused the most important democratic potential among the political forces of the time to remain effectively immobilized. This passivity and the incapacity to create a constructive policy have their root largely in the unresolved leadership and structural problems of the SPD. They caused its 'conservatism' and made it impossible to develop forward-looking political and economic policies at a time of crisis.

This also explains the party's incapacity to steer a clear and popular course against the rising tide of radicalism among its own following and against the threat of Communist competition. Rather, the party largely wasted its strength in a desperate attempt to integrate divergent ideological forces within itself.

All this was nothing new because the inherent weaknesses of Social Democratic policy, which became clearly visible in the period of economic crisis, can easily be detected in all previous phases of the Republic, starting with the Government of People's Deputies.

We have now reached the point where we can ask the decisive question, namely how much significance is to be attributed to traditional patterns of behaviour in the SPD's policies. This question seems much more useful for our purposes than an examination of ideological disputes within the party, i.e. whether its policies contained too much or too little 'Marxism'. For it must be admitted that Marxism as an ideology was merely an irrelevant label which explained nothing about the party's substance. The question of the traditional patterns of behaviour, on the other hand, can also help to focus our attention on the fact that never throughout the Weimar period did the Social Democrats succeed in gaining a real understanding of political power. They were trapped in their old habits of legal opposition to an alien authority and did not grasp the need to impose their own solutions on a nation which was in a state of social and political turbulence. This means that we shall have to modify Neumann's thesis: It was the SPD's dilemma that by and large it remained the old pre-war party in spite of its changed position in the constitutional system. This is why even the 'state party of the Republic' has to bear a share of the responsibility for the instability of democracy in Germany and its ultimate failure.

CHAPTER 4

PARLIAMENTARY GOVERNMENT IN WEIMAR GERMANY, 1924-1928[1]

MICHAEL STÜRMER

Writing about parliamentary government in Weimar Germany at the end of 1923, Arthur Rosenberg, a candid political observer whose histories of the period have stood the test of time better than most, declared that no one would then have given more than five *Rentenmark* for the survival of the Weimar Constitution.[2] Yet, despite good grounds for such pessimism, the unexpected happened. By the spring of the following year the Republic had recovered from the crisis of the *Parteienstaat* and, albeit in a rather undramatic fashion, had re-established the routines of parliamentary government. The Enabling Law of the first Marx cabinet (1923-24) expired without the government having taken the oportunity once and for all to strip the *Reichstag* of its powers, a course advocated by some ministers.[3] Similarly the military state of siege, by means of which the more thoughtful nationalists hoped to provide the country with a solidly authoritarian form of government, was abandoned.

[1] For help in translating this article the author is very much indebted to Dr Volker R. Berghahn, University of East Anglia and to Dr John C. G. Röhl, University of Sussex. My thanks are also due to Dr Erich Matthias, University of Mannheim, and to Anthony Nicholls, St Antony's College, Oxford, for their critical comments and encouragement.

[2] Arthur Rosenberg, *Geschichte der Weimarer Republik* (reprinted Frankfurt-on-Main, 1961), p. 154

[3] Michael Stürmer, Koalition und Opposition in der Weimarer Republik. (Beiträge zur Gesch. d. Parl. u.d. pol. Parteien, Bd. 36, Düsseldorf, 1967), pp. 33-8

This unexpected revival of parliamentarianism was, of course, anything but an accident. Rather it can be seen as the indirect result of the currency reform of November 1923, which eliminated the chaos of inflation by creating the *Rentenmark*.[1] It was also affected by the preparedness of the US State Department to view the hitherto largely unsolved reparations question as a financial problem – rather than accepting French insistence that it was an issue of power politics. Such were the preconditions of the Dawes Plan in 1923-24. The gradual return to parliamentary government was also due to the fact that, although there existed innumerable plans to unhinge the Republic, none of those in power were prepared to stage a full-scale *coup d'etat*.

The ensuing stability lasted for more than half a decade. Yet the extent to which the political climate depended on economic prosperity is demonstrated by the fact that, with the beginning of the Great Depression in 1929, the days of the last parliamentary cabinet were also numbered. Parliamentary government in the classical sense can therefore be studied only during what have euphemistically been called the 'golden years' of the Republic. In fact they were by no means so golden as has been imagined, but were haunted by a host of unsolved economic, ideological, and political problems. Up to 1923, and after the great crash in 1929, Germany found herself in a state of latent civil war which threatened to explode into open fighting at almost any moment. There may have been opportunities for a gradual return to parliamentary government even after Brüning had been called to the Reich Chancellorship, but if so they were neglected.

Before turning to examine parliamentary government in Germany from 1924 to 1928, there is a more technical point which should be borne in mind when discussing the dilemma of Weimar democracy. This is that in 1919 three-quarters of the electorate had voted for the parties which supported the 1917 peace resolution and which formed the first parliamentary cabinet of October

[1] See Karl-Bernhard Netzband/Hans-Peter Widmaier, *Währungs-und Finanzpolitik der Ära Luther 1923-25* (Veröff. d. List-Gesellschaft, Bd. 32, Basel, 1964)

1918. Those were the political groups which later came to be associated with Weimar – i.e. the 'Weimar coalition'. They were the Social Democrats, Democrats and the Catholic Centre Party. But in less than a year the Weimar parties, having survived the Kapp *Putsch*,[1] suffered a heavy defeat at the polls. When the first *Reichstag* was elected in 1920[2] they were only supported by a minority of the voters. Germany had become what an observer called a 'republic without republicans'. After 1920 a solid majority in the *Reichstag* could not be formed unless one of the parties to the right of the Weimar coalition was included.

This gave a key position to Stresemann's moderately right-wing German People's Party (DVP) which slowly drifted from intransigent 'national opposition' to some sort of understanding with the Weimar constitutional system and with the Social Democrats. But the alliance with the SPD, whenever it came about, remained unable to overcome the dominant class conflict; it was never extended to include economic and social legislation. A grand coalition – a cabinet including both Social Democrats and the industrialist DVP – came into existence only at the height of the domestic crisis in the summer of 1923. That this was possible was due to the fact that the Social Democrats were prepared to face the responsibility of giving up passive resistance in the Ruhr area and very soon abandoned what was left of their orthodox economic programme. Consequently, it was not so much economic pressure which brought about the end of the grand coalition in November 1923, but rather the extensive use of *Reichswehr* troops against the Left in Saxony and Thuringia. Henceforth a minority of the moderate bourgeois parties took office in Berlin. Such a grouping was forced to manœuvre constantly between the Nationalists (DNVP) – who fiercely opposed the policy of fulfilment – on the one hand, and the Social Democrats who were openly hostile

[1] See Johannes Erger, *Der Kapp-Lüttwitz-Putsch. Ein Beitrag zur deutschen Innenpolitik 1919/20* (Beiträge zur Gesch. d. Parl. u.d.pol. Parteien, Bd. 35, Düsseldorf, 1967)
[2] For a detailed account of election results see Alfred Milatz, *Wähler und Wahlen in der Weimarer Republik* (Schriftenreihe der Bundeszentrale für pol. Bildung H. 66, Bonn, 1965), pp. 29-39 and *passim*

whenever the government sided with agrarian and industrial interests – on the other.

This means that when the era of stability began parliamentary government was faced with a number of problems which had been insoluble in the past and remained so throughout the period. These questions may be listed briefly. First, the preponderance of conflict over consensus in political life or, to be more precise, the striking imbalance of government and opposition. Second, the power of the government parties *vis-à-vis* the cabinet. Third, the lack of political cohesion; there were in the *Reichstag* different kinds of majorities, namely a majority for the conduct of foreign policy, a majority for social policy, and majorities based on agrarian and industrial interests; but these majorities were mostly incompatible with one another. Consequently, with no solid majority in existence in the *Reichstag*, there was neither consistent government, nor consistent opposition.

When, after 1923, economic stabilization began, a gradual change became apparent. Without an authoritarian government having assumed power, both the parties of the Right (DVP and DNVP) came to consider it vitally important to make their influence felt in the executive, in Prussia as well as in the Reich. This was not particularly difficult for the DVP, as the *Vernunftrepublikaner*[1] had taken control of it in 1920.[2] But with the Nationalists it turned out to be another matter. The DNVP had been hoping up to the end of 1923 – and even beyond – to gain power, not by means of a parliamentary majority, but in close alliance with the *Reichswehr*[3] which, after the Kapp *Putsch*, had been purged of most officers and men who had been unwise enough to show Republican sympathies during the decisive days of March 1920. After their dreams of an authoritarian solution had proved vain,

[1] Perhaps best translated as 'Republicans of the Intellect': they lacked any emotional commitment to the new regime.

[2] Henry A. Turner, *Stresemann and the Politics of the Weimar Republic* (Princeton, 1963), pp. 68-113

[3] Lewis Hertzman, *DNVP. Right-Wing Opposition in the Weimar Republic* (Lincoln, 1963); Stürmer, 'Die konservative Rechte in der Weimarer Republik', *Politische Parteien in Deutschland und Frankreich*, ed. O. Hauser (Wiesbaden, 1969), p. 40

the Nationalists started in 1924 to negotiate seriously for entry into the cabinet.

All these problems came to the surface during the Dawes Plan debate, which set the tone for German politics in 1924. The Nationalists, though fighting the Plan as just another extension of Versailles, were extremely keen on having a say in the subsequent distribution of the financial burdens which would mainly take the form of taxes and import duties. However, the agrarian and industrial pressure groups which directed the party's economic policies did not worry very much about the ideological content of foreign policy as long as it did not interfere with their basic aims. Their main interest was in gaining the maximum economic benefit from the Dawes Plan, including a sound basis for credits and a handsome settlement of the tariff issue. They could not do this, however, without having some hand in the government's policies. Thus the *Reichslandbund*[1] chairman said bluntly: 'The main thing is that we join the government. This is why we should accept the Plan if there is no way out.'[2] It was a fine example of pressure-group thinking, the more so as the agrarians intervention proved to be successful.

But it was not only this sort of cold-blooded reasoning which determined the DNVP's unsteady course. The Nationalists also feared that they might lose voters unless they left the ranks of the opposition. This was emphasized by one of the party's ideologists in a letter to Count Westarp, the party leader: 'The Republic is about to become more stable and the German people is about to reconcile itself to what has happened. This is the moment at which we must hesitate no longer!'[3]

Finally, the Nationalists feared – and perhaps quite rightly – that the party would fall to pieces unless it proved to its members that it was, after all, a useful political instrument. The

---

[1] The most important agrarian pressure group in Germany, representing especially the interests of large landowners in Eastern Germany.

[2] Quoted in Stürmer, *Koalition und Opposition*, p. 250

[3] Lindeiner-Wildau to Westarp, September 22, 1924, quoted in Roland Thimme, *Stresemann und die Deutsche Volkspartei* (Lübeck/Hamburg, 1961), p. 89

correspondent of Westarp was convinced 'that our party, as it now stands, cannot be held in unconditional opposition in the long run. If we want to remain an influential and vigorous right-wing movement we must have a share in the Government's powers now!'

This, after all, was a goal which was not very different from that of the middle-of-the-road parties. But whereas the Nationalists wanted to occupy the key positions in the executive – namely the *Reichswehr* Ministry and Reich Ministry of the Interior, as well as the Prussian premiership – the main aim of the other parties was to include the Nationalists in the government only as far as was necessary to render them harmless. Stresemann, for example, was convinced that the Nationalist Party, once in office, would not be strong enough to dominate the others. On the contrary, their entry into the cabinet would, he said, 'lead to a crisis within the Party and hence to its *convalescence*. This process must be furthered in the interests of the Republic.'[1]

On the Left the failure of the grand coalition in 1923 had convinced the Social Democrats that their wisest policy was to abstain from government.[2] As a result of this decision only two types of cabinet were possible between 1924 and 1928: those supported only by the moderate parties and those which included the parties of the Right. The former commanded only a minority vote in the *Reichstag* and were forced to govern by making compromises with the Right and Left. They attempted to hold a balance with even-handed concessions to both sides. However, whenever they had to face really important issues – such as the financial legislation after the Dawes settlement in August 1924, or the regulation of working hours in 1926 – these moderate admini-strations usually looked to the Right for help.[3]

[1] Cabinet minutes of October 15, 1924, quoted in Stürmer, *Koalition und Opposition*, p. 76

[2] Erich Matthias, 'Der sozialistische Einfluss in der Weimarer Republik', *Politische Parteien in Deutschland und Frankreich*, pp. 116-27

[3] Josef Becker, 'Die Deutsche Zentrumspartei 1918-1933', supplement to *Das Parliament* 11/1968

Right-wing cabinets, on the other hand, enjoyed greater numerical support in the *Reichstag*, but this did not necessarily make them any more powerful. The fact was that a minority government was weak because it lacked the requisite parliamentary support, but a right-wing majority cabinet was also weak because, despite its parliamentary majority, it was made up of too many divergent and often conflicting forces. Hence, even in the favourable atmosphere of stabilization, governments remained at the mercy of shifting *ad hoc* alliances in the *Reichstag*.

As far as foreign policy was concerned, Stresemann's supporters ranged from the trade unions and the SPD to his own DVP and German export industry. By and large these groups supported Stresemann's conduct of foreign policy and, what is equally important, his export-oriented trade policy. They furnished the Foreign Minister with a steady parliamentary backing, while the Nationalists, on the whole, were entrenched in an intransigent all-or-nothing opposition. The agrarians, as another *ceterum censeo*, put forward their demand for tariff reform.

It was principally the moderate majority which secured the passage of the Dawes Bills in 1924 and which continued to function below the surface of parliamentary politics throughout the following year, when Luther's right-wing government was in office. In fact, Stresemann's Locarno policy of 1925 and his work for Germany's entry into the League of Nations (1926), was heavily bombarded by the 'National Opposition' whether it was in or out of office. To a large extent Stresemann's success depended on the willingness of the various moderate groups to accept almost unconditionally what Stresemann, pursuing a long-standing German tradition, called the primacy of foreign policy over domestic problems. Thus, the *Primat der Aussenpolitik* became a vitally important formula in German politics. Stresemann's parliamentary majority allowed him greater freedom of action on the international scene, while at the same time, when negotiating with the Entente powers, he was perfectly justified in pointing to the importance of reconciling the 'National Opposition' at home – a useful argument when it came to obtaining political

E

concessions.[1] The reverse side, however, was a constant split in the government. This was accentuated by the fact that the Foreign Minister could pursue his policies without really having to bother about the views of half his cabinet colleagues. The moderate parliamentary alliance showed little coherence, however, on domestic issues like tariff reform and social legislation. The gulf between the industrialists and the agrarians, on the one hand, and organized labour, on the other, remained unbridgeable. The parliamentary mouthpiece of industry was the DVP which in this respect continued the tradition of the old National Liberals under Wilhelm II. In 1925, one in every three deputies of the DVP was listed by the Reich Association of German Industry as being a trustworthy friend of industrial interests, while only 9 per cent of the DNVP's Reichstag delegation were representatives of industry.[2] At the opposite pole, the organized working class outside parliament was led by the General Federation of German Trade Unions (ADGB), which maintained close relations with the Social Democrats. In Parliament, the Christian trade unions held a much more important position. Although by and large they were affiliated to the Catholic Centre Party, they could, by means of their inter-party links, stimulate a broadly based opposition to food tariffs – even in the Nationalist camp – and could exert considerable pressure on all questions of working hours and social security.

Perhaps the strongest of these coalitions in and out of the *Reichstag* was that backed by agrarian interests. Their constant demand was that the food tariffs, which had been cut in 1914, should be restored on a scale which came near to the Bülow tariffs of 1902. In 1919 the Versailles Treaty had barred the way for revival of protectionist policies for five years. The demand for wholesale tariff legislation was therefore put forward with ever-increasing intensity during 1924 and led to a regrouping within the Nationalist Party. It was the DNVP especially which made the

---

[1] This applies especially to Stresemann's attitude towards a militant nationalist organization such as the *Stahlhelm*. Cf. Volker R. Berghahn, *Der Stahlhelm. Bund der Frontsoldaten* (Beiträge zur Geschichte des Parl. u.d. pol. Parteien Bd. 33, Düsseldorf, 1966), pp. 75-91

[2] Cf. Stürmer, *Koalition und Opposition*, p. 286

interests of the great landowners of the Eastern provinces its own. No less than half the party's deputies were members of the *Reichslandbund*, the most powerful agrarian pressure group and successor of the radical *Bund der Landwirte*.[1] More than one-third were farmers or officers of agrarian organizations. Because no other group would stand up for its demands with equal vigour and equal conviction that what was good for it was good for the nation, the great landowners of the East could to a large extent determine the course the Nationalists took in the *Reichstag*. But their never-ending demand that the party should join the government at any cost was also among the main causes of the deep rift between pragmatism and dogmatism which first split the DNVP over the Dawes issue and finally led, step by step, to the self-destruction of the party after 1928. It was a split between a somewhat old-fashioned conservative *Gouvernementalismus*, on the one hand, and a rigid 'National Opposition' on the other.

The heavy pressure of agrarian demands also endangered any long-term co-operation with the industrial elements in the DVP. Being the foremost spokesman of German light industry, Stresemann's party did everything to secure maximum exports. This of course conflicted with the farmers' call for protection from foreign imports, especially from low-price agrarian countries such as Spain and Poland. The bargaining over trade treaties with these countries occasionally developed into a duel between German industry and German farmers (as in 1925 and 1927). Whenever this conflict arose, it was bound to weaken the position of the Nationalists *vis-à-vis* their parliamentary allies, since the other parties were exposed to agrarian pressure to a much lesser degree and, unlike the DNVP, were not dependent on the *Reichslandbund's* electoral machine and financial subsidies. Moreover, the moderate parties could always threaten to go with the socialists through thick and thin, whereas the Nationalists, of course, could not.[2]

[1] Ibid., p. 285

[2] It should be remembered that in 1926, shortly after the settlement of the *Eisenkartell*, even some of the leaders of the powerful *Reichsverband der Deutschen Industrie* openly came out in favour of a coalition with the Social Democrats.

Under these circumstances, there can hardly be a convincing answer to the question as to whether economic growth and political tranquillity, had it lasted for a longer period of time, would finally have resulted in a fully fledged consolidation of the Weimar *Parteienstaat*. Certainly, what might be called the governmental structure needed reform, either by a regrouping of the parties, as was tried several times, or by an agonizing redefinition of governmental and parliamentary powers. No doubt a genuine change in the distribution of power could only have resulted from close co-operation between the government and the *Reichstag*. But apart from various far-reaching projects for *Reichsreform*[1] and apart from almost innumerable proposals from outside the *Reichstag*, there were in fact very few serious attempts to redefine the relationship between Parliament and the cabinet.

Since some of the plans for reform coming from within the executive to a large extent reflected the characteristic weaknesses of parliamentary government in the Weimar period, it is instructive to examine four reform projects which were significant enough to leave at least some traces in the *Reichskanzlei* files and especially in the cabinet minutes. Two of these plans were in fact not far from a silent *coup d'état*. The circumstances in which they were formulated were dissimilar, though all four projects would have involved far-reaching constitutional changes. The first two cases occurred in 1924, the other two in 1926. This is significant in so far as they coincided with the existence of weak minority governments, which were inclined to behave like drowning men clutching at straws.

When Marx's first cabinet took office in December 1923, its political authority was based on the recently passed Enabling Law and the emergency powers in the hands of General von Seeckt, the chief of the *Reichswehr* and probably the most powerful figure on the domestic scene. In January 1924 a sharp conflict arose between the cabinet and its *Reichstag* majority when the parties

[1] Cf. Gerhard Schulz, *Zwischen Demokratie und Diktatur. Verfassungspolitik und Reichsreform in der Weimarer Republik, Teil I, 1919-1930* (Berlin, 1963)

declined to prolong the Enabling Act unless the government accepted several amendments to the third emergency decree on taxes (*Steuernotverordnung*), a stern austerity measure. The cabinet felt that the new emergency decree, which was based on Article 48 of the Weimar Constitution and which imposed heavy taxes and other deflationary measures, should at all costs be maintained. The ministers therefore soon came to consider a 'fight with the *Reichstag*' inevitable.[1] If the parliamentary parties could not be prevented from tabling motions to modify the decree or from refusing a prompt renewal of the Enabling Act, the *Reichstag*, it was thought, ought to be dissolved at once.

This meant in practice that the cabinet confronted the major parties with the unpleasant choice of either excluding themselves from control of events or of being excluded as a direct result of the dissolution. It was Count Kanitz, Minister for Food and Agriculture – called the 'Red Count' by his bewildered friends – who at this point bluntly summarized the cabinet's view: 'It is impossible to work with the *Reichstag*. This applies to the present as well as to a newly elected *Reichstag* which, presumably, will be even less constructive than the existing one. We should get used to the idea of carrying on without the *Reichstag*.'

As its immediate aim the cabinet wanted to leave the Enabling Act unchanged so that the government was guaranteed freedom from parliamentary interference. The condition was, however, that the *Reichswehr* maintained the 'state of siege' and worked hand-in-glove with civilian authority. In this the calculation failed. A few days later, the plans for bypassing the *Reichstag*, if they had ever been taken seriously, had to be dropped altogether. In the middle of February 1924, General von Seeckt, mainly in order to prevent a further loss of coherence and of military effectiveness among the troops and contrary to the wishes of almost all right-wing politicians and the bulk of the generals, announced that he was going to hand back his emergency powers to the President of the Republic. He intended, as he put it, 'to prevent the state of emergency being allowed to crumble (*versacken zu*

[1] Cabinet minutes February 6, 1924, quoted in Stürmer, *Koalition und Opposition*, pp. 35-6; Schulz, *Zwischen Demokratie und Diktatur*, pp. 453-4

lassen) and to withdraw the *Reichswehr* from politics as soon as possible'.[1] He had realized that there existed more subtle ways of wielding political power and, as he pointed out to Count Westarp, he was convinced that under the present circumstances 'nothing could be done anyway'.[2]

In consequence, the cabinet, facing a parliamentary majority which refused to tolerate its further existence, decided to dissolve the *Reichstag* at once. Some cabinet ministers hoped that elections for a new *Reichstag* could be put off for some time. This proved legally impossible. For a while, the dissolution of Parliament served the same aims as the extension of the Enabling Act, which the *Reichstag* had declined. But in the long run, the ministers had to anticipate the emergence of a *Reichstag* with a new mandate.

The second case which seems worthy of discussion occurred at the end of 1924 when, as a result of the failure of all attempts to create a right-wing coalition after the passage of the Dawes Plan, another election had to be called (December 7, 1924). Once again the distribution of the seats did not change sufficiently for a clear-cut right- or left-wing majority to be formed. By the end of 1924 all negotiations between the Nationalists and the Centre Party had again reached a deadlock. While the commander-in-chief of the Bavarian *Reichswehr* division toyed with the idea of a military dictatorship, General von Seeckt conferred with Friedrich

---

[1] To General von Tschischwitz (February 21, 1924) who had urged his commander-in-chief to uphold the state of siege in order to facilitate a military regime, quoted in Stürmer, *Koalition und Opposition*, p. 36

[2] Quoted in Stürmer, *Koalition und Opposition*, p. 36. Francis L. Carsten, in *Reichswehr und Politik 1918-1933* (Cologne, 1964), p. 217, has argued that Seeckt did this mainly in order to pave the way for his prospective candidacy in the presidential elections of 1925. But this, it seems, is a much too subtle explanation. Seeckt's reasons were solidly military, accentuated perhaps by the consideration that it would not particularly please the American bankers, who stood behind the Dawes proposals, if the country were under military rule. The argument of Hans Meier-Welcker in his recent biography of Seeckt, pp. 434-6, that the general remained dependent on the cabinet throughout the period of virtual military dictatorship misses the point. E. Meier-Welcker, *Seeckt* (Frankfurt, 1967).

Ebert, the Social Democratic President of the Republic. Ebert confessed to the general that he saw no way out. If there was to be neither a parliamentary cabinet nor a 'government of personalities', he [Ebert] had 'to decide on something new'.[1] The evidence of this talk, of which no word ever reached the press, helps to confirm the fact that it was with Ebert's consent that, at the end of 1924, a small circle of ministers met to discuss new and unconventional ways of overcoming the current crisis.[2] The meeting was highly confidential, and the Democratic Party Ministers were not even invited. Moreover, the protocol was never filed with the other cabinet minutes. Such precautionary measures were not taken without justification. For it soon became clear that the politicians present sought a solution which was not strictly on parliamentary lines; the ministers intended to form a new cabinet consisting mainly of experts and civil servants – a possibility which had been under discussion for some time.

The project rested on the idea that the constitution did not expressly comment on the role the parties were to play in forming and supporting the government. Constitutional theory therefore permitted the formation of a cabinet of personalities – or whatever label might be attached to such a construction – provided it managed to win a *Reichstag* majority. Accordingly, the ministers present agreed that the Democratic Party's cabinet members, whose resignation was thought inevitable, should be replaced by 'personalities close to the German National People's Party' – as Stresemann put it. It also turned out that the Centre Party, which

---

[1] Quoted in Meier-Welcker, *Seeckt*, pp. 457-8; it is interesting to note that Ebert not only allowed himself to be influenced in favour of proposals which were, strictly speaking, not in tune with constitutional practice, but even went so far as to take the initiative in putting them forward. The evidence on Ebert's role in the crisis of 1924-5 renders inconclusive some of the arguments which Peter Haungs has recently presented in a study on presidential influence in Weimar Germany: *Reichspräsident und parlamentarische Kabinettsregierung. Eine Studie zum Regierungssystem der Weimarer Republik in den Jahren 1924 bis 1929* (Opladen, 1968), p. 277.

[2] The Protocol of the meeting on December 19, 1924, has been published in Otto Gessler, *Reichswehrpolitik in der Weimarer Zeit*, ed. K. Sendtner (Stuttgart, 1958), annex 21; cf. Stürmer, *Koalition und Opposition*, pp. 81-3

in public had time and again denied any such intention, was in fact willing to join such a cabinet, provided a formula could be found which was constitutionally plausible and acceptable to the party as a whole. A cabinet under the *Fachminister*[1] flag, it seemed, could bridge the gap between the Centre and the right-wing parties, while otherwise there was no chance of ever winning a majority. Thus the old idea of competent and independent ministers with a civil service career or an industrial background and without explicit party affiliation celebrated a revival.[2] It has even been maintained that of all the Weimar governments, Luther's 'expert' cabinet was the one most in tune with constitutional theory[3] – a view which sheds an interesting light on the latter.

The myth of the *Fachminister* dated back to Imperial days and was rooted in the traditional view of the state, according to which the government was 'above the parties' (or, better perhaps, as one historian remarked, 'above the parties, but to the right'). Under the Weimar Constitution, however, the function of expert ministers must be seen in a different light. Whereas the old-style Imperial or state secretary – as long as he was conservative by birth or conviction – was not, as a rule, bound by party loyalty and not subject to a vote of no-confidence, the expert minister serving under the auspices of a parliamentary government was in fact an anachronism. Yet expertise was apparently some kind of authoritarian fetish which most of the *Reichstag* parties were only too willing to worship. The *Fachminister* therefore was usually called upon whenever it became necessary to fill the gap between constitutional theory and political expediency. In the case under discussion the conventional practice was now altered in so far as the *Fachminister* idea was to serve as a fig-leaf for a cabinet which was actually dependent on Nationalist support.

This compromise had hardly been worked out when the

---

[1] 'Expert Minister', implying a contrast with 'party' ministers. The *Fachminister* also fitted into the traditional German concept of government.

[2] For the ideological and social background see John C. G. Röhl, 'Higher Civil Servants in Germany, 1890-1900', *Journal of Contemporary History*, Vol. 2, November 3, 1967, pp. 101-21

[3] Haungs, *Reichspräsident und parlamentarische Kabinettsregierung*, p. 278

ministers who wanted some kind of *Reichsreform* decided that it was still unsatisfactory. The new government of 'experts' was therefore merely to have a transitory character and was to pave the way for more comprehensive constitutional changes. In view of this ultimate goal, the *Reichswehrminister*, Gessler, demanded 'a strong *Staatsautorität*, a strong central executive equipped with powers which will make such crises and the helplessness we witness today impossible'. One would have to strengthen either the rights of the *Reich President* or the position of the cabinet in the *Reichstag*, once the government was in office. 'It would have to be the task of the new personalities and the new cabinet to enact, with strong determination, a constitutional reform on this point.' Gessler met with opposition only when he argued that a cabinet independent of the *Reichstag* would be in a better position to solve this problem than a parliamentary one. On the other hand, everybody agreed that time was running out. The almost permanent crisis in domestic politics endangered the consolidation of the Republic as a whole. Stresemann added: 'There are wide circles in the population which follow this muddle and these never-ending government crises with glee and comfort because it helps them to explain to their supporters the bankruptcy of parliamentary government. In this fashion the Nationalists have always gained new followers, and if there is no improvement, they will hold 200 seats in the next *Reichstag* mainly because the voter is getting sick and tired of ever-lasting crisis-mongering and difficulties in forming the cabinet. Similarly, people are gaining ground . . . who want to achieve reform by illegal means.'[1]

It is perhaps important to note that Stresemann's statement, while agreeing in principle with the outlines of the reform project, explicitly stressed the psychological importance of reform and its repercussions on the middle-class vote.

The short-term result of this discussion was the formation of the first Luther cabinet early in 1925, formally based on the *Fachminister* ideology, but in fact being the first conventional coalition cabinet of the Right. The long-term institutional reform never materialized. The immediate difficulties facing the Luther cabinet

[1] See above, footnote on 2 p. 71

left no time for projects which needed very thorough preparation. In addition it would have multiplied the difficulties facing the Luther government to push through legislative measures which were designed to cut the *Reichstag's* powers. Moreover, the rightwing Reich government would have found it almost impossible to overcome opposition from the solidly left-wing Prussian cabinet.

The third attempt at redefining the relationship between cabinet and parliament adopted a functional approach. It began with Luther's resolution, after he had taken office as Chancellor, to reinforce the cabinet's powers. He wanted to establish firm control over the majority parties through a steering committee of party leaders. Although by and large he failed, owing to the unwillingness of the major parties to disclaim their highly prized sovereignty by making themselves dependent on the cabinet, the struggle for power continued in 1926 with the revival of the *Interfraktioneller Ausschuss*. This was an inter-party committee, composed of the government parties, which was to be responsible for a constructive co-ordination of policy. The difficulty was that this committee, although it institutionalized mediation between the government and the majority, ultimately failed to bridge the gulf between the two.

The committee's duties were defined by a formal agreement between the Chancellor and the party leaders. It was to hold together the coalition, to facilitate close co-operation in the *Reichstag's* committees and, finally, to secure support for the cabinet's policy. Firm control was to be exercised by the cabinet, especially over private members' bills involving financial measures. In theory the committee was to be guided by the *Reichskanzlei*, the Chancellor's secretariat. The cabinet pledged that it would make 'every effort to negotiate matters of importance with the parties beforehand', but it neither stated what these matters were nor what should happen if the parties found no common ground. Finally, the parties bound themselves not to go ahead with interpellations and bills without having previously consulted the cabinet.[1]

It is not quite clear from the evidence available to what extent

[1] Cf. Stürmer, *Koalition und Opposition*, pp. 200-2, 292-3

this agreement ever really worked. One fact, however, is beyond dispute, namely that both sides interpreted the various clauses of the document in a sense most favourable to them but detrimental to the alliance. Luther thought it gave him a free hand in parliamentary politics, while the government parties firmly believed that the Chancellor was bound to do exactly what they had in mind. This discrepancy contributed heavily to the sudden rebellion in the *Reichstag* which broke out in May 1926 and which ended with the fall of Luther. Instead of guaranteeing stability the inter-party committee merely accentuated the rivalry already existing between the government and the various parties on which it was dependent. After having fallen into well-deserved oblivion for almost a year, the committee took up its functions again in the spring of 1927, when a second right-wing cabinet had assumed office and the inter-party committee suddenly developed into a 'parallel cabinet' – to quote the secretary of state in the *Reichskanzlei*, Dr Pünder.[1] The new cabinet only regained its supremacy when the majority parties found it increasingly difficult to arrive at a common policy in the committee, and had to ask the cabinet for a decision. This was the end of the autonomous existence of the committee. When in spring 1928 the fourth Marx cabinet was about to collapse, the inter-party committee, instead of cementing it together, could do nothing but report on what had happened.

The final case of attempted administrative reform is interesting only in so far as it foreshadowed constitutional – or rather unconstitutional – practice after March 1930. At the end of 1926 a conflict over the statutory limitation of hours of work and the issue of political control over the *Reichswehr* had split the Social Democrats and swept away the majority government which had for six months worked smoothly with what was described at the time as a 'silent grand coalition'.[2] *Reichspräsident* von Hindenburg,

---

[1] In a letter to Stresemann, February 24, 1927, quoted in Stürmer, op. cit., p. 201

[2] The 'grand coalition' was one which included DVP and Social Democrats. The significance of the 'silent' grand coalition was that it formally excluded the Social Democrats but could rely on their tacit support

elected in 1925 in an upsurge of nationalist feeling, did all he could to create a solidly right-wing cabinet. To this end he even went so far as to threaten the continuous use of Article 48 as the source of authority for an openly anti-parliamentary government. During the crisis a memorandum was drafted by Hindenburg's versatile Secretary of State, Otto Meissner, which reflected the President's intentions and which envisaged only three alternatives as being acceptable. The first and most attractive course was a firm majority from the Centre to the Nationalists. The second would be a minority cabinet of the Right, tolerated by the moderate parties but, because of this, obviously dependent on 'the Centre's grace'. The third possibility was a 'government of personalities', as it was called in imitation of Luther's evasive formula. This one, however, was not to be an ordinary parliamentary cabinet in disguise, but was to depend exclusively on the President's authority. It seemed viable only if the President 'backs this cabinet for the dissolution of the Reichstag and any special measures which may then become necessary'.[1] Meissner's memorandum was far from being isolated from political events. It coincided with a similar project which owed its existence to Colonel von Schleicher, the enigmatic political expert of the *Reichswehr*, and which was written in the style of a general staff memorandum, taking into account all possible moves by the enemy, i.e. the left-wing parties.[2] The aim was to bring the Nationalists into the government by constitutional means if possible, but, if not, by a gradual ousting of the *Reichstag*. Should parliamentary government produce nothing better than left-wing majorities, Germany was to be governed against her Parliament.

When the outlines of this policy were announced in a cabinet meeting it put the Centre Party into a dilemma. The party chose what it regarded as the lesser evil. The threat of going ahead with an extensive use of Article 48 remained in the background, but did in fact contribute considerably to the gradual shift to the right

[1] Stürmer, op. cit., pp. 180-1
[2] Josef Becker, 'Zur Politik der Wehrmachtabteilung in der Regierungskrise 1926/27' (Dokumentation), *Vierteljahrshefte für Zeitgeschichte*, 14 (1966), pp. 69-78

which took place in the Catholic Party.[1] On these lines, and not without a long period of intrigue and manœuvring which helped to save the Centre from a split, a new cabinet of the Right based on a comparatively solid majority took office in January 1927. Article 48, while not being actually used, had proved to be an extremely helpful instrument in forcing the views of the President's entourage on to the party politicians.

To conclude these comments on the state of parliamentary government in Weimar Germany one could say that in the period of economic resurgence after 1924 the middle-of-the-road parties, the Social Democrats and even the Nationalists were on the whole sufficiently flexible to be able to find some common interests as far as parliamentary politics were concerned. But by and large, *all* coalitions remained what they had been before: compromises on a very limited scale between vested interests, and alliances over specific issues. These had little permanence in view of the deep ideological and socio-economic rifts which class conflict, accentuated by the reparations question and the distribution of its financial burdens, produced in the *Reichstag*. Any continuity of government policy in economic, fiscal and foreign affairs was permanently in jeopardy because of the fluctuating state of coalition and opposition. The parties showed enough flexibility to allow marginal shifts. But, if parliamentary government was to have a future, a reappraisal of values and practices and a thorough reform had long become overdue. It could have been effected either by a regrouping of the major political parties or by alterations in the distribution of power between president, government, and *Reichstag*. Before this reform could take shape, however, the ill-fated Weimar Republic broke down under the impact of the Great Depression, which presented a new and decisive political advantage to those who allied themselves against parliamentary government in Germany.

[1] Becker, 'Joseph Wirth und die Krise des Zentrums während des IV. Kabinetts Marx (1927-28)', *Zeitschrift für die Geschichte des Oberrheins*, 109 (1961)

77

CHAPTER 5

ARTICLE 48 OF THE WEIMAR CONSTITUTION, ITS HISTORICAL AND POLITICAL IMPLICATIONS

HANS BOLDT

Article 48 of the Weimar Constitution, which referred to the emergency powers available to the President of the Republic, recently became the subject of sharp debate in the German Federal Republic, when the Bonn Government amended the constitution by introducing extensive emergency legislation. The opponents of this legislation, who feared that the laws might be abused by the authorities, frequently referred to Article 48 and its use during the critical years 1930-3. They claimed that the employment of Article 48 had brought about the collapse of Germany's democracy. The supporters of the emergency laws, on the other hand, argued that this article and its application had been very useful as a last resort and had nearly led to success.[1] One might well ask what sort of success they had in mind. However, it is interesting in this connection that some experts claimed Article 48 to be a genuinely democratic device because it facilitated a far-reaching intervention by the executive similar to what was conceived to be English martial law.[2]

There were, however, fundamental differences between what

[1] On this controversy see Adolf Arndt and Michael Freund *Notstandsgesetz –aber wie?* (Cologne, 1962), and Jürgen Seifert, *Gefahr im Verzug* (Frankfurt am Main, 1963). For the Weimar Republic consult Karl Dietrich Bracher, *Die Auflösung der Weimarer Republik* (Villingen, 1955; third ed. 1960)

[2] See Professor Hesse in *Die öffentliche Verwaltung* (Stuttgart, 1955) p. 741f

79

was sometimes loosely referred to as 'martial law' in Britain and the powers given to the German Government under Article 48 of the Weimar Constitution. At the root of these differences lies the contrast between the character of English Common Law on the one hand and the continental legal system – derived from Roman civil law – on the other. Article 48 was firmly in the continental tradition.

(i)

Before 1914 martial law in England was a matter for academic discussion rather than practical application. Victorian historians of the British legal system – such as Dicey and Stephen – took a considerable interest in the differences between the British conception of martial law, as it was revealed in the practice of earlier centuries, and the so-called 'state of siege' which existed on the continent. Dicey and Stephen[1] both came to the rather comforting conclusion that martial law could only be invoked in England when there existed a state of war – i.e. in the case of invasion or insurrection. In this case, any person was authorized to repel force by force and servants of the Crown were even obliged to do so. Above all it was the duty of the armed forces to take action against the enemy or the rebels after martial law had been proclaimed. They were authorized to do whatever was necessary to suppress insurrection. But their action had to be justified by reasonable necessity; that is, they had to try not only to end the insurrection as quickly as possible but also to end it with a minimum of disturbance to the people. There was to be no excessive use of force in re-establishing public order. For this purpose military authorities were allowed to do everything except establish military tribunals (courts-martial) and try rebels. This had been proclaimed illegal since the famous Petition of

[1] Sir James F. Stephen, *A History of the Criminal Law of England*, 3 vols (London, 1883), I, pp. 207-16. A. V. Dicey, *Lectures Introductory to the Study of the Law of the Constitution* (second ed., London, 1886), p. 296f. See also Charles M. Clode, *The Administraton of Justice under Military and Martial Law* (London, 1872)

Right of 1627.[1] There could always be a judicial examination of measures taken by the authorities. It was not soldiers who pronounced the verdicts, but judges. They could also pass judgment on the actions of the military.

Obviously this brought a good deal of uncertainty into the policies of those who were obliged to defend the country in periods of martial law. Under these circumstances it was difficult for an official to decide what was to be done. Nobody could guarantee that his measures were both reasonable and necessary. It was possible that he could be condemned by the courts because he had failed to act reasonably. Alternatively, he might be made responsible by his superiors because he had failed to do everything that was necessary. To paraphrase Dicey: a soldier had the awkward choice between being shot if he disobeyed an order of his superior and being hanged by a judge if he obeyed it.[2] To avoid this dilemma Parliament in most cases passed an indemnity act for actions which seemed acceptable to it. Parliament 'legalized illegality', as Dicey said.[3] But even in this case the judges retained their right of reviewing individual cases.

(ii)

This traditional English method of meeting emergencies was very different from the continental one. The so-called state of siege was first developed in the mother-country of continental legalism, namely France, and was subsequently adopted by the Germans, with Prussia in the lead.[4] The state of siege was also directed against war (invasion) and insurrection. To pinpoint the difference between the state of siege and British practice it is

[1] See also Habeas Corpus Act (1679) and the Bill of Rights (1689)
[2] Dicey, op. cit., p. 311   [3] Dicey, pp. cit., p. 46
[4] See Carl Schmitt, *Die Diktatur* (second ed., Berlin, 1928), and Hans Boldt, *Rechtsstaat und Ausnahmezustand* (Berlin, 1967). Especially for the French state of siege, see Paul Romain, *L' État de Siège Politique* (Albi, 1918). A good survey of the development of martial law, state of siege and modern emergency legislation can be found in Clinton Rossiter, *Constitutional Dictatorship* (Princeton, 1948), and in Ernst Fraenkel (ed.), *Der Staatsnotstand* (Berlin, 1965)

important to stress two points. Firstly, on the continent constitutionalism is a matter of a written constitution and the law is a system of statutes authorized by Parliament, which regulate life and public order in a general way. The continental system aims at an *a priori* regulation of all conceivable contingencies including problems which by their very nature are irregular, such as a state of national emergency. The second point is that the continent, unlike England, had developed strongly established governmental authority created in an absolutist tradition which had triumphed over the medieval corporations and medieval common law. For the continentals it had therefore been very difficult to limit the prerogatives of the monarchs at the end of the eighteenth century and the beginning of the nineteenth. The aim of written constitutions was to reserve a sphere of liberties for individual citizens with which the monarchical state was not allowed to interfere unless it had received *a priori* legal authority to do so. In the same fashion the separation of powers was introduced to protect these liberties. Consequently, continental constitutionalism was a matter of formal competences and of a division of spheres of influence. Above all it involved a distinct delimitation of the field of action of the State as against that of private persons. When dealing with a case of emergency, therefore, it became difficult for the continental law-maker to grant wider, generally valid and theoretically justifiable powers to the executive and at the same time to maintain any constitutional limitations on state action at all.

The legal solution found for this problem was typical of the nineteenth century, as can be seen from the examples of France and Prussia.[1] Put into a nutshell the general line was as follows: taking the Roman dictatorship as a precedent (the *bellum et seditio*), it was stipulated that a state of siege could be proclaimed in cases of war or insurrection if 'public security' (*securité publique, öffentliche Sicherheit und Ordnung*) was in danger. This declaration already had a different legal meaning from the British

[1] 'Loi sur l'état de siège', August 9, 1849, revised April 3, 1878. 'Gesetz über den Belagerungszustand', June 4, 1851. (Texts in Hans Boldt, op. cit., note 8)

concept of martial law, the proclamation of which did not possess a constitutional validity. The intervention of military forces was justified exclusively on the grounds of an actual condition of emergency.

The continental state of siege, on the other hand, had to be declared explicitly, and nothing could be done without such a declaration. But the other side of the coin was the fact that the army could interfere whenever such a declaration was made, however unjustified it might be – even if there was no actual danger to the public safety. Moreover, the state of siege only involved military authorities. They took over the rights and powers of the civil authorities – in Prussia even those of the cabinet. The intervention of the army implied the suspension of a number of basic individual rights, such as the inviolability of residence, *habeas corpus*, freedom of assembly and of the press. The military authorities were also able to establish military tribunals; in Prussia they could even court-martial rebels and condemn them to death in the style of ancient *Standgerichte* (courts-martial with the power of summary process, i.e. sentence and execution *stante pede*).

It was, of course, very difficult to control these powers. In France such control was exercised by Parliament, which declared the beginning and the end of a state of siege. Thus Parliament had immediate control over the emergency powers. Moreover the cabinet, and especially the Minister of War, who supervised the army, was responsible to it. This parliamentary authority did not exist in Prussia or, later on, in the German Reich. Here it was the Kaiser who proclaimed the state of siege and the military were responsible only to him. The Prussian Minister of War had no supervisory powers and consequently the head of the cabinet, the Reich Chancellor, could not be responsible to Parliament for actions over which he himself had no control. Neither in France nor in Germany was there a judicial control of the declaration of a state of siege, for laws and so-called 'acts of government' could not be challenged in the courts. Therefore the state of siege might be declared without an insurrection, or any actual danger to public security. Judges could merely consider the formal authority for the action of the armed forces, i.e. whether the declaration of a state of siege was formally valid. It was irrelevant whether the measures taken were considered necessary and reasonable.

Here we come to the most important difference between the English and the continental legal tradition in this matter. According to the latter the acts of authorities were not treated in the same way as were the acts of a private person. A line was drawn between the State and society. What mattered was not the purpose of the action but its formal legality and whether it fell within a formally described sphere of competence. The emergency regulations were seen exclusively from the point of view of the State. In cases of emergency, the constitutionally limited State tended to re-assume its pre-constitutional position. This view is demonstrated also by the military direction of a state of siege designed to uphold public order and security, i.e. police order and security. Emergency action in Anglo-Saxon countries, on the other hand, was bound by the idea that the functions of the courts had merely been suspended, a concept advanced by Justice Davis of the Supreme Court of the United States in 1863: the so-called 'open-court-theory'.[1]

To this characteristic difference one should add that in the so-called *bürgerlicher Rechtsstaat* in the nineteenth century public order and security simply meant a condition in which the police protected the interests of the bourgeoisie, and preserved the characteristics of the middle-class State. A state of siege was to be proclaimed, *wenn der Aufruhr der Pöbelmassen Kirche und Staat zu vernichten droht, indem er in entfesselter Leidenschaft vererbte Sitten und Unantastbarkeit des Eigentums mißachtet*[2] (if an uprising of the mob threatens to destroy Church and State by

---

[1] 'ex parte Milligan' (4 Wall 2 1866), see E. Fraenkel, op. cit., p. 199

[2] Hermann Bischof, *Das Nothrecht der Staatsgewalt* (Giessen, 1860), p. 113. See also Lorenz von Stein, *Geschichte der sozialen Bewegung in Frankreich von 1789 bis auf unsere Tage, 1849/50* (Darmstadt, 1959), III, p. 62. (Stein defines (public) 'order' as the subordination of the workers to the regime of the capitalists.)

disregarding, in its fury, established mores and the inviolability of property). This was typical of the nineteenth century; emergency powers to protect both morality and private property.

(iii)

There is another factor of historical importance for an understanding of Article 48: namely that since the First World War, during a period of repeated economic crises, the problem of a state of emergency has come to assume rather a different dimension, in which private property is no longer regarded as inviolable. Between 1914 and 1918 it had been a question of organizing the war economy. After 1918 this war economy had to be re-adjusted to peace-time conditions. The government had to cope with an economic crisis and with the political radicalism of the unemployed. It is understandable that the old-styled state of siege was not really equipped to deal with such problems. The task was no longer to bring the revolutionary heroes of 1830 and 1848 down from their barricades and to put soldiers into action according to the maxim, *Gegen Demokraten helfen nur Soldaten* (Soldiers are the only cure for democrats). The task was much more to re-establish normal economic and financial conditions through official measures, laws or decrees. This was above all a matter of legislation – of legislative, not of executive or administrative dictatorship.[1] The trouble was that for various reasons Parliament could not fulfil this role (because it was incapable of taking rapid, unpopular decisions), and therefore it passed so-called enabling acts which led to a dictatorship of the cabinet more or less under parliamentary control. This happened not only in France and Germany but also in Great Britain and in other countries. And this situation is a proper starting point for a discussion of Article 48.

[1] This is the basic distinction in the modern theory of emergency powers. See Rossiter (note 7), and Frederick M. Watkins, 'The problem of Constitutional Dictatorship', *Public Policy*, ed. Carl J. Friedrich and Edward S. Mason, Vol. 1, (Cambridge, Mass., 1940), pp. 324f

(iv)

Article 48 itself read as follows:

'If a *Land*[1] does not fulfil the obligations laid upon it by the Reich Constitution or by the Reich laws the Reich President can compel it to do so with the help of armed force.

'If public security and order in the German Reich are seriously disrupted or threatened the President can take the necessary steps to restore public security and order, when necessary with the aid of armed force. For this purpose he may temporarily abrogate all or part of the fundamental rights set out in Articles 114, 115, 117, 118, 123, 124, and 153 of the Constitution.

'The Reich President must immediately inform the *Reichstag* of all measures taken on the authority of sections 1 and 2 of this article. The measures are to be abrogated at the request of the *Reichstag*.

'If there is danger in delay a *Land* government may, within its own territory, take exceptional measures of the kind set out in section 2. The measures are to be abrogated on the request of the Reich President or the *Reichstag*.

'A Reich Law will provide a more detailed definition of this article.'

This part of the Weimar Constitution was based on the experience of the revolutionary troubles of 1918 and 1919 and of the emergencies of the First World War as well as on the traditions of the Prusso-German state of siege. The terms of this article which are important in this context are contained in sections 2 and 3. Whereas section 1 covered the case of the failure of one of the *Länder* to fulfil its obligations – an important stipulation in a federal system – section 4 provided that a Land could, if danger was imminent, apply the emergency powers of the Reich prophylactically and on its own initiative. The details of these powers were specified in section 2.[2]

[1] Member-state of the German Reich.

[2] For Article 48 and its legal interpretation consult the above-mentioned books by Clinton Rossiter and Carl Schmitt, and Gerhard Anschütz, *Die*

ARTICLE 48 OF THE WEIMAR CONSTITUTION

This section rehearsed the conceptions underlying the pre-1918 state of siege. First among these was again the *Gefahr für die öffentliche Sicherheit und Ordnung*. The difference was, however, that the application of emergency powers was no longer restricted to cases of war or insurrection. Nevertheless the government could still use force and was allowed to suspend the same basic rights as in the old state of siege, these now including the right to private property.[1] This did not mean that Article 48 was designed specifically to cope with an economic crisis. Rather the opposite is true; there was a tendency in the National Assembly to model this article on the old state of siege.[2] It might conceivably have been more restricted in scope if the Reich Law, referred to in section 5 had been ratified at the same time. Nor was the fact that the Reich President now had the power to pronounce the *Ausnahmezustand* (State of Emergency) an innovation.

In this respect the Weimar Constitution was rather a curious constitution. It contained parliamentary elements, stipulating, for example, that the government required the confidence of the *Reichstag* (Art. 54). But the constitution makers shied away from strengthening Parliament more than necessary. This is why a counter-weight was created in the form of the Reich President. He nominated and dismissed the cabinet (Art. 53). He was empowered to dissolve the *Reichstag* (Art. 25), and finally he could exercise the emergency powers continued in Article 48. The President had thus more or less taken over the position of the Emperor and was considered to be an *Ersatzkaiser* (Substitute emperor).[3]

Verfassung des Deutschen Reiches (commentaries on the Weimar Constitution), fourteenth ed. (Berlin, 1933); Richard Grau, *Die Diktaturgewalt des Reichspräsidenten* (Berlin, 1922) and *Handbuch des Deutschen Stattsrechts*, ed. G. Anschütz and R. Thoma, Vol. 2 (Tübingen, 1932), p. 274f. The best survey of the political problems involved is Gerhard Schulz, 'Artikel 48 in politischer und historischer Sicht', E. Fraenkel, op. cit., p. 39f
[1] For military tribunals see Article 105 of the Constitution.
[2] Eduard Heilfron (ed.), *Die Deutsche Nationalversammlung im Jahre 1919*, Vol. 5 (Berlin, 1919), pp. 3236-64 (fourteenth meeting, July 5, 1919)
[3] Theodor Eschenburg, *Die improvisierte Demokratie der Weimarer Republik* (Laupheim, 1954), p. 42

To be sure, there were a number of decisive differences between the two. The President was elected by popular vote for a seven-year term (Arts. 41, 43). His decisions required the counter-signature of the responsible minister, even when these decisions were made on the basis of Article 48 and referred to the army (Art. 52). Another difference was that the army was now under the control of the *Reichswehrminister*, who was normally a civilian. Thus the general assumption in the National Assembly of Weimar was that it was not dangerous to entrust a democratic president with emergency powers because he would use them democratically. Indeed, it seemed better to give him powers which were too wide rather than too narrow. It was only Dr Oskar Cohn, representing the Independent Social Democrats, who warned against giving too much authority to the President.[1] He argued that one day a man less democratic than the Social Democrat Friedrich Ebert might wield the powers granted by Article 48. What, he continued, would happen if a puppet of the Hohenzollerns, a general perhaps, became the first representative of the Reich? This was indeed prophetic, although there was a precedent for it in the French Third Republic, when MacMahon, who had been a general under Emperor Napoleon III, became President in 1877 and began to toy with the idea of using the state of siege against the Republic. But in 1919 the Germans were not so far-sighted. On the contrary, the *Reichstag* never thought of securing for itself the right to proclaim the state of siege, a right on which the French Assembly had always insisted. The German parliamentarians were satisfied with the stipulation in section 3 which ordered the President to inform the *Reichstag* of his decisions and which empowered the *Reichstag* to request the abrogation of the measures he had taken. In practice this meant that all the *Reichstag* could do was to intervene indirectly and only after the event. What is even more curious, however, is that Article 48, unlike the pre-war emergency provisions, did not contain any rules about the form the declaration of the state of siege should take. Parliament not only abdicated responsibility for proclaiming the *Ausnahmezustand* but even

[1] Heilfron, op. cit., p. 3242

refrained from regulating the manner in which emergency powers were set in motion. The President could use the powers of Article 48 whenever he and the cabinet considered public security and order to be in danger. No prior announcement was needed. Not even the courts could consider whether the use of these powers was actually justified. The whole arrangement was typical of continental rather than Anglo-Saxon practice. Nor did the application of Article 48 in the early post-war years differ from the manner in which the state of siege had been used before the Republican Constitution had been established.

Between 1919 and 1924 Germany was shaken by a number of separatist movements and right-wing and left-wing *Putsches*, starting with the Spartacist Rebellion of 1919 and ending with the Hitler-*Putsch* of 1923. Moreover, there were numerous acts of political terror. The assassinations of Erzberger and Rathenau, Eisner, Rosa Luxemburg, and Karl Liebknecht are cases in point. Finally, there was the unrest resulting from French occupation of the Ruhr in 1923.

In such cases Article 48 was applied very liberally and without legislative ratification. First of all the President frequently proclaimed the *Ausnahmezustand* over individual *Länder* or the entire Reich in a fashion similar to that of the pre-revolutionary state of siege. Basic rights were suspended, 'order' was restored by the military and courts-martial were established. The implementation of the state of siege was either in the hands of a civilian commissioner who was named for this specific purpose or – as in Imperial times – in the hands of a military commissioner.[1] This exercise of emergency powers by the democratic President, Ebert, and his various cabinets turned out to be very successful. There was only one case in which it was touch and go, namely when units of the army revolted against the government in the Kapp *Putsch*. It was on this occasion that General von Seeckt, the Chief of the *Reichswehr*, replied to the war-minister's request to mobilise the army against the rebels with

[1] For its application between 1919 and 1924, see Fritz Pötzsch-Heffter, 'Vom Staatsleben unter der Weimarer Verfassung', I, *Jahrbuch des öffentlichen Rechts*, Vol. 13 (Tübingen, 1925)

the words: '*Reichswehr* does not shoot upon *Reichswehr*'. No such inhibitions existed, however, when it came to suppressing uprisings by workers in Saxony, Thuringia or in the Ruhr. Nevertheless, there is no doubt that the Republic could scarcely have been defended against its adversaries in the post-war era had it not been for Article 48. Thus, in the first years of its existence Article 48 was a stabilizing factor for the Republic.[1]

Apart from employing Article 48 along the lines of the pre-war state of siege, another mode of application soon became common. From 1922 onwards the Article was used not only to suppress rebellion or public disturbance but also to prevent the imminent collapse of the currency. At first there were a number of decrees on foreign exchange.[2] These were no longer classical measures of emergency – demanding the use of military force – but decrees of a more general administrative kind. They were no longer compatible with the old state of siege, but bore some resemblance to the former right of the monarch in some constitutions of German *Länder* to issue decrees in the case of imminent danger and at a time when Parliament was not assembled. The monarch had been authorized to issue emergency decrees, the so-called *Notverordnungen*, valid until Parliament had been re-assembled and ratified them or demanded that they be annulled.[3] It was in this sense that Article 48 was now being employed.

The difference between its use and that of the classical *Notverordnung* was that the latter had never been a measure of financial or economic restoration and had been issued only when Parliament had been unable to act. Now the *Notverordnung* based on Article 48 began to be used extensively without regard to the rights of Parliament. Of the total of sixty-seven decrees which the President issued between October 1922 and 1925, forty-four

[1] Number of decrees based on Article 48 issued by the President in 1919:— 5; 1920, 37; 1921, 19; 1922, 8; 1923, 24; 1924, 42; 1925, 1; 1926-9, none (F. Pötzsch, op. cit., p. 144)
[2] Pötzsch, op. cit., p. 141
[3] Walther Schönborn, 'Die Notverordnungen', *Handbuch des Deutschen Staatsrechts*, Vol. 2, p. 300f. See note 2, p. 86.)

were devoted to economic, fiscal and social problems. In that way Article 48 had become an instrument of emergency legislation for the executive. It was equally important that the *Reichstag* accepted what in practice was an infringement of its rights. Only once did it demand the cancellation of a decree.[1]

It is even possible to say that the *Reichstag* actually furthered the government's legislative activity by decree in that it surrendered its own legislative rights in a number of enabling acts in order to facilitate measures to end the chaos of inflation in 1923. The powers then given to the government were far-reaching indeed. For, on the basis of enabling laws, steps were taken which had no connection with the actual crisis at all. One decree, for example, authorized a measure of judicial reform.[2] In many cases the powers granted by Article 48 and by enabling acts overlapped one another. If, for example, a problem had been tackled with the help of an enabling act and if this act then expired the same matter might be disposed of with the help of the government's other legal authority, Article 48. From the purely legal point of view such use of Article 48 as an instrument of legislation remained rather dubious. This was even admitted by one Reich Chancellor, Luther, who in 1928 wrote, with the benefit of hindsight: 'It has to be admitted that when Article 48 was drawn up its use was only envisaged in cases which needed police action or similar measures designed to uphold public order. However, this Article actually proved to be very useful in cases of extreme urgency when economic measures – and especially the imposition of taxes – had to be carried out.'[3]

One might say that the successes justified the means. In 1925 the Republic was more firmly established from the economic and financial point of view than ever before. There was no further need of Article 48 until 1930.

By 1930 Germany was being shaken by the repercussions of the Great Depression. This, in conjuction with Brüning's deflationary policy, quickly led to mass unemployment. In the face

---

[1] Pötzsch, op. cit., p. 149   [2] Pötzsch, op. cit., p. 131
[3] Quoted by Arthur Rosenberg, *Entstehung und Geschichte der Weimarer Republik* (Frankfurt am Main, 1955), p. 476

of the unrest that resulted the government once again had re-course to Article 48. It was sometimes used to suppress revolutionary violence; for example when the government banned Hitler's SA in 1932. But above all it was again used for economic legislation, including such petty problems as protection of amateur gardeners against being evicted (*Kündigungsschutz für Kleingärtner*) and for the regulation of discount benefits for shopkeepers (*Rabattwesen im Einzelhandel*).[1] The most curious thing of all is that these decrees were never annulled and that several of them are force to this day. Some of these decrees, in fact, could in themselves fill a whole volume, such as the four lengthy decrees to strengthen the economy and finances (*Verordnungen zur Sicherung von Wirtschaft und Finanzen*), which covered taxes, tariffs, salaries, commercial, agricultural and other questions. There was a saying that the ministerial bureaucracy of the Reich seized this crisis as a golden opportunity to empty its drawers and to put everything into the President's decrees, since it otherwise had no hope of getting its meticulous drafts passed into law through the *Reichstag*.

Of course, Article 48 had already been applied rather widely during certain periods of Ebert's presidency. But this extensive application became almost customary after 1930. Between 1930 and 1932 the *Reichstag* passed twenty-nine relatively unimportant bills as against the 109 emergency decrees which were ratified by the President. But even this replacement of Parliament in its legislative role was not the most important divergence from previous practice. It was much more significant that this practice was no longer supported by the *Reichstag* and by enabling acts. Brüning's policy was based on the rejection of any attempt to find a parliamentary majority which included the Social Democrats. Instead he was vainly hoping to win some Nationalist support for his programme. For a short time he could be thankful that he was 'tolerated' by the Social Democrats, in order to avoid a vote of no confidence. That was no adequate base for parliamen-

[1] For its application from 1930 to 1933 see Fritz Pötzsch-Heffter, 'Vom Staatsleben unter der Weimarer Verfassung III', *Jahrbuch des öffentlichen Rechts*, Vol. 21, 1933/4

tary legislation. But Brüning did not need the support of the *Reichstag* at all as long as President Hindenburg – precisely that Hohenzollern general whose advent Dr Cohn had foreseen in 1919—put Article 48 at his disposal. With Hindenburg's help Brüning could realize his governmental programme. It is true that a *Reichstag* majority could demand the revocation of a decree issued on the authority of Article 48. But even then the executive had a remedy. With the aid of the President the Chancellor could dissolve the *Reichstag* and then renew the emergency decree which he had just been forced to annull. Thus even the supervisory power of the *Reichstag* was practically eliminated, and this had been the only effective control it had possessed.

Of course it was no longer a matter of emergency legislation in an economic crisis, but an attempt to govern without Parliament under the pretext of an emergency. The governmental authorities could hardly maintain that Parliament was not able to pass the necessary bills to avert the depression, although this argument has often been advanced to defend Brüning. In fact he did not try to find a majority in Parliament at all, and the inability of Parliament to pass resolutions had been largely brought about by the government itself, which dissolved the *Reichstag* again and again, only causing an increasing radicalization of the legislature. Thus the government intensified the crisis by its own action[1]. Hindenburg's and Brüning's style of policy was not without precedent in Germany. King Wilhelm I and his Prime Minister, Bismarck, had governed in a similar manner during the so-called *Verfassungskonflikt* (constitutional conflict) in Prussia, 1862-6.

Considered as a whole, it was a new style of anti-parliamentarian and authoritarian government, in which Article 48 played

---

[1] On political problems created by the application of Article 48 see K. D. Bracher, op. cit., and Klaus Revermann, *Die stufenweise Durchbrechung des Verfassungssystems der Weimarer Republik in den Jahren 1930-1933* (Münster, 1959). See also Gerhard Schulz, *Zwischen Demokratie und Diktatur*, I. *Verfassungspolitik und Reichsreform in der Weimarer Republik* (Berlin, 1963), and Erich Matthias and Rudolf Morsey *Das, Ende der Parteien 1933* (Düsseldorf, 1960). Memoirs: Arnold Brecht, *Prelude to Silence* (New York, 1944), and Otto Meißner, *Staatssekretär unter Ebert – Hindenburg – Hitler* (Hamburg, 1950)

an important part. The cabinet was no longer responsible to Parliament. It legislated by the authority of the *Reichspräsident*[1] and Hindenburg dissolved the *Reichstag* whenever the cabinet risked a vote of no confidence. For example, the argument which was used to justify the dissolution of Parliament on July 18, 1930, ran as follows:

'Because the Reichstag today demanded that my decree of July 16th issued on the base of Article 48, should be revoked, I dissolve the Reichstag in virtue of Article 25 of the Constitution.'[2]

In 1932, under Chancellor von Papen, Hindenburg even dissolved the *Reichstag* simply because there was a mere danger that it would refuse an emergency decree. To sum up, the decisive organ on the Weimar Republic was no longer the *Reichstag* but the *Reichspräsident*. This can be demonstrated by the following facts:

Whereas in 1930 the *Reichstag* had 94 full sittings, in 1931 there were only 41 and in 1932 – at the height of the crisis –13! The increase of decree laws from 1930 to 1932 was 5, 44, 60. On the other hand parliamentary legislation in 1932 amounted to only five laws.[3] The result was not only that the cabinet was now exempted from parliamentary responsibility but that it was also completely subjected to the will of the Reich President. According to the Constitution the President nominated and dismissed the Chancellor and his ministers. Until now the President had been limited in his personal decisions by the power of Parliament. After having scrapped this restraint, he could nominate and dismiss the cabinet just as he liked: first Brüning, then Papen, finally Schleicher. This was the anti-parliamentarian system of the last years of the Weimar Republic, the so-called 'Presidential-regime'.

Hindenburg had grown up believing in respect for authority.

---

[1] On this second method of legislation by the president (*ratione necessitatis*) see Carl Schmitt, 'Legalität und Legitimität', 1932 (reprinted in *Verfassungsrechtliche Aufsätze* (Berlin, 1954), p. 263f) and Carl Schmitt, *Der Hüter der Verfassung* (Tübingen, 1931)

[2] Pötzsch-Heffter, III, p. 127   [3] Pötzsch-Heffter, III, pp. 110 and 127

He had learnt that Parliament was the enemy of good government. It is claimed that he had read the constitution of the Republic for the first time when he became President and that he then had underlined all passages concerning the rights of Parliament with a red pencil and the passages concerning the authority of the President with a blue one. It was in this fashion that Hindenburg understood his role as President. Indeed, many people in Germany at this time longed for such an authoritarian government. There was a widespread yearning for a 'Strong Man', and at first Hindenburg filled the role. This one-man government opened the way for a *camarilla*, a *ministère occulte*, which greatly influenced Hindenburg. And so he governed inconstantly with Brüning, Papen, Schleicher and Papen, until finally he accepted Hitler. One result of this 'strong man' government was the 'rape' of Prussia in July 1932. This action was officially *based* on Article 48, sections 1 and 2.

Did this authoritarian style of government under Article 48 cause the fall of the Weimar Republic and the rise of Hitler's dictatorship? There is no simple answer to that question. One must take into account the fact that, with the help of the presidential regime, it was hoped to control the government of Hitler. This government seemed to be unavoidable in the eyes of Hindenburg and his advisers, for without nominating Hitler to be Chancellor, people would not follow the conservative regime of Papen and his 'barons', and might be attracted to the rising Communist Party. Thus Hitler as the 'drummer' for Hindenburg and Papen was to become Chancellor of the Reich and was to be watched by Papen as 'Vice-Chancellor'. Moreover, Hitler would be restrained by the President's control of his powers under Article 48. If Hitler disobeyed Hindenburg, the President could withdraw the legal basis of the new government, and, if the worst came to the worst, dismiss him as he had dismissed Brüning and Schleicher. At the beginning of 1933 Hitler had no majority in Parliament and was therefore bound to the will of the President.

This, of course, was a false conclusion. After the burning of the *Reichstag* in February 1933 Hitler terrorized the Communists and the Social Democrats with the help of two emergency decrees granted to him by Hindenburg. The terror influenced the *Reichstag* elections in March. The newly elected *Reichstag*, without the Communists and against the votes of the Social Democrats, granted him an enabling act to end the crisis. On the basis of this enabling act of March 24, 1933, Hitler could take measures against the constitution itself and establish his dictatorship in a legal way. He was no longer subjected to the President's emergency powers, but was a 'dictator in his own right'.[1]

Did Article 48 play an important role in this catastrophic development? In the opinion of this writer there is no doubt that it did. Of course, no constitutional clause can by itself initiate political events. But the way in which it is used can be indicative of important political tendencies. These tendencies had a great influence over developments in Germany from 1930 to 1933.

First of all, there was the continental, and particularly the Prussian-German, tradition of emergency powers which left the measures of the government, emperor or president uncontrolled by the courts. Secondly, there was the broad interpretation of the terms of Article 48 which conferred the power of government by decree upon the president. Article 48 was thereby used as a second method of legislation – legislation without and even against Parliament. Thirdly, the application of Article 48 was combined with the habit of dissolving Parliament in order to prevent it controlling the activities of the government. This can be seen as an attempt to destroy the parliamentary system and smuggle in a presidential regime. Hence the Weimar Republic had already been led far down an authoritarian path by the time Hitler came to power. When he appeared, democracy possessed no reserve powers with which to resist him. On the contrary, the theory of German law and the attitudes prevalent in the public mind tended to support an authoritarian regime. Even in Parliament such a regime enjoyed considerable popularity. Fourthly, Article 48 was used directly to establish Hitler's dictatorship. Helped by the emergency decrees issued after the *Reichstag* fire in February

[1] Pötzsch-Heffter, III, p. 102 and note 28

1933, Hitler took arbitrary measures against his enemies and prepared the ground for the enabling act. The slippery slope on to which Brüning and Hindenburg had ventured in 1930 was to end with the rapid descent into *Gleichschaltung* and the victory of National Socialism.

CHAPTER 6

HITLER AND THE BAVARIAN BACKGROUND TO NATIONAL SOCIALISM[1]

ANTHONY NICHOLLS

The historian of Bavaria in the Weimar period is bound to find himself paying a good deal of attention to the early history of the Nazi Party. Munich was sometimes described in Nazi terminology as the capital of the movement (*Hauptstadt der Bewegung*) and for most of the Republican era this was literally true. However far Hitler might travel in Germany rallying support, his roots remained in Munich. His attachment to this Bavarian base upset many North German Nazis, some of whom disliked the *Führer's* Bavarian associates – Esser and Streicher were particular targets of abuse – and felt that Hitler ought to have his headquarters in a Protestant, Prussian province. Nevertheless, Hitler resisted all attempts to woo him away from his unsavoury Bavarian environment into healthier Northern climes.[2]

Munich had been the birthplace of Hitler's party and provided

[1] A revised version of a lecture delivered at the University of Mannheim in February 1969.
[2] Hitler was constantly in difficulties over his association with Esser and Streicher in Bavaria as well as elsewhere. Cf. Alan Bullock, *Hitler, a Study in Tyranny* (London, Penguin, 1962), pp. 122–3; W. Maser, *Die Frühgeschichte der NSDAP* (Frankfurt/Athenäum, 1965), p. 271. For the hopes of Nazis in Hanover and Göttingen that Hitler could be wooed away from Munich, see J. Noakes, *The NSDAP in Lower Saxony 1921-1933: a study of National Socialist Organization and Propaganda* (Oxford, D.Phil. thesis, 1967), p. 57

him with an early nucleus of rank-and-file members, thus giving him an important advantage over many of his rivals in the amorphous German *völkisch* movement. It was in Munich that the party had drawn up its political programme – for tactical reasons to be declared immutable in 1926 – and had created its organization. Although amateurish, improvised and often confused, this organization was to be of the greatest importance to Hitler. It was thanks to the ability of Max Amann and his industrious colleagues that Hitler's brilliant but undisciplined leadership was able to exercise such an impact on the dedicated activists who later carried the Nazi Party to its triumphs in the 1930 and 1932 elections.

There might seem to be some grounds for claiming that National Socialism appeared in Bavaria as the result of an historical accident – namely that Adolf Hitler happened to be in Munich in 1914 and joined the Bavarian Army. There is no reason to suppose that he would have found service in the Prussian Army any less congenial, or that he would not then have found his way into a North German *Freikorps* after the war. Bavaria had no monopoly of violent, anti-semitic and anti-Republican movements, and Hitler could have sought a political home elsewhere. The National Socialist Party as it developed in Munich was very much his own creation, even if he was not its founder. It is impossible to imagine that Anton Drexler or Karl Harrer would have made their mark on German history if they had not been able to recruit Hitler as their chief propagandist. Even assuming that, given the social tensions and political neuroses to which the Weimar Republic was subject, some form of Fascist movement was inevitable in Germany, there is no doubt that its path to victory would have been much less certain without the extraordinary gifts which Hitler demonstrated as its leader. This is not to endow him with mystical powers; it is simply to recognize that, at certain moments in the party's development, he took decisions which were vital to it and which helped to win allies whom no other extremist politician in Germany could have been expected to attract.

In addition, when questioning the significance of the Bavarian background to National Socialism, one may point to the fact that, although the formative years of the party associated it with Bavaria, its break-through to victory came elsewhere in Germany. A glance at the electoral statistics shows that, whereas in the *Reichstag* elections of 1928 6·8 per cent of the Bavarian electorate voted Nazi as against a 2·6 per cent average in the Reich as a whole, in 1930 18·3 per cent of German voters were choosing Hitler's party, but the Bavarians were lagging behind with 17·9 per cent. In the two elections held in 1932 the Bavarian Nazi vote was substantially – if not dramatically – below the Reich average. The reason was not far to seek. Nearly 70 per cent of Bavaria's population was Roman Catholic. Although this confessional characteristic was by no means conclusive so far as party loyalties were concerned, and although before 1914 Bavarian Roman Catholics had always been marginally less likely to vote along confessional lines than their co-religionists in Northern Germany, the Bavarian People's Party – like the Centre elsewhere – succeeded in resisting Nazi electoral pressure far better than middle-class parties of a secular or Protestant complexion. Bavaria was not one of the German *Länder* where Hitler came to power by democratic means.

Nevertheless, when all these qualifications have been made, Hitler's Bavarian experience remains a crucial and seminal period in his career. If one cannot imagine the Nazis succeeding without Hitler, it is difficult to imagine Hitler succeeding without the unusual advantages presented to him by that curious phenomenon known in the early 1920's as *Ordnungszelle Bayern*. Had Hitler tried to establish himself in any other German capital in 1919 it is almost inconceivable that he could have achieved the same results. In Berlin, for example, he could probably have found right-wing radical organizations similar to that which he exploited in Bavaria. Munich had no monopoly of anti-semites, currency cranks and purveyors of the *Dolchstosslegende*. But nowhere else was the atmosphere so completely suited to their activities.

To treat this on its crudest level, it is difficult to believe that Hitler would have been able to build up his party in a *Land* where its natural and most energetic opponents, the Social Democrats, were not hamstrung by hostile police and officials. It is inconceivable that he himself would have been allowed such liberties elsewhere as those accorded to him by the authorities in Munich. In Prussia he would certainly have been arrested after Rathenau's murder, if not earlier, and his party was actually banned there in November 1922. Nor is it likely that Prussian justice officials would have been as reluctant as their Bavarian colleagues to press for Hitler's extradition to Austria.

Even after the so-called Beer Hall *Putsch* of November 1923 had hardened the attitude of the Bavarian authorities towards Hitler and his followers, his control of his Bavarian base remained important to him. It was the prestige he won for himself in the *Putsch* and at the subsequent trial which lifted him above his rivals in the *völkisch* movement. It was the party machine he controlled in Munich which enabled him to defeat attempts – weak and confused though they were – by North German Nazis to challenge the policy he was imposing on the party.[1]

Perhaps even more important than the Nazi *Apparat* itself was the fact that, had Hitler operated elsewhere in Germany, his fortunes might have been bound up more closely with an appeal to the urban working class than was the case in a *Land* like Bavaria. The anti-capitalist element in the party's programme was something Hitler always treated with caution. Exploited with too much vigour it would have ruined his chances of achieving power. In Bavaria he was not tempted to make too much of it, since his supporters there were unlikely to welcome attacks on private property unless it was of a Jewish or 'alien' character.

Bavaria's hospitable attitude towards the nascent Nazi Party can be attributed to two inter-dependent factors: the conservative character of politics in the country, which weakened resistance to extremist opponents of the new Republican regime, and the obsession with the threat of Bolshevism which encouraged over-compensation by government authorities. The latter obsession was conditioned by Bavarian experience of revolution and turmoil in the period between November 8, 1918, when Kurt Eisner

[1] For an interesting discussion of this episode see Joseph Nyomarkay, *Charisma and Factionalism in the Nazi Party* (Minneapolis, 1967), pp. 78-89

established a Bavarian Republic with the support of workers' and soldiers' councils, and May 1, 1919, when a communist-led soviet republic in Munich was suppressed with considerable brutality by North German troops and counter-revolutionary Bavarian *Freikorps*.[1]

What might perhaps be described as the traditional interpretation of these events is one which in some respects approximates to the Nazi explanation of the November Revolution. This presents the Eisner regime and its successors as being the work of alien or alienated intellectual forces – the *Künstlerproletariat* of Munich – which, by their bizarre and violent proceedings, created a series of radical oscillations and upheavals in a country previously remarkable for its political stability, liberal institutions and harmonious social relationships. The result of such turbulence was an intense fear of communism and a willingness to tolerate or even encourage extremist forces ready to oppose it. Such a view implies that Bavaria itself contained little in its own history or political or social make-up to suggest a Fascist tradition, and that the events of the November Revolution both represented and provoked a tremendous break with the past.

As against this there is the now more fashionable view that the concepts and attitudes which characterized National Socialism had been present in Germany for a long time before Eisner or Leviné ever appeared on the scene, and that even if Hitler's extremism was not shared by the average German judge, police commissioner, university professor or army officer, his attitude towards parliamentary democracy was far from unusual among opinion-forming circles in the Wilhelmine Empire, or, for that matter, in Wittelsbach Bavaria.

[1] The best account of the revolutionary period in Bavaria is that given by Alan Mitchell in his book *Revolution in Bavaria 1918-1919. The Eisner Regime and the Soviet Republic* (Princeton, 1965). For a recent discussion of pre- and post-revolutionary conditions in Bavaria see the collection of essays *Bayern im Umbruch. Die Revolution von 1918, ihre Voraussetzungen und ihre Folgen* (Munich and Vienna, 1969) edited by Karl Bosl. Carl Landauer's article 'The Bavarian Problem in the Weimar Republic, 1918-1923', *Journal of Modern History* (June and September, 1944), is still of considerable interest.

So far as the first of these interpretations is concerned we know enough about the Bavarian Revolution to realize that alien (*Landesfremd*) elements could not have created it alone. The workers', soldiers' and peasants' councils – confused and hesitant though they were – did express ill-formulated discontents and aspirations of native Bavarians, although the more ambitious revolutionary conceptions were often championed by intellectuals of a *Landesfremd* character. On the other side of the political coin there are enough examples of right-wing crankiness in pre-revolutionary Munich to suggest that Fascism did not appear there entirely unheralded after the collapse of the Soviet Republic. The Pan-German League had begun to expand its activities in the city in the years before the war, and in 1917 patriotic Bavarians were not backward in joining the *Vaterlandspartei*. Annexationists and last-ditchers were vocal among Munich's professional classes. On the lunatic fringe there were racialist organizations like Rudolf von Sebottendorff's *Thule Gesellschaft* and even Anton Drexler's Munich branch of the Committee for a German Workers' Peace, established in March 1918.

Nevertheless, the radical Right was not noticeably stronger than in many other parts of Germany. Drexler's Committee, for example, was lamentably unsuccessful in combating war weariness among the working classes in Munich, and the main centres of political anti-semitism before the war had been outside Bavaria. Theodor Fritsch's *Hammerbund* had found Bavaria a very unsuitable region for its activities prior to 1914.[1] Readers of the comparatively respectable *Süddeutsche Monatshefte* might be told by Paul Cossmann in October 1918 that the English would ruthlessly exploit a German willingness to make peace and that the Germans would be forced to live on roots and grass like Indians and the Irish,[2] but at a time of crisis belligerent statements of this kind were not unusual, and were by no means confined to Germany, let alone Bavaria.

What was important about the November Revolution in

[1] R. Phelps, 'Before Hitler Came: Thule Society and Germanen Orden', *Journal of Modern History*, Vol. XXXV, 1963, p. 248
[2] *Süddeutsche Monatshefte*, October 1918, p. 67

Munich was that, owing at least partly to the relative weakness of the orthodox working-class party in Bavaria – the SPD – it was able to assume forms which were at once more radical and more frightening to the propertied, conventionally educated classes than was the case in Northern Germany. If one takes the Nazi model of the November Revolution one can see that, superficially at least, it fitted the image created for Bavarian citizens by the events which took place in Munich between the fall of the Wittelsbachs on the night of November 7, 1918, and the collapse of the Soviet Republic the following April. To its enemies the revolution was the work of men who had been working to sabotage the German war effort by undermining morale on the home front, and who had delivered Germany up to the vengeance of her enemies by suggesting that she – and not they – had been responsible for starting the war. The revolutionaries were portrayed as Jews and Bolsheviks who had set one class fighting against another and introduced a reign of terror into a peaceful society.

So far as the SPD leadership in Berlin was concerned such accusations were difficult to substantiate, although this did not prevent their dissemination. In Bavaria the situation was different. Kurt Eisner and his USPD colleagues undoubtedly had tried to foment industrial unrest to hinder the war effort in January 1918 and had been held in detention as a result. Eisner's chief interest in joining the Independent Social Democratic Party had been to end the war and to cleanse the German Government of those politicians whom he felt to be responsible for it. His most controversial act as Bavarian Prime Minister was the publication of Bavarian official documents which demonstrated German complicity in Austria-Hungary's ultimatum to Serbia. It became part of the whole anti-war-guilt campaign waged by the German Foreign Office and most of the German press to demonstrate that Eisner had falsified the documents he had published and that his action had been deliberate treason.[1] In actual fact the documents had

---

[1] See, for example, *Bayerische Dokumente zum Kriegsausbruch und zum Versailler Schuldspruch*, ed. P. Dirr (Munich, 1922), especially pp. iii-viii and 93-8. Dirr's publication was the result of a report by a committee of the

simply been shortened to facilitate their reproduction in the press and subsequent revelations fully justified Eisner's judgement. Nevertheless, the campaign against him went on long after his assassination. In autumn 1922 there occurred what can almost be described as a show trial at which his private secretary, Felix Fechenbach, who happened also to be Jewish, was accused of having played a major part in this publication and of having passed similar documents on to the French press. Fechenbach was sentenced to eleven years' imprisonment and the attitude of the court towards him was not dissimilar to that of Hitler, who always declared that the November revolutionaries were guilty of treason rather than insurrection.[1]

The extent to which this judgment was shared even outside the ranks of *völkisch* extremists or indignant officials of the former regime can be illustrated from a speech made on September 1921 by Georg Heim, the founder of the Bavarian People's Party and the most influential farmer's leader in the whole of Bavaria. Speaking before the *Christlicher Bauernverein* (Christian Farmers' League) at Tuntenhausen, he bemoaned the changed fortunes of the good Bavarians he saw before him, many of whom had helped to found the Tuntenhausen *Verein* twenty-three years earlier. In his gloomy review of recent events he said:

'There is no longer any question about who was guilty of starting the World War. We saw the King of England travelling round in all countries, all the newspapers wrote about the policy

Bavarian *Landtag*. In April 1922 Fechenbach brought an action against Paul Cossmann, editor of the *Süddeutsche Monatshefte*, in the course of which experts testified to the distorted and damaging nature of Eisner's publication. In fact, many passages in the despatches not published by Eisner were equally embarrassing from the point of view of assessing German policy in 1914. This point was well made by Professor Quidde, who appeared on behalf of Fechenbach. See also *Der Münchener Prozess um die sogenannte Eisnerische Fälschung* (Munich, n.d.), pp. 33-7

[1] Documents relating to this trial can be consulted in the Staatsarchiv für Oberbayern in Munich (*Fechenbachprozess*, 93/1684). For the court's verdict and judgment at the trial see *Münchener Neueste Nachrichten*, No. 433, October 21, 1922. See also Gerhardt Pohl, *Deutscher Justizmord* (Leipzig, 1924), pp. 15-16 and *passim*

of encirclement; our enemies were arming themselves to destroy us. Only contemptible wretches, born of German mothers and grown up on German soil, could have had the gall to suggest that we were guilty of the war. Then came the saddest time of all, when it was just a question of holding out for a few more weeks and when men, corrupted by enemy gold, undermined the Fatherland from within.'

He went on to claim that 'German honour is dead and dishonour is enthroned'.[1]

Heim himself was very far from being a Nazi. In the same speech he warned the farmers against the National Socialists and similar extreme groups. Nevertheless, he was one of the most influential politicians in the country and his attitude towards the November Revolution and war guilt reflected feelings which were very widespread among the Bavarian farming population, as well as the academic community and the civil service.

If Bavarian reactions to Eisner made the 'stab-in-the-back' legend and the controversy over war guilt even more fierce in Munich than elsewhere in Germany, the actual course of the revolution there also seemed to conform very closely to the Nazi model of a Jewish/Marxist terrorist conspiracy, and took on more frightening forms than in Berlin or the Ruhr, for example. It seemed inconceivable that the old and stable Wittelsbach monarchy, with its apparently liberal institutions, should be overthrown by a radical Jewish journalist like Eisner and that his ministry should be followed by assassinations, Soviet dictatorship and civil war. Furthermore, the leaders thrown up in this astonishing convulsion were almost tailor-made for *völkisch* propaganda purposes; they included *verkrachte Akademiker* like the hapless Dr Franz Lipp, a mentally unbalanced political dilettente who became Foreign Minister in the first Bavarian Soviet; Jewish anarchists like Gustav Landauer and Erich Mühsam; Russian-born communists like Max Levien, Eugen Leviné and Tobias Axelrod. Although the success of their activities was very limited they had mounted an assault on property and established institutions which – though it

[1] *Bayerischer Kurier*, September 19, 1921. Bundesarchiv Koblenz (Hereafter BA) R43T 2229, folio 261

was more remarkable for its ambitious claims than its practical effects – was enough to provoke a neurotic fear of Bolshevism among the country's educated classes for many years after the revolution.

The importance of this development for the Nazis can be summed up as follows: there is nothing unusual about the idea of an international conspiracy, be it Communist, Freemason, Jesuitical or Jewish. This is a concept which had been common to politically illiterate and unbalanced groups for many decades. The Protocols of the Elders of Zion demonstrated how easy it was to fabricate evidence of such a conspiracy for those who wished to believe in it. But in the Bavarian case events occurred which even relatively sophisticated or so-to-say respectable people felt the need to explain in terms which sounded like the usual nonsense of anti-semitic myth. It is unlikely, for example, that the speech which Rudolf von Sebottendorf claimed to have made on November 9, 1918, in which he declared that 'in place of our Princes linked by ties of blood our deadly enemy is ruling us . . . Juda',[1] would have found a wide or very receptive audience at that time. Six months later its tone might still have been considered extreme, but the content would have been more generally accepted.

To be sure, blame for the Soviet Republic was usually placed on 'Eastern' Jews or alien intellectuals rather than on Munich's own Jewish community. Obsession with the dangers of foreign elements in Munich's intellectual life had been a feature of the Munich police authorities before the war. But so staggering had been the nature of the upheaval in Munich that the wildest rumours about the revolutionaries were current and resistance to *völkisch* extremism was correspondingly weakened.

In this respect the intellectual climate of Bavaria was favourable to the growth of National Socialism, even if the tradition of right-wing extremism there was no stronger than in other parts of Germany. It is of course, well known that the political environment was exceptionally beneficial to the Nazis. Hitler's debt to the

[1] R. *v.* Sebottendorff, *Bevor Hitler kam* (Munich, 1934), pp. 57-60, cited in Georg Franz-Willing, *Die Hitlerbewegung. Der Ursprung, 1919-1922* (Hamburg, 1962), p. 29

Bavarian Army, for example, was very great. The obsessive fear of a new Bolshevik rising led the military and civilian authorities to encourage political movements of a nationalist character, and after the Kapp *Putsch* Gustav von Kahr's government employed a state of emergency to restrict socialist parties and encourage 'anti-Marxist' ones.

Kahr, himself a state official who made no secret of his monarchist loyalty, came to power largely as the result of his influence over the Bavarian *Einwohnerwehr*, a home guard organization designed to combat subversion of the kind which had led to the Bavarian Soviet. Officially non-political, it was a thorn in the side of the Republican Government in Berlin. The administration of law in Bavaria encouraged the migration to that country of various nationalist and anti-Republican elements, many of them, like those led by Captain Hermann Ehrhardt – the most decisive leader in the Kapp *Putsch* – of a very violent character.

There was more to these developments than the miscalculation of over-enthusiastic soldiers and policemen trying their hands at politics after the party politicians had failed in their task during the revolutionary period. The experience of the revolution, in which of course Bavarian national pride had suffered as much as Bavarian political stability, tended to bring to the surface those anti-liberal features in right-wing political thought which had always existed very strongly in the country but which had been masked by an appearance of social harmony before the war. The Bavarian Centre Party, for example, had never been enthusiastic about Parliament exercising power under the control of powerful political parties. When the revolution came a momentary conversion to democracy soon gave way to the sort of ideological anti-Republicanism which appealed to the provincial German *Mittelstand* with increasing magnetism throughout the Weimar period. If, for example, one examines the working programme of *Orgesch*, the political organization of the Bavarian *Einwohnerwehr* which enjoyed the full backing of Kahr, one finds marked similarities between the attitudes it expresses towards politics and society and those expressed in the Nazi Party programme of February 1920. *Orgesch* itself was directed on the basis of the 'leadership principle' and among the points in its working programme were the

'Reawakening of the national ideal in all classes of the people among all Germans at home and abroad . . . strengthening of the authority of the state and its organs. The furtherance of a cleansing of the civil service to restore its old capacity for work. . . . Struggle against Bolshevism and National Bolshevism. . . . Nurturing of an idealistic attitude to life instead of materialistic *Weltanschaung* . . . promotion of will to work and protection of the freedom to work. . . . Compromise between employers and workers . . . overcoming of social conflicts, maintainance and strengthening of the middle class; closer relationships between town and country . . . moral and corporal training of youth; education to regard the duty to work as a national necessity: examination of the possibility of a year's compulsory work service . . . we should win over German women and in particular German mothers to promote our aims in the family.'[1]

These objectives, which were those of a semi-official and supposedly non-political organization, help to explain what many Bavarian officers and civil servants found so attractive about the Nazi Party. Hitler claimed that he could bridge the gap between the nationally minded section of the population – more specifically the ex-officers and students – and the masses. As Rudolf Hess, who was himself both a former officer and a student at Munich University, wrote to Kahr on May 17, 1921, at Hitler's meetings 'class differences are bridged over; the artisan converses with officers and students'.[2] The same sort of experience had affected members of Bavarian *Freikorps* fighting against communists in North Germany or Poles in Upper Silesia. At Hitler's trial in 1924 Dr Friedrich Weber of *Freikorps Oberland* described how deeply moved he had been in the spring of 1921 to find among his comrades in the struggle against the Poles a real spirit of

---

[1] Günther Axhausen, *Organisation Escherich. Die Bewegung zur nationalen Einheitsfront* (Berlin, 1924), p. 24

[2] Ernst Deuerlein, *Der Aufstieg der N.S.D.A.P., 1919-1933 in Augenzeugenberichten* (Düsseldorf, 1968), p. 132-3

brotherhood between men of different classes, despite two and a half years of 'revolution'.[1]

It is therefore not surprising that, even when Hitler's official contacts in high places became less influential after the fall of Kahr and his Munich police president, Ernst Pöhner, in September 1921, the nature of his movement and its programme were such that most non-socialist parties were inhibited in their criticism of it.

It was, for example, apparently more in sorrow than in anger that the leaders of the *Christlicher Bauernverein* publicly took issue with the Nazis on January 15, 1923, and pointed out the errors in their programme. They objected to the Nazi attack on interest rates, claiming that this might damage agriculture by restricting credit. They attacked the Nazi proposals to nationalize co-operatives and expropriate land for communal purposes. The Nazi attitude towards religion and Nazi insistence on a strong German central government were naturally unattractive to them, as was the proposal that national health might be improved by banning child labour. The latter, they pointed out, was essential to a healthy rural economy. But in making this attack the *Bauern-verein's* leaders were careful to recognize and approve the efforts of the Nazi Party to arouse feelings of national honour among the masses, and especially among the urban workers. They ended their comments by pointing out that:

'Like the National Socialists we also fight against the Jewish-materialistic spirit. However, we do not do this in the fashion of rowdy anti-semitism (*Radauantisemitismus*) but in comradely concentration of Christian elements. . . .'[2]

Such qualifications in their critique of the Nazi movement, whose attacks on their own Bavarian People's Party were often of a virulent and scurrilous kind, illustrate how cautious the *Bauernverein* leaders felt they had to be in opposing a National Socialist campaign, the uninhibited nature of which was likely to prove attractive to their own followers. Perhaps even more remarkable is the comment made at almost the same time by

[1] *Hitler Prozess, Stenographisches Protokoll*, p. 137 (typed pagination)
[2] *Bayerischer Kurier*, January 15, 1923, BA R431 2681, folio 130

Dr Eduard Hamm, a Bavarian member of the Democratic Party who had been one of the most liberal ministers in the post-war period and who was well-informed about the nature of right-wing extremism in the country. Hamm, who had become a State Secretary in the Berlin *Reichskanzlei*, wrote to Wolff of the *Berliner Tageblatt* about the Nazis, and agreed that they gave cause for concern. He claimed, however, that: 'There are decent emotions which lead misguided people to the Nazis – men who honourably desire to serve their people and their state'. It was necessary, he wrote, 'to channel their idealism into more healthy outlets'.[1]

All this helps to explain how, even when the police authorities in Bavaria were becoming increasingly irritated by Hitler's violence and disrespect for law, nothing very effective was done to restrain him. It also indicates that the programme and tactics of the Nazis were themselves very deeply affected by the environment and political atmosphere in which they had built up their movement. This applies to Hitler as well as to his followers. It is a process which can be illustrated by reference to the way in which both the party and the Bavarian authorities reacted to the crisis which faced Germany in 1923. During that year both groups tried to put into practice the lessons they had learned – or thought they had learned – in the years since the November Revolution.

Their activities culminated in the Hitler *Putsch*, an event which, like the revolution itself, was immediately to become the subject of highly speculative and politically motivated interpretations. The trial which followed it was scarcely calculated to settle doubts about its origin and political significance, especially since important parts of the proceedings were held in secret. It was in the interests of many on both sides of the court to blur the record, or at least to weight the evidence in such a way that the picture of events obtained by the public was distorted.[2]

---

[1] Hamm to Wolff, January 3, 1922. BA R431 2681

[2] The reluctance felt by the Chairman of the Court, *Landgerichtsdirektor* Neithardt, to press Hitler and his Nationalist colleagues too hard, is well known. The Bavarian military authorities were also very embarrassed at the prospect of revelations about their own part in organizing anti-republican

Recent historiography has discounted some of the cruder views of the *Putsch* put about in the period after its suppression and partly accepted by historians after the Second World War. The most obvious myth about the *Putsch* was that which was propagated not so much by Hitler as by Ludendorff – namely that the events in 1923 in Bavaria had been characterized by a conflict between Roman Catholic separatist Wittelsbach supporters on the one hand and greater German Nationalists in the *Kampfbund* on the other. This was a point of view which was given some encouragement by the Social Democratic opponents of the Bavarian People's Party, who, in their eagerness to unmask the undoubtedly anti-Republican nature of the Bavarian authorities, sought to associate them with anti-national causes in order to make them more widely unpopular. In this way a needlessly complicated web of intrigue was hinted at, and the myth of a strong separatist movement in Bavaria, a myth which the Nazis themselves accepted, for different purposes, was allowed to distort the historical record. Evidence available to historians has enabled this particular misunderstanding to be cleared up. It is now clear that genuine separatists in Bavaria were few and that their activities were rarely important. Particularism, that is to say the belief that the Bavarians had a duty to retain their special character and even to save the rest of Germany from herself, was a much stronger sentiment, but this was by no means confined to any one political party, or, for that matter, to one social or confessional group.

Another and more lasting belief about the *Putsch* was that it conditioned Hitler's own attitude towards the manner in which he should come to power in Germany. The failure of his *coup* in Munich was thought to have made him realize that he could only achieve success in collaboration with state authorities rather than by taking up arms against them. This again has been disproved by a more careful look at the evidence. It is now realized that Hitler was determined to march with the army and the police in 1923, and had no idea of fighting them. As his biographer, Alan

forces in 1923 – hence the authorities' insistence that part of the trial be held in secret. As a result of this the entire proceedings were recorded by an official stenographer.

Bullock, puts it, 'the last thing Hitler wanted, or was prepared for, [on November 9th] was to shoot it out with the army.'[1] It is natural that such a shift in emphasis has caused many historians to stress the extent to which Hitler's movement in 1923 formed part of a wider nationalist front in Germany which had its most powerful elements in Bavaria, but which looked for aid and comfort to allies – some of them very influential allies – in the North. Bavarian politics were seen as part of a movement for national liberation which might well culminate in a war against France. The ideas which Hitler presented in his speeches and embodied later on in *Mein Kampf* were in harmony with the environment in which he found himself in Munich from 1919 until 1923, and the situation in that country undoubtedly conditioned his own reaction to political events in the world outside.

Georges Bonnin, who in his book *Le Putsch de Hitler* was one of the first historians to make use of the full transcripts of the Hitler trial, has pointed out that in 1923 – as in 1933 – Hitler's appeal to the masses lay not in any hypnotic or demoniac characteristic which he possessed, but in his ability to crystallize an existing state of mind into effective but uncomplicated words.[2] By the same token, talk of Hitler's own prophetic vision becomes less convincing when one takes into account the extent to which Hitler thought of the future in terms of his own Bavarian experiences. One may point to the famous passage in Hitler's closing speech to the court at his trial when he says:

'The army we have formed is growing from day to day. . . . I nourish the proud hope that one day the hour will come when these rough companies will grow to battalions, the battalions to regiments the regiments to divisions and that the old cockade will be taken from the mud, that the old flags will wave again, that there will be a reconciliation at the last great divine judgement which we are prepared to face. . . .'[3]

[1] Bullock, *Hitler, A Study in Tyranny* (Penguin, 1962) p. 114
[2] Georges Bonnin, *Le Putsch de Hitler a Munich en 1923* (Les Sables D'Olonne, 1966). See also Bonnin's article 'Les Leçons du Putsch de Hitler de 1923' in *A Century of Conflict: essays for A. J. P. Taylor* (London, 1966), p. 202   [3] Bullock, *Hitler*, p. 119

This was not a mere pipe-dream. It was simply a rehearsal of the plans which had been formulated in Bavaria for the mobilization of the *Reichswehr* and the para-military formations. It was the realization of this dream which had been expected day by day among Hitler's *Kampfbund* until November 1923, and it was the dashing of these hopes which caused Hitler to revile his former colleagues in the Bavarian army as traitors to the national cause. The extent to which Hitler's Bavarian experiences determined his political strategy in later years is a matter for discussion, but there can be no doubt that the peculiar conditions of *Ordnungszelle Bayern* helped to produce some of the attitudes towards domestic and international policy which remained with him for many years. Sometimes in the past the origin of Hitler's thought has been sought in individual thinkers or writers with whom he is known to have come into contact. Dietrich Eckart, for example, and the White Russian emigrés in Munich in the early 1920s[1] are seen as having had an important influence on his political attitudes, and the even more obscure figure of Adolf Lanz has been brought forward with the claim that he was the man who 'gave Hitler his ideas' in Vienna.[2] Similarly, on the international front, Hitler is supposed to have been greatly influenced by the geopolitical ideas of Professor Haushofer, ideas which were incorporated in *Mein Kampf*, although they had probably been known to Hitler before the crisis of November 1923.[3] Hitler's career and character are not those of a man who was easily fired with the ideas of others. He was more likely to accept those parts of any theory which coincided with his own prejudices or inclinations. The convictions Hitler held were, in his own mind at least, the results of experience; experience of frustration in Vienna, experience of

[1] See, for example, W. Z. Laqueur, *Russia and Germany, A Century of Conflict* (London, 1965), pp. 55-6. An interesting account of Hitler's antisemitic views is given in R. Phelps, 'Hitlers "grundlegende" Rede über den Antisemitismus', *Vierteljahrshefte für Zeitgeschichte*, Vol. 16, October 1968, p. 390

[2] Wilfried Daim, *Der Mann, der Hitler die Ideen gab* (Munich, 1958). For details about Lanz's origins see p. 42

[3] Wolfgang Horn, 'Ein unbekannter Aufsatz Hitlers aus dem Frühjahr 1924', *Vierteljahrshefte für Zeitgeschichte*, Vol. 16, July 1963, p. 284

elation and despair in the war, experience of political struggles in
Munich. It is no coincidence that his writings, speeches, and
recorded conversations contain many references to his early
struggles and present him as the hero of a sort of *völkisch* saga,
a personification of the brave, honourable, but sadly ill-treated
German patriot. Even when Hitler did try to make his own
contribution to Nazi ideology in *Mein Kampf* he chose to do so in
autobiographical and historical form. His own experiences in
youth and the struggles of his party – not the written works of
others – are presented to the reader as the determining factors in
his thought. His critics tend to see this as an example of his
arrogance and plagiarism. It is just as likely that Hitler was never
conscious of a debt to any intellectuals – with the possible exception of Dietrich Eckardt, whom he seems to have admired more
for his eloquence and artistic vigour than for the originality of his
mind. Hitler was in his own eyes a pragmatist – a man who based
his beliefs on what seemed to him to be the lessons of his own
experience. Since his early years of struggle in the Nazi Party
represented his most exhilarating personal triumph after an early
life of frustration and disappointment, it is not surprising that he
looked back on them with nostalgia later, nor is it fanciful to
suppose that many of the lessons he drew from that period
remained important to him long after the objective situation in
which he found himself had changed very radically.

One example, which is not particularly unusual but which
illustrates in a very broad way the relationship between Hitler's
everyday conflicts in Bavaria and his wider conceptions about
political life, is the record of remarks made about Hitler in
December 1922 – that is to say, before the Ruhr occupation and
the reactions which that provoked – by the Bulgarian Consul in
Munich, Eduard August Scharrer. Scharrer had talked to Hitler
shortly after Cuno became Reich Chancellor. He was acquainted
with Cuno, and after talking to Hitler wrote to the Chancellor to
inform him about Hitler's movement and its growing strength
in Munich.[1]

Hitler claimed to Scharrer that parliamentary government in

[1] BA R431/2681 folios 85-93. Scharrer to Cuno

Germany was on the point of collapse. The parliamentary leaders were controlled by their parties and had no following among the people. Dictatorship would come and had to come. The only question was whether it would be of the Right or the Left. In North Germany the Left was so well organized that in Frankfurt, for example, the police would support a left-wing *Putsch*. The army could be neutralized in Northern Germany as it had been in November 1918. Nationalist organizations in Northern Germany were mostly bluff. The leaders of these organizations were politically compromised and the organizations themselves existed only on paper. Their problems were exacerbated by the fact that the big cities of the North were controlled by the Left and the nationalists there were not armed. In addition they faced the danger of a general strike. In Bavaria, on the other hand, the situation was quite different. The Nazis had been growing for three and a half years and were sure of victory. He claimed that the Nazi Party had seventeen *Hundertschaften* in Munich alone, that thousands joined the party every week, that the Munich *Sicherheitspolizei* was 75 per cent Nazi and that the situation among the rank and file of the city police was even better.

This estimate of the Nazi strength was, of course, exaggerated, but it was by no means absurd. Hitler was correct in claiming that his particular strength as a *völkisch* politician lay in the relatively strong local following he had built up, first of all in Munich and its surroundings and later in other parts of Bavaria. Although the Nazi Party had its sympathizers in Northern Germany, its real strength was concentrated south of the Maine. Hitler's sneer at his rivals did reflect the fact that many of them were more concerned with the creation of grandiose umbrella organizations than with recruiting a large rank and file. Others were more interested in academic discussion of *völkisch* theories than in rallying mass support; it is partly for this reason that Streicher had broken with the DSP in Nuremberg and come over to Hitler. Hitler was also correct in stressing the contrast between the political environment in Bavaria and that in North Germany – especially Prussia and the central German States. By December 1922 his own party had already been banned in many of these.

The benevolent attitude adopted by the Bavarian authorities towards Hitler's movement in its early days is well known, and even though the situation had become less favourable for Hitler with the resignation of Kahr as Bavarian Prime Minister on September 11, 1921, his boast that he had sympathizers in the Munich police was not an idle one. But in addition to this, Hitler's view that Bavaria represented a secure basis for nationalist resistance to revolution was by no means unusual to him. It was a commonplace among Bavarian politicians who stood to the right of the Democratic Party. It had been one of the earliest claims of George Heim, the founder of the Bavarian People's Party in December 1918, even though the disaster of the Munich soviet had made this view seem laughable only a few months later. It was the justification for the type of government which Gustav von Kahr had imposed upon his fellow-countrymen, with the support of a parliamentary majority, after the Kapp *Putsch*. And it was to be the article of faith to which the Bavarian Government clung during the critical months in 1923 when the conflict between Bavaria and the Reich seemed about to burst out into civil war.

There is plenty of evidence that Hitler's own model for the future of events in Germany owed a great deal to Bavaria's recent past. In his conversation with Scharrer he explained the methods which would be used by the Left to obtain control of North Germany. He argued that after Cuno had been forced to resign the first step would be for the congress of works' councils (*Betriebsrätekongress*) to establish itself as a parallel source of authority with the existing government (*Nebenregierung*). This development was not a sudden invention of Hitler's. The Communist Party eagerly sought to increase the political power of the *Betriebsräte*, in which they felt themselves to have their most effective support.[1] In Munich the possibility was likely to be taken more seriously than it deserved because it revived memories of actual occurrences in April 1919. The Communist-led second

[1] See, for example, Werner T. Angress, *Stillborn Revolution, The Communist bid for Power in Germany, 1921-1923* (Princeton, 1963), pp. 302-3 and 407-9. In August 1923 the Reich government in Berlin dissolved the central organization of the factory councils.

Munich Soviet Republic had in fact based its authority on the assembly of local *Betriebsräte*, which had been kept in session in the *Hofbräuhaus*. The concept of a *Nebenregierung* had been popular among Bavaria's left-wing radicals ever since the time of Kurt Eisner. He had encouraged the Congress of Workers' and Soldiers' Councils in Bavaria to regard itself as a so-called *Nebenparlament* which would function alongside the more conventionally elected *Landtag*. It was in the reaction against this kind of political experiment that Hitler had been given his opportunity to embark on a political career under the patronage of the Bavarian army. The belief that what had happened in Munich could happen again elsewhere in Germany was widespread among Bavarian officials and military men. It had apparently received confirmation in the aftermath of the Kapp *Putsch*, when Bavarian *Freikorps* had gone to suppress left-wing violence in the Ruhr, and in March 1921, when communist-supported disturbances had broken out in central Germany.

It comes as no surprise to find that when, in February 1924 Hitler explained to his judges what his attitude had been towards Berlin before the *Putsch* of November 8, 1923, he began by referring back to the Munich Soviet Republic. Addressing the court in closed session he said,

'Never in the history of the world has a nation been cleansed of infection by the actions of a capital city which was itself infected. You have one classic example here in Munich. We should never have freed ourselves from the Red era if recovery had not emanated from the healthy section of the people.'[1]

He went on to cite the examples of ancient Rome, Kemal's Turkey, Primo de Rivera's Spain and Fascist Italy. Speaking of the Turkish example he said:

'Salvation could not come from the decayed centre, from Constantinople. Just as in our case this city was without patriotism, infected by democratic, pacifistic, internationalized people who

[1] *Hitlerprozess. Stenographisches Protokoll*, p. 368. Secret session, February 28, 1928

were no longer capable of action. It [salvation] could only come from the countryside.'

Hitler's conception of the need to liberate 'decayed' metropolitan centres by mobilizing the rural community reflected one of the current myths about the Bavarian revolution according to which Munich had been freed from Red terror in 1919 by the efforts of Bavaria's own peasantry organized in *Freikorps*. In actual fact the brunt of the fighting had been borne by North German forces sent in under the orders of Noske, and the strength of the *Einwohnerwehr* had only been developed after the real danger from the Communists had passed.[1]

The belief that in Northern Germany Marxists and internationalists had succeeded in subverting state authority was, of course, shared by many in the Bavarian official establishment who were not themselves Nazis, and some of whom regarded the Nazis with suspicion. On October 22, 1923, for example, at a time when the dispute over General von Lossow's insubordination had caused relations between Bavaria and the Reich to reach the point of a major crisis, Kahr inspired an article in the *Münchener Zeitung* in which he justified the attitude of the Bavarian authorities towards the government in Berlin. Speaking of the need to overthrow a Reich coalition which was, at that time, headed by Stresemann, the leader of the German People's Party, he declared that in Prussia 33,000 men of Marxist persuasion had been given official posts and that 'as a result domestic politics are purely Marxist; that is to say they are directed against the natural order of things and are orientated towards compulsion, agitation, demagoguery and street fighting. Foreign policy is becoming internationalized and those who control it are careful to ensure that Germany never becomes powerful again'.[2] There was nothing in

[1] The part played by the Epp *Freikorps*, in particular, tended to be exaggerated. For a detailed account of the fighting at the end of April 1919, see K. Deuzinger, *Die Niederwerfung der Räteherrschaft in Bayern, 1919* (Berlin, 1937)

[2] Article in the *Münchener Zeitung*, No. 291 of October 22, 1923. BA R431 2264. The accompanying legation report refers to Kahr's probable inspiration of the article (folio 154)

this statement which would not have fitted into Hitler's picture of German politics, and its conclusion – that Bavaria had to fight for the German cause – is identical with that which Hitler had drawn to Scharrer the previous December.

So far as Hitler was concerned, his forecast of events in December 1922 was also of interest for the light it shed on his attitude towards the mechanics of establishing a dictatorship and the probable course of a civil war in Germany. He told Scharrer that once the *Betriebsräte* had established their position the German people would be told that a dictatorship was needed, and Gustav Noske, who for some reason enjoyed the trust of officers and officials in Germany, would be appointed to fill the post. Once Noske's authority had been used to crush the German national movement he would be replaced by an out-and-out Bolshevik. This would all be what Hitler described as a 'more or less legal' development; middle-class parties would be dissolved, whilst democratic ones would only be allowed to exist so long as they suited the Bolsheviks. No serious opposition to this was to be expected in Northern Germany.

In order to form the basis of national resistance, Bavaria would have to seal herself off hermetically and organize a counter-revolution. To do this she would have to be ready to launch an offensive across her frontiers within two weeks of the outbreak of the conflict, because otherwise coal and bread shortages would cripple her. In this respect Hitler showed an interesting continuity of thought with the leaders of the Bavarian Soviet in 1919, who had been greatly exercised by the blockade of food and raw materials imposed by the Reich Government.

The Bavarians would have to put themselves under the leadership of a dictator, who should be a man 'ready, if necessary, to march across fields of blood and corpses' – which meant that he should not be a parliamentarian. Hitler did not imply that he himself aimed at this position, and later experience in September 1923 showed that his candidate would probably have been Ernst Pöhner, the former Munich police president. Hitler remarked rather grimly that the Left in Bavaria would not enjoy the protection of the dictator. On the one hand this reflected the notoriously lop-sided administration of law and police powers in Bavaria, with which Pöhner himself had been closely associated. Nazi violence against Social Democrats had been treated with remarkable leniency by the Munich police, as well as by the state officials in other parts of the country – notably Commissioner Gareis in Nuremberg. At the same time the idea that the dictator should hold the ring while the 'National' movement destroyed its left-wing enemies foreshadowed the tactics which Hitler actually put into effect when he did come to power in 1933.

Hitler then, like many other political leaders on the right of the political spectrum, expected that there would be civil war in Germany in 1923. He therefore had to consider what role Germany's neighbours would have to play in this particular struggle and how the international situation could be turned to the advantage of the national forces. He told Scharrer that it would be necessary to seek aid from sympathetic European powers. England was the most likely source of help. She would not want to see Germany go under, leaving France the greatest continental power. The British could not publicly offer to help Germany, but they would see to it that Germany did in fact receive assistance. From the German point of view the most important development would be the withdrawal of the Allied control commissions, a withdrawal that would enable German industry to start work in 'the national sense and for the benefit of national defence'. Otherwise Britain would give Germany a free hand in her conflict with the French. It is worth observing here that Bavarian experience in the years since Kahr's elevation to the prime ministership in March 1920 had been apparently indicative of the relative leniency with which Britain regarded Germany in comparison with the hostile attitude of France. The Bavarians were indignant at what they took to be the open encouragement of separatism by French authorities in the Bavarian Palatinate. Bavarian separatists were also thought to be a target of French subversion. Great indignation had been aroused when the French insisted on sending their own diplomatic representative, M. Dard, to Bavaria, and in encouraging him to gather information about para-military formations tolerated by Kahr's government. Later on, in a scarcely impartial political trial, Count Leoprechting was claimed to have taken money from Dard to further Bavarian separatism, and French military intelligence was accused of financing treasonable activities among Bavarian separatists.[1] In the summer of 1921 the British were thought to have taken a warmer line towards Germany over the Upper Silesian question, and certainly British officers were less partial towards the Poles than their French counterparts. This issue aroused particular feelings in Bavaria because a Bavarian *Freikorps, Bund Oberland*, was involved in some of the most colourful episodes of the Upper Silesian conflict. There were, of course, more general reasons for believing that Britain would be more friendly to Germany than the French. The policies of fulfilment pursued by Chancellor Joseph Wirth until his fall from power in November 1922 had demonstrated that, on the reparations issue at least, the British would welcome a compromise settlement and a reduction in their tiresome continental commitments.[2]

Hitler was naturally more pessimistic about the attitude to be adopted by the French. He expected that they would invade the Ruhr. He argued that the Germans must do their best to make sure that any Ruhr occupation was a joint Entente operation so that the French would be held back from too chauvinistic a policy by their allies. Hitler, then, was not unduly optimistic about the international outlook – he thought that there would be French intervention, and he did not expect the Anglo-Saxon powers to do much more than avoid committing themselves to any anti-German action. He claimed that the United States would not be very concerned about the conflict but would be impressed by a people waging war on Bolshevism and Marxism, the dangers of which were no longer unknown on the other side of the Atlantic. In this context it is worth remembering that early in 1923 rumours that the Nazis were being helped by Henry Ford became sufficiently strong to warrant a visit by the American

[1] Documents relating to the trial of Leoprechting are in the *Geheimes Staatsarchiv*, Munich. *Gesandtschaft Berlin 200*

[2] See, for example, Ernst Laubach, *Die Politik der Kabinette Wirth, 1921-1922* (Lübeck, 1968), pp. 128-9 and 258

Consul in Munich, Robert Murphy, to enquire what the situation actually was. Although Hitler denied receiving help from Ford he did pay tribute to the contribution to Nazi funds made by Germans living in America.[1] Hitler was not entirely ignorant of the USA – he had, after all, a self-styled friend of that country in Putzi Hanfstaengl – even though his view of it was of a distorted kind.

Hitler had even more positive views about two of Germany's other former enemies in the World War. The first of these was Italy. He felt that Italy would show interest in the German cause and must not be discouraged from doing so by German claims on Austria. In particular Mussolini wanted the South Tyrol question eliminated from all discussions. Hitler said that Italian goodwill was very important to Bavaria because if she were cut off from Northern Germany, coal, raw materials and food could only come through Italy. There is, of course, no doubt that Hitler regarded Italy with favour owing to the complexion of her Fascist Government, but it is none-the-less worth noting that his enthusiasm for Italy as an ally was based on a specific strategic objective in the forthcoming German civil war.

The last country to come under consideration was Soviet Russia. Hitler had, of course, no faith in the Rapallo policies favoured by diplomatic and military circles in Berlin. He argued that once the Bolsheviks had consolidated their power in Russia they would probably turn their efforts against Germany. Therefore the war against Bolshevism in the German Reich must be extended to crush the threat from Russia. To quote from Scharrer's account of Hitler's views:

'With the defeat of Bolshevism in Germany the dictator must rule with an iron hand. Diplomatically Germany must follow a purely continental policy avoiding any damage to British interests. Attempts should be made to dismember Russia with the aid of Britain. Russia should provide enough land for German settlers and a broad field of activity for German industry. Britain would not interfere with Germany when it came to a settlement of accounts with France.'

[1] Robert Murphy, *Diplomat among Warriors* (London, 1964), pp. 40-1

These ideas about international policy have been examined in some detail because they lead to two conclusions. The first is that they confirm the view that Hitler's ideas about possible alignment with Britain and Italy and, more important, his belief in the colonization of Eastern territories, were developed in his mind well before the collapse of the Munich *Putsch* and his incarceration in Landsberg prison. The second and more important conclusion is that these ideas about the nature of international relations and Germany's place in the world were conditioned by the circumstances in which Germany found herself in 1922 and, more especially, by the position Hitler felt Bavaria to be in as the result of impending civil war. One of the questions put to Hitler by the State Prosecutor during the secret session of his trial for high treason on February 28, 1924, was whether he had considered the very serious international reactions which a march on Berlin such as that contemplated by the Nazis and their allies on November 8, 1923, would be bound to call forth. Hitler replied that, of course, he had realized that France would try to interfere, but that even under the most favourable circumstances it was clear that France would oppose a national government in Germany, and he implied that this was a fact of political life which had to be faced.[1] It seems clear that Hitler himself had already reckoned with it long before the *Putsch*, and had assumed that Germany would be strong enough to withstand French pressure so long as it was not supported by Britain or Italy.

In fact, one is struck by the accuracy of Hitler's forecasting, and by the extent to which it seemed that his own judgments were being reinforced by the turn of events during 1923. The French behaved much as he had foreseen, even without the provocation of a German civil war. They occupied the Ruhr in January 1923, but did so without the support of Britain. The German Government refused to allow the Allied military control commission to continue its activities, and the *Reichswehr* began to train para-military volunteer formations in readiness for a general mobilization should passive resistance

[1] *Hitlerprozess. Stenographisches Protokoll*, p. 368. See also Bonnin, *Le Putsch de Hitler*, p. 149

against the French in the Ruhr have to be transformed into all-out war.

The Bavarian *Reichswehr* and the Bavarian Government wholeheartedly supported this activity, and the flagrancy with which the Bavarian authorities flouted the disarmament limitations of the Versailles Treaty caused Berlin – not for the first time – considerable embarrassment. On August 16, 1923, Gessler wrote to General von Lossow telling him he could no longer cover up for the military authorities who were training volunteer forces outside the *Reichswehr*. He claimed that this activity was enabling the French to win British and Italian sympathy for their demands that there should be more rigorous control over the German armed forces.[1] So far as the Bavarian civilian and military authorities were concerned such restrictions on the part of the Government in Berlin were simply another demonstration of weakness of the Reich leadership. Cuno's fall from office on August 11, 1923, had been regarded with dismay in Munich and the Bavarian cabinet had no faith in his successor, Gustav Stresemann.[2]

By September 1923, the situation which Hitler had foreseen was apparently coming to pass in Germany. The Bavarian authorities themselves, represented after September 26th by Gustav von Kahr as State Commissioner, accepted the view that Northern Germany was in the hands of Marxist or Marxist-dominated politicians who were selling Germany out to the Entente. The threatening noises being made by Communist and Left-wing Social Democratic parties in Saxony and Thuringia, coupled with the evident enthusiasm of Russia's Comintern leaders for a left-wing revolution in Germany, seemed to confirm Hitler's belief that civil war between Left and Right was only a matter of time, and that Bavaria would have to act as the bastion of the nationalist movement against 'Marxism'. This was the sense in which Kahr and Lossow interpreted the conflict between Bavaria and the Reich over the orders given by Seeckt to the Bavarian *Reichswehr*

[1] B. A. Freiburg WKVII 4577, Gessler to Lossow, August 16, 1923
[2] See Ernst Deuerlein, *Der Hitlerputsch, Bayerische Dokumente zum 9. November 1923* (Stuttgart, 1962), p. 159

in October 1923. Both men declared that the whole matter of the suppression of the *Völkischer Beobachter* and Lossow's dismissal was a pretext to justify the emasculation of the 'National' forces built up in Bavaria. As Kahr put it in his famous speech to Bavarian officers on October 19th, the real issue between Munich and Berlin was related

'to the great struggle between the two *Weltanschauungen*, which are of decisive importance for the fate of the whole German people, the international Marxist-Jewish conception and the national-German conception. The choice is, on the one hand German, on the other un-German. Every officer and every German must choose. Bavaria has been selected by fate to take over the leadership in this struggle for the great German objective. . . .'[1]

The conception behind Kahr's *Generalstaatskommissariat*[2] in September 1923 and that of Hitler's national dictatorship were not dissimilar. In his conversation with Scharrer, Hitler commented on the future state form to be adopted in Germany once the threat of Bolshevism had been crushed. He suggested that there should be what he termed a '*Lord Protektorat*' which might eventually be replaced by a monarchy. In all probability Hitler referred to the monarchy to please his obviously monarchist interrogator, but one is reminded of Kahr's own insistence the following November that his participation in the *Putsch* should be regarded as *Statthalter der Monarchie* – a position which already existed in Hungary, whose Regent, Admiral Horthy, was regarded with great sympathy by nationalists in Bavaria.

Even the economic measures which Kahr tried to introduce during his period in office as State Commissioner were very similar to those proposed by Hitler when discussing a possible national dictatorship. Kahr's fulminations against the *Misswirtschaft* organized in Berlin and the need to eradicate *Schieber and Wuchertum* (black marketeering and corruption) were very similar to Hitler's statement to Scharrer that 'Die Wirtschaft wäre

[1] Ibid., p. 238
[2] A form of *Land* dictatorship exercised by Kahr in Bavaria, authorized but not effectively controlled by the Bavarian Government

neu zu organisieren und von den Schlacken zu reinigen'.[1] Hitler claimed that the *Unproduktivität der Staatsbetriebe* would have to be eliminated and Kahr was equally inclined to support private enterprise against nationalized industry. Hitler spoke of introducing a new currency, and there is strong reason to suppose that Kahr hoped to introduce a reformed currency into Bavaria during his period as State Commissioner. This is not to suggest that Kahr drew his ideas from Hitler or that Hitler took Kahr as the model of a Bavarian National dictator – an Oliver Cromwell in *Wittelsbacher Staatsdienst*. Indeed, we know that Hitler regarded Kahr with contempt as a weak man who went back on his promises to resist the 'Marxist' pressure from Berlin.[2] The fact is that Hitler's ideas about the methods of combating Bolshevism and of resisting France were entirely consistent with those of the nationalist consensus which existed on the Right in Bavaria and which were directly attributable to what Bavarian military and civil service leaders felt to have been the lessons of the November Revolution.

I think it is not too much to claim that Hitler never entirely gave up his 'Bavarian' way of looking at politics. Both from the point of view of his internal policy, with its stress on the need for a free hand to eliminate internal enemies by semi-legal means, and in his conceptions about foreign policy he revealed an attitude of mind which had been shaped in the extraordinary circumstances of *Ordnungszelle Bayern* and was designed to meet the needs of a South German State struggling against the twin threats of Republican Reich power and international intervention.

[1] See footnote 1, p. 116. Literally: 'The economy is to be reorganized and cleansed of dross'.

[2] Hitler claimed in 1924 that he had ceased to respect Kahr after he had allowed the *Einwohnerwehr* in Bavaria to be disbanded in the summer of 1921, despite having promised a Nazi deputation that he would never do so. (*Hitlerprozess. Stenographisches Protokoll*, p. 54).

CHAPTER 7

JULIUS STREICHER AND THE ORIGINS OF THE NSDAP IN NUREMBERG, 1918-1923[1]

ROBIN LENMAN

On the evening of October 20, 1922, the first Nuremberg branch of the National Socialist German Worker's Party was founded at a meeting in the Ludwig Gate Tower by the primary-school teacher Julius Streicher. It was an occasion of some significance, for in time Nuremberg was to establish itself as the centre of *völkisch* politics in the favourable recruiting ground of Protestant Franconia; beyond this, it came eventually to overshadow

[1] This chapter is based mainly on three collections of unpublished documents. (*a*) the *Nachlass Streicher*, now to be found in the West German Federal Archive in Koblenz. It consists of 126 large folders containing a mass of private correspondence, judicial records and photographs covering most of Streicher's political career, as well as much of the right-wing pamphlet literature upon which his articles and speeches were based. (*b*) The *Nachlass Luppe*, the surviving papers of the Democratic Mayor of Nuremberg, also in the German Federal Archive. It is the remains of a much larger collection which was heavily depleted by the Gestapo and by Allied bombing during the war, but it contains much interesting material, including reports of legal proceedings and two versions of an autobiography written by Luppe while in retirement after 1933. (*c*) The *NSDAP Hauptarchiv*, on microfilm in St Antony's College, Oxford. The most important sections of this were the reports compiled by the *Polizei-Direktion Nürnberg-Fürth* (Reel 84ff.) and the correspondence between the Nuremberg SA and the Munich Party leadership between May and September 1923 (Reel 16).

Abbreviations: *HAF* NSDAP Hauptarchiv film
                 NL   Nachlass Luppe
                 NS   Nachlass Streicher

even Munich as the symbolic home of National Socialism for both Germans and foreigners: the scene of its mass rallies, its early racial legislation and the trials of its surviving leaders. This first meeting was undoubtedly a personal triumph for Streicher. Among those who came to hear his three-hour dedication speech were many longstanding personal followers from all over North Bavaria who were later to found other branches of the NSDAP under his guidance. For a long time to come these outlying groups continued to look to Streicher rather than Hitler for advice and leadership, a tendency which added fuel to the organizational disputes of the following months. Later on, as *Gauleiter* of Mittelfranken and editor of the violently anti-semitic newspaper *Der Stürmer*, Streicher continued to hold a dominant position in Northern Bavaria. And even after his downfall and retirement in the autumn of 1939 he still ranked internationally among the most hated and notorious of the Nazi leaders. For this reason it is interesting to glance briefly at his personality and career, especially in relation to the earlier *Völkisch* predecessors of the Nuremberg NSDAP.[1]

Streicher was born in February 1885, the ninth child of a Roman Catholic primary school teacher in the Northern Bavarian village of Fleinshausen. Very little is known of his early life beyond the fact that he too became a teacher and in 1909 obtained a post in the Nuremberg suburb of Gleisshammer. As the result of a particularly distinguished war record he eventually reached the rank of lieutenant, and this in spite of the fact that as a one-year volunteer before the war it had been expressly stated in his pay-book that he was never to be given a commission. After demobilization, Streicher returned to Nuremberg and began to play an increasingly prominent part in the revival of right-wing politics in the city. It was only after considerable activity as an editor and political publicist and after many quarrels with his early *völkisch*

---

[1] Streicher became *Gauleiter* of Mittelfranken in 1925, was dismissed in September 1939 and on October 16, 1946 was hanged for incitement to racial hatred. For an extremely biased account of his early career, see H. Preiss, *Julius Streicher und die Anfänge der völkischen Bewegung in Franken*, Erlangen diss., (Wilmy, 1937)

allies that he finally decided to throw in his lot with Hitler in the autumn of 1922.

It is extremely hard to give a fair or accurate picture of Streicher's personality, as the fanatical, almost religious,[1] devotion of his followers was matched by the utter loathing he aroused in all who opposed him. Both before and after 1933, his presence in the party leadership was undoubtedly a major discouragement to many moderate and conservative Germans who were beginning to see National Socialism as a solution to the nation's problems. In spite of a certain bluff joviality towards friends and supporters, Streicher was hardly a very attractive individual by any standards. Even Hitler, who always remained remarkably loyal to him, admitted that his sexual appetite bordered on mania[2] and the pornographic ingredients of his propaganda probably explained much of his popularity among certain types of people. Like Hitler, Streicher liked to be seen with a heavy whip in public and seems to have delighted in brutality and violence. From the very beginning his speeches and writings were full of sadistic imagery and the advocacy of force as the universal solution to Germany's problems; as *Gauleiter* he personally helped to beat up helpless political opponents.[3] Although willing to heap the foulest abuse on his enemies, he was abnormally touchy about any criticism of his own character or conduct: anyone, for instance, who questioned his war record at a political meeting was liable to unleash a paroxysm of rage.

Historians have sometimes suggested that Streicher was actually mad. This was probably not true in any really useful sense, but he was certainly a man with powerful obsessions which bordered on the psychopathic. So at least thought the doctor of Landsberg prison, where Streicher spent two months early in 1924, and his view seems to be supported by Streicher's total inability either to compromise or even to understand that any of his opinions

[1] One of Streicher's anonymous admirers in Nuremberg hailed him as 'the new Luther', urging him to 'pray industriously' and to campaign against drinking and smoking. See letter of May 1922 in *NS* 81
[2] *Hitler's Table Talk*, ed. H. R. Trevor-Roper (London, 1953), p. 155
[3] *The Trial of German Major War Criminals*, Vol. XII, p. 321

might be mistaken.[1] This was shown over and over again throughout his career by the quarrels he waged within the Nazi Party, but also, and most significantly of all, by the dominant obsession of his life, anti-semitism. 'Through the study of books, as well as by a great many observations and experiences' explained the Nuremberg *Landesgericht* in December 1925,[2]

'he acquired the conviction that the Jews were the originators and manipulators of the war and the Revolution and so were guilty of the entire distress of our people. In his view the Jews, whether baptized or unbaptized, are active in all nations and parties in pursuit of the aims of 'Pan-Israel'.'

Scolding him for his criminal libels and his incitements to racial hatred, the Bavarian courts seldom failed to comment on Streicher's obvious and absolute belief in the truth of what he said and wrote, and it was a belief which remained completely fixed until the end of his life. At his trial in Nuremberg in 1946, Streicher presented himself as 'a fanatic in the cause of truth' and claimed that '80 or 90 per cent of what I assert with conviction was the truth'. When asked by the court whether he had ever felt uneasy about ignoring those Jewish qualities which could be described as great, he replied, 'I did not understand that question, perhaps I did not hear it correctly' and added that as an anti-semite he was not interested in the good traits 'which you or some others find in the Jews'.[3]

Yet in spite of this, and although he openly admitted that his approach to politics was irrational, it would be highly misleading to see Streicher's career and ideas solely in terms of his psychology. In fact, his utter lack of originality makes it particularly easy to relate him to his environment. Not only his racial theories – almost all of which can be directly traced to the influence of Theodor Fritsch and other writers active at the end of the nine-

[1] The report of the Landsberg doctor is now lost, but was mentioned in the MS. version of Dr Luppe's *Memoirs*, p. 377

[2] Verdict of *Schwurgericht des Landgerichts Nürnberg*, December 16, 1925, in *NS* 10

[3] *Nuremberg Trial*, Vol. XII, pp. 301, 302 and 317

teenth century, or even to medieval anti-semitic superstitions –
but his entire complex of attitudes stemmed from the *völkisch*
movement which had grown up in Germany and Austria long
before the war. His religious beliefs are a good example of this.
He saw Catholicism and Christianity itself as products of Jewish
legalism alien to German racial experience and himself professed
a kind of vague Germanic mysticism. 'This tragedy can only be
grasped' he told his judges in 1946, explaining the significance
of recent events, 'by those whose vision is not limited to the
purely material, but who can perceive those higher vibrations
which can be felt even today'.[1] Like many other *völkisch* 'intellectuals' he disliked urban civilization, was devoted to the
German landscape and wrote articles in favour of herbalism and
Nordic fairy-tales. He composed a number of quite attractive
little pre-industrial lyrics and fancied himself as a watercolour
painter, a creative Germanic *Naturmensch* forced by harsh events
to struggle for the salvation of his country.[2]

In case Streicher's maudlin sentimentality and his utter ruthlessness towards the Jews seem too grotesque a combination, it
should be understood that this was perfectly consistent with the
Völkisch world view held by a great many people. According to
this, the Jews were agents of formlessness and decay and as such
an implacable threat to the cultural integrity of the German race.
Taken to its logical extremes, this meant that their removal, even
by the most fiendish methods, could be seen as something essentially positive and good, a means of restoring society to its
supposed equilibrium. Although Streicher's extremism was certainly exceptional when measured against German society as a

[1] Ibid., p. 301
[2] A number of Streicher's poems survive in *NS* 54 and a series of sketches
made in Landsberg prison in early 1923 are in *HAF* Reel 97. The clearest
guide to Streicher's *völkisch* beliefs is the series of commentaries and review
articles he wrote as editor of the newspaper *Deutscher Sozialist*. For general
surveys of the whole intellectual background, see G. L. Mosse, *The Crisis
of German Ideology. Intellectual Origins of the Third Reich* (New York, 1964);
P. G. J. Pulzer, *The Rise of Political Anti-Semitism in Germany and Austria*
(New York and London, 1963); N. Cohn, *Warrant for Genocide. The Myth
of the Jewish World Conspiracy* (London, 1967).

whole, it is worth remembering that even he was less ferocious than the friend of animals and small children who actually led the National Socialist movement. 'Streicher is reproached for his *Stürmer*' Hitler remarked in December 1941. 'The truth is the opposite of what people say: he *idealized* the Jew. The Jew is baser, fiercer, more diabolical than Streicher depicted him.'[1]

In his long speech at the founding of the Nuremberg NSDAP, Streicher paid tribute to the earlier right-wing movements in and around the city and these can be described very briefly. Already before the war there had been a local branch of Theodor Fritsch's *Hammerbund*, connected with most of the other early *völkisch* organizations and in particular with the important white-collar trade union, the *Deutschnationaler Handlungsgehilfenverband*. Before 1914, the Nuremberg *Hammerbund* had been extremely small and ineffective,[2] but after the war and the revolution several of its members returned to play a part in the local revival of right-wing politics: first of all in the *Freikorps* and the *Schutz-Trutz-bund*,[3] then in the early *völkisch* parties and finally in the NSDAP.

Streicher had had nothing to do with the foundation of the Nuremberg branch of Brunner's *Deutsche Sozialistische Partei* in November 1919 but was invited to join in the following January and from then on became increasingly prominent in both the local and national activities of the party. Above all, membership of the DSP gave Streicher his first experience as a political journalist, since it was he who undertook to edit the party newspaper, the *Deutscher Sozialist*, which first appeared just before the *Reichstag* elections of June 1920.[4] Although perpetually hampered by lack of money, the paper brought Streicher into contact with

[1] *Hitler's Table Talk*, p. 155
[2] The founder of the Nuremberg *Hammerbund* was Julius Rüttinger, who reappeared after the war. See autobiographical fragment and notes on meetings in *NS* 31. There were only twenty-six members in 1913.
[3] Minute-book of the Nuremberg *Schutz-Trutzbund* in *NS* 119
[4] DSP Congress minutes in *HAF* Reel 4; Nuremberg City Council to State Police Office, August 2, 1920, *HAF* Reel 84. In spite of an expensive campaign, the Nuremberg DSP did so badly in the election that it was ranked in the official returns with the small group of splinter parties which together only obtained 1973 votes, 1·2 per cent of the ballot.

völkisch personalities from all over the German-speaking world and gave him privileged access to the flood of right-wing antisemetic literature which had appeared in Germany since the war. In the late summer of 1921, however, Streicher broke with Brunner, seceded from the DSP and took the *Deutscher Sozialist* and the Nuremberg branch with him. Before this, apparently, he had already begun to work with another *völkisch* organization, Dr Otto Dickel's *Deutsche Werkgemeinschaft des Abendländischen Bundes*. This was so named because Dickel, an Augsburg schoolmaster, had written a refutation of Spengler's *Untergang des Abendlandes* which had been reviewed in the *Deutscher Sozialist* in May 1921. This new association, which seems to have brought a considerable increase in Streicher's political activity, lasted almost exactly a year and ended once again in disillusionment and strife. A violent quarrel with Dickel and his friends was the immediate prelude to Streicher's letter of October 8, 1922, to Hitler, in which he offered himself, his numerous followers in North Bavaria and the newspaper (by this time renamed the *Deutscher Volkswille*) to the NSDAP.[1]

There were a number of reasons behind these early shifts and changes. Certainly one of the most important of these was chronic shortage of money: the worsening inflation and Streicher's lack of any administrative talent raised obstacles at every step and the situation was immeasurably aggravated by Streicher's reckless enthusiasm for lawsuits with political opponents, regardless of the cost. In view of this, it is significant that there were evidently considerable financial incentives for the transfer to both the *Werkgemeinschaft* and the NSDAP. In the summer of 1921, Dickel was able to offer money to the hard-pressed Nuremberg branch and a year later quarrels over a large debt contributed to the break-up of the alliance. The payment of this debt, together with an initial grant towards propaganda expenses and a loan with which to bring over the *Deutscher Volkswille*—in all amounting to some 70,000 Marks – was the major concession requested and evidently obtained by Streicher from Munich when he wrote to Hitler in October 1922.[2]

[1] *HAF* Reel 84   [2] Ibid.

Streicher's personality was also important, for he was an exceptionally quarrelsome and headstrong individual who reacted violently against any kind of restraint on his own initiative and supremacy. As far as the DSP was concerned, the Franconian section rapidly outgrew the struggling branches north of the Main, while Streicher himself demanded a more decisive voice in the making of policy and absolutely refused to share his exclusive control over the newspaper.[1] Similar problems arose with both Dickel and Hitler, and Streicher's continuing touchiness about his own independence in the first half of 1923 very nearly wrecked the new branch of the NSDAP as well. It was only in the late summer of that year, after a series of long and bitter quarrels, that a workable solution was reached: Streicher continued to enjoy considerable freedom as an agitator while the party leadership was at last able to insist effectively on its control over the SA.

But perhaps the most important reason of all was the difference in method between the *völkisch* groups, even though it must be emphasized that this was not due to any serious difference in ideas. There were certainly disagreements within and between groups about the precise meaning of 'socialism' and the merits of various economic policies, but that was all: *völkisch* men were all in varying degrees anti-semitic, nationalistic and more or less distrustful of orthodox Christianity. Their deep antipathy to urban society and civilization frequently went with various kinds of eccentricity – herbalism, vegetarianism and so on. And this general similarity of outlook was reinforced by a close interconnection of membership between groups: it was quite usual, for instance, for someone to belong simultaneously to the DSP, a branch of the *Schutz-Trutzbund* and to one or more of the many para-military organizations. In all these groups the same atmosphere and type of person was to be found, as also in the comparable organizations in Austria and the Sudetenland.

What really divided the *völkisch* movement was the question of tactics and emphasis. On the whole, the *völkisch* intellectuals – very often doctors, schoolmasters, minor professional men and civil servants – who had formed these early groups were mostly

[1] Minutes of the Leipzig Congress of the DSP, August 1920, in *NS* 9

JULIUS STREICHER AND THE ORIGINS OF NSDAP

interested in the peaceful discussion of economic and antiquarian problems and had little desire to enter the whirlpool of mass politics. In particular they were anti-semitic in a theoretical, nineteenth century way and were genuinely taken aback by the absolute fanaticism and ruthlessness of Streicher's campaign against the Jews.[1] This was the essential reason for Streicher's break with Brunner and the DSP. His rabidly anti-semitic articles in the *Deutscher Sozialist* had aroused increasing criticism from other party members who wanted the paper to be a forum for semi-scholarly cultural debate. Brunner himself admitted[2] that he had no talent for public speaking and his last letter to Streicher showed quite clearly that he saw the DSP as a discussion group for the *völkisch* elite and not as the nucleus of a mass organization.[3] One reason why Streicher did not at this stage turn towards Munich was that Drexler and his friends in the DAP were hardly different from Brunner in this respect. Indeed, they were trying to negotiate with him in an attempt to outflank Hitler and the other radicals in their own camp. Streicher had opposed these negotiations, not because he admired Hitler or even knew him very well, but probably in order to prevent any strengthening of the moderate faction in the DSP at his expense.[4]

In spite of a more promising start, much the same happened in the *Werkgemeinschaft*. Dickel and his friends were clearly alarmed by Streicher's radical methods, which not only alienated

[1] Ibid. See also F. L. Carsten, *The Rise of Fascism* (London, 1967). Streicher's relations with Bavarian conservatives were also poor – see for instance the letter of March 7, 1922, *NS* 105, from Dr Erich Kühn, sharply criticizing Streicher's demagogic methods and accusing him of identifying himself with chaos and turmoil in what ought to be the *Ordnungszelle Bayern*.

[2] Brunner to Streicher, March 13, 1921, *NS* 9

[3] Brunner to Streicher, November 30, 1921, *NS* 9

[4] It is hard to disentangle the aims of the various groups at this time, but in the spring of 1921 Streicher was apparently more in favour of combining with the *Völkisch* groups in and around Berlin and regarded National Socialism as an enemy. In May he apparently met Hitler but by the autumn was sharply attacking him in the *Deutscher Sozialist*.

their more moderate followers but also brought them into conflict with the authorities. Again, it soon became obvious that the *Werkgemeinschaft* was more interested in cultural and economic discussions than in violent and disorderly mass meetings. But Streicher refused to modify his views in any way. 'In the treatment of the Jewish question' he wrote, explaining his eventual secession, 'I have always considered myself to be a "radical" and I cannot weaken my conviction on this matter in the future'.[1]

By this time, Streicher had clearly begun to see the NSDAP as the most suitable framework for his kind of politics. The meeting of October 20, 1922, was a triumph for his personal viewpoint and he made his intentions absolutely plain. Earlier movements had failed, he said, because they had renounced the need for struggle: the aim of the NSDAP was not 'pious and peaceful reconstruction' but revolution: an entire transformation of Germany based on the belief that the Jewish question lay at the root of all her problems. The first and fundamental aim was power.[2] Even now, however, the question of absolute extremism versus relative moderation was not entirely eliminated. In the first half of 1923 there were still complaints that Streicher's attacks on his enemies went beyond what was acceptable even in the overheated atmosphere of Nuremberg politics.[3] And the appearance, in May 1923, of Streicher's sensational broadsheet *Der Stürmer* apparently aroused dismay not only within the branch but even at Party Headquarters in Munich.[4]

October 1922 was a highly appropriate time for the appearance of National Socialism in Nuremberg. Partly as a result of the murder of Rathenau in June and the general crisis of the summer, the SPD and the Independent Socialists were at last reunited at a great rally held there on September 24th. Although too late to recover the numbers already lost to Communism, reunification

---

[1] Streicher to the leadership of the Nuremberg *Werkgemeinschaft*, September 19, 1922, *NS* 81

[2] Report in *Deutscher Volkswille*, October 20, 1922

[3] A number of letters from local Party members illustrate this. See for instance Eisenbeiss – a local SA leader – to Streicher, March 28, 1923, *NS* 81

[4] Max Amann to Streicher, August 16, 1923, *NS* 105

certainly improved morale and at least temporarily reduced the bickering on the moderate Left. But at the same time it undoubtedly reinforced the anxiety of all those whose whole political outlook was based on fear and hatred of Socialism. This was particularly true in Nuremberg. Although the city had been highly industrialized ever since the end of the previous century, many of its earlier craft enterprises still survived and in 1925 21 per cent of its working population were employed in units of less than six men. For artisans, small tradesmen and other self-employed people, shaken by the collapse of Imperial Germany and severely threatened by the inflation, the situation had hardly been improved by the local government elections of June 1919, by which the combined socialist parties had won 31 out of the 50 seats on the City Council. The fact that the elderly party bureaucrats and trade union secretaries who dominated the left-wing bloc seldom initiated anything really radical was beside the point. The mere existence of a socialist majority created the fear in many minds that wartime economic controls would now be transformed into full-scale public ownership or that co-operatives and large enterprises would be favoured in the allocation of scarce municipal contracts. There were rumours, too, that with the urgent need to rationalize the city administration, politics played a part in the dismissal of officials.

All this helps to account for the undeniable fact that in the Nuremberg NSDAP and its predecessors, the leadership at least was overwhelmingly dominated by the petty bourgeoisie. Of the 21 separate individuals belonging to 5 successive branch committees of the DSP, the *Werkgemeinschaft* and the NSDAP, there were 2 doctors, 1 schoolmaster (Streicher), 1 army officer, 1 technician, 1 white-collar employee, 4 officials of various grades, 5 tradesmen, and either 5 or 6 artisans. There was only one man who might have been termed a 'worker' in the usual sense.[1] This was why, apart from relentless anti-semitism and the vilification

---

[1] See report of founding meeting of the Nuremberg DSP in *NS* 9; Nuremberg City Council memoranda of February 8, 1922, October 20, 1922 and March 7, 1923, in *HAF* Reel 84; the same picture emerges from a list of thirty-one leading members of the local *völkisch* movement in *NS* 114.

of his personal enemies, the vast bulk of Streicher's propaganda was dedicated to the economic anxieties and anti-socialist paranoia of the 'little man', regardless of the fact that serious abuses and actual radicalism in the city government were extremely rare. But there was also another, much more immediate, reason why the founding of the Nuremberg NSDAP was likely to make a particular impact at this time. Only a few days previously, a Jewish doctor who had allegedly poisoned two local girls with a dangerous contraceptive was acquitted of manslaughter by a Nuremberg court. This caused an immediate outcry in the city and the mixture of pornographic sensationalism and racial hatred offered by the incident was something ideally suited to Streicher's peculiar tastes and talents as a propagandist. On October 19th, the evening before the founding of the Nazi branch, he held a public meeting attended by about a thousand people which was entirely dedicated to the affair. After impassioned speeches against the Jews and the existing legal system, a resolution was passed which declared that German women protested against being delivered up to the lust of aliens under the eyes of German courts. The crude melodrama of this was typical of Streicher and highly significant for his future tactics. For he realized above all that successful propaganda must be fed not only by national crisis but also by local scandal and the vilification of local scapegoats. It was upon his ability to pose effectively as 'representative of the public' within a particular community that much of his later support was to depend.[1]

The new branch grew rapidly in the first months of its existence. The anxieties of the inflation drew large numbers of middle-class people to Nazi meetings, where Streicher regaled them with the arguments of racial hatred rather than of economics.[2]

[1] See Verdict of *Schöffengericht des Amtsgerichts Nürnberg*, May 12, 1924 and report of the Government of *Kreis Mittelfranken* to Bavarian Ministry of the Interior, November 21, 1922, *HAF* Reel 22A

[2] Police reports of Nazi meetings of December 12 and 21, 1922, *HAF* Reel 84. According to Streicher, the Jews were engineering the inflation to destroy the German middle-classes – the same method they had used to ruin the Canaanites and the Romans.

Shortage of food, shortage of housing, rising unemployment and external events like the March on Rome at the end of October all added to the appeal of a party which offered simple solutions even – indeed particularly – to the most complex problems. On their own chosen level, Streicher and his men showed themselves equal to every opportunity; by the end of the year, the political sound barrier had been broken and the party was arousing widespread attention. 'The National Socialist movement' reported *Staatskommissar* Gareis, the head of the State Police Office, on December 22nd, 'thrusts itself more and more into the focus of public interest: a result of the Party's activity, of good management and, not least, of great successes'.[1] At the centre of all this was Streicher's own unflagging determination to attack and humiliate his opponents – the Jews, the Socialists, the Democrats and the Mayor – by every possible means, of which public meetings were only one. All kinds of functions and demonstrations were organized; in December, Streicher personally prevented a performance of Arnolt Bronnen's 'obscene' play *Der Vatermord* and the previous month he had boasted that he had no less than seven libel actions pending.[2]

The intense energy of the Nuremberg Nazis is vividly illustrated by a fragment of a young SA man's diary preserved among Streicher's papers.[3] Even when condensed to a few figures, the material it contains is extremely impressive: between January 8 and March 11, 1923, the period covered by the fragment, the anonymous author mentioned or was personally involved in no less than sixteen mass meetings, one special members' meeting, four expeditions to neighbouring towns, two rallies in Munich, three SA parades, four field exercises and one riot. He also received at least one serious injury. And, if anything, this level of activity actually increased during the following summer and

[1] *Staatskommissar* Gareis to Bavarian Ministry of the Interior, December 22, 1922, *HAF* Reel 22A
[2] See Preiss, op. cit. Streicher correctly regarded court cases as an excellent form of propaganda, whether successful or not, though they were a crippling burden on party finances.
[3] *NS* 133. The fragment is in the form of a later typescript copy.

autumn. In the first twelve months of the branch, in Nuremberg alone, according to a report dated October 1923, there had been twenty-nine restricted meetings of various kinds, twenty-six discussion evenings, forty-six public mass meetings and one Christmas celebration.[1] This was in addition to a public commemoration of Leo Schlageter in June, the spectacular *Deutscher Tag* in September and assistance in founding a substantial number of new branches in the towns and villages around Nuremberg.

The ceaseless propaganda accompaniment to all this activity was fed from many sources. Of these, one of the most important and fruitful was 'inside' information about the working of the city government, as the hardships of post-war life as well as the usual discontents of any bureaucracy ensured that there were always people with real or imaginary grievances which could be exploited. Some had simply lost temporary wartime jobs as the result of de-control; others had been dismissed for misconduct or embezzlement; and Streicher's chief lieutenant, Konrad Raschbacher, was an ex-municipal official who had been prematurely retired for mental instability. Yet in supporting these people, it was not simply a question of the Nazis protecting their own. Many of them had originally been liberals or even socialists; they were united solely by economic anxiety and resentment against their former employers. When the Mayor finally decided to sue Streicher for libel, his lawyer commented in court that the latter's witnesses looked like 'a society of the discontented and the reprimanded'; there can be no doubt that a great many other National Socialists exactly fitted this description. Idealism certainly played its part, but otherwise the party clearly drew much of its early strength from the aggrieved and the disorientated, to say nothing of adventurers and obvious lunatics.[2]

Streicher's methods of presentation, both as a speaker and journalist, are also interesting. More perhaps than Hitler, Streicher combined the instincts of a political fanatic with those of a

[1] Branch report of October 20, 1923, *NS* 124

[2] See the reports of the long series of libel suits between Streicher and Dr Luppe, in the papers of both. Streicher received a very large number of complaints and appeals, some of them very pathetic indeed.

born comedian and impresario. He was furious when the socialist *Fränkische Tagespost* referred to his meetings as the '*Variété Streicher*', yet this was an extraordinarily apt description. 'One could compare the occasion to a cabaret' commented a senior police officer in May 1923.[1] Indeed, whatever the advertised theme, Streicher's performances usually offered something for everybody: utopian promises and violent threats; crude sentimentality and heroic offers of martyrdom; the emotional intensity of a revivalist meeting relieved by the jokes and repartee of a music-hall. And the object was always the same: every kind of theatrical and psychological effect – patriotic music, uniforms, the ostentatious exclusion of Jews – was employed to convert ordinary political participation into an act of total emotional commitment and to endow large numbers of anxious and excited people with a collective identity.

Yet progress did not go unimpeded. And the danger came neither from the socialists, whose counter-measures tended to be more noisy than effective, nor from the Bavarian authorities, which were either neutral or positively sympathetic.[2] The real threat was the series of acrimonious quarrels which broke out within the branch itself less than a month after its foundation and which was to continue intermittently until the late summer of 1923. The central dispute, from which others developed, arose from the personal rivalry between Streicher himself and the editor of the *Deutscher Volkswille*, Walther Kellerbauer. Although they had worked together in Nuremberg since the autumn of 1921,[3] and Streicher had warmly recommended Kellerbauer to Hitler in his letter of October 8, 1922, relations between the two began to break down little more than a month later and soon became so bad that they threatened to disrupt the entire branch and the SA.

[1] Police report of meeting of May 17, 1923, *HAF* Reel 84
[2] This emerges from police reports at almost all levels, though official sympathy became more strained as the radicalism of the Nazis became more obvious.
[3] He had been recommended to Streicher by Dickel: Dickel to Streicher, September 3, 1921, *HAF* Reel 97. He had taken over management of the newspaper in the summer of 1922.

The exact causes and course of the quarrel were too trivial and infantile to be worth discussing in detail. For behind the financial squabbles, the complaints about Kellerbauer's editorial policy and a host of other charges and counter-charges lay a straightforward struggle for power within the branch. Kellerbauer was nine years older than Streicher, an ex-naval officer and an able journalist and speaker in his own right. In view of his intolerance of any interference or restraint and Streicher's drive for domination it was hardly surprising that Nuremberg soon became too small a place for both of them.

The significance of the quarrel was more than merely local or personal however, for it exposed not only the organizational vagueness of the Nuremberg branch but also Hitler's inability to impose a satisfactory settlement from outside. In fact, his repeated failure to remedy the situation in Nuremberg in the spring and early summer of 1923 did much to mar the successs of the party rally held in Munich at the end of January. The problem of controlling the branches was one that had to be solved if the NSDAP were not simply to split into separate fragments as its membership increased. Events in Nuremberg show very clearly that such a solution could not be imposed by arbitary decree from Munich or even by Hitler's personal intervention, but only by a gradual process of reorganization lasting many months.

By December 1922, the deadlock in Nuremberg made some kind of outside intervention unavoidable. Streicher and the branch committee had broken off relations with Kellerbauer, refusing to pay the debts he claimed and boycotting the *Volkswille*. Kellerbauer simply refused to accept their jurisdiction, claiming, as he later emphatically put it, that he represented 'the *cause* of the *whole Party* and the *general* interests of National Socialism'.[1] Both sides appealed to Munich, Streicher taking the additional precaution of mobilizing his supporters in the Franconian branches outside Nuremberg.[2]

[1] Kellerbauer to Hertlein, February 28, 1923, *NS* 105
[2] Josef Kolb (Hersbruck) to Nuremberg branch leadership, December 22, 1922, *NS* 81

Hitler now had to tread extremely carefully. Kellerbauer was the editor of a party newspaper and a useful speaker; he also had supporters and appeared to have a good deal of right on his side. Yet it was Streicher who had built up the Franconian movement and to alienate him would mean splitting it altogether. All this no doubt encouraged Hitler to attempt a compromise solution when he visited Nuremberg on January 3, 1923. After addressing 2,000 party members and their guests on the theme 'We Have Become Racially Dishonourable',[1] he evidently proved to his own satisfaction that Kellerbauer was innocent of the charges against him and proposed that a court of honour be set up to clear his name.

What followed vividly illustrated the limits of Hitler's authority. For no sooner had he left than Streicher re-opened his campaign against Kellerbauer with renewed venom: not only did the boycott of the newspaper continue but the branch committee now expelled Kellerbauer from the party, and when he protested at a public meeting he was beaten up and thrown out.[2] Kellerbauer continued to maintain his immunity as a 'party official' and the quarrel also began to spread to the SA. A further visit from Hitler in February was equally fruitless; other local right-wing organizations were drawn in and the affair dragged on for weeks to come at political meetings, in the press and finally in the law-courts.[3]

It was not surprising that Kellerbauer's reliance on Hitler's support in order to maintain himself should soon have raised the whole issue of local versus central authority in an acute form. As early as the beginning of February there were signs that some party members including Bürger, Streicher's immediate deputy, were even contemplating complete secession from Munich.[4] Streicher was therefore in an embarrassing position: he obviously

[1] Police report in NS 8
[2] Kellerbauer to Nuremberg branch leadership, January 12 and 13, 1923, NS 105
[3] See the correspondence between Streicher and his lawyers in NS 77 and 78; the legal ramifications of the affair continued at least until September.
[4] Kurt Schuhmann to Ferdinand Bürger, February 3, 1923, NS 81

K

found Hitler's support for Kellerbauer intolerable, yet for political and perhaps also for financial reasons he could hardly afford to go on his travels again. The NSDAP was clearly the ideal setting for his kind of agitation and a complete break would probably have left Kellerbauer, his supporters and the *Deutscher Volkswille* as a permanent source of irritation and rivalry. This no doubt explains why Streicher, after some hesitation, decisively repudiated separatism and carried out a thorough reorganization of the branch committee at the beginning of March.[1]

The immediate result was the explosion of another furious quarrel, for the purged members began a violent propaganda campaign against Streicher, held a special public meeting to denounce him and even leaked information to the *Fränkische Tagespost*.[2] This was the occasion for yet another development in Streicher's career as an agitator. On April 20th, a notice appeared all over the city addressed to 'all those who seek the truth' and announcing Streicher's reply to the 'lies and slanders': a new polemical broadsheet named *Der Stürmer*. After quoting Bebel's claim that the glory of the SPD was its ability to wash its dirty linen in public without loss of stature, the notice ended with the promise that 'We National Socialists will emerge whiter than before when the wash is over'.[3]

Der Stürmer – 'a broadsheet for the struggle for truth'[4] or 'pornographic colportage literature of the worst kind',[5] according to one's political and aesthetic standpoint – bore little resemblance in its early days to the prosperous national newspaper it later became. Coming out irregularly and similar in format to an ordinary political pamphlet, it was mostly dedicated to issues far too parochial to interest anybody outside Nuremberg. But its appearance did mark a further stage in Streicher's emancipation

[1] Nuremberg City Council Memorandum, March 7, 1923, *HAF* Reel 84. The new members were distinguished mainly by their fanatical personal loyalty to Streicher. The latter's unwillingness to break finally with Bürger seems to be supported by the fact that his place was left vacant until the middle of April.

[2] Report in *Nürnberger Anzeiger*, April 16, 1923
[3] Poster in *HAF* Reel 84
[4] *Der Stürmer's* official subtitle.   [5] Luppe, *Memoirs*, MS., p. 377

from the more restrained type of *völkisch* agitation and his progress towards the peculiarly extreme and horrible forms of propaganda for which he was to become internationally notorious. Although *Der Stürmer* was initially produced as a weapon against Streicher's enemies within the *völkisch* camp, the events of the early summer soon widened its scope. On May 1st, Hitler tried unsuccessfully to browbeat the Bavarian Government into banning the left-wing Labour Day demonstrations. And even though Streicher himself was in fact with the other party leaders in Munich there were also repercussions in Nuremberg, where for some weeks the Mayor and City Council had been concerned about rumours of a right-wing *Putsch*. These seemed to be confirmed when, in the early hours of May 1st, the police raided the Nazi *Lokal* in the *Beckengarten*, discovered a number of firearms and arrested several people, including a sergeant of the municipal police. As the weapons belonged to the local *Einwohnerwehr*, the Mayor, Dr Hermann Luppe, at once assumed that they had been issued with the connivance of *Staatskommissar* Gareis and that therefore, as he had suspected, the Bavarian authorities were supporting a right-wing *coup* against the Republic. Fearing an imminent march on Nuremberg, Dr Luppe telephoned straight through to the *Reichskanzlei* in Berlin to ask for help. In actual fact, although Gareis was blatantly hostile to the Left and enjoyed much the same reputation with the Nazis as Pöhner had done in Munich[1] he had had nothing to do with this particular incident, which was probably planned with the vague idea of supporting whatever might happen in the South rather than of starting anything in Nuremberg itself.[2]

The whole affair and the events that followed it give a remarkably vivid picture of the political atmosphere in Bavaria at this time. Although the police sergeant arrested in the *Beckengarten*

[1] Röhm, E., *Geschichte eines Hochverräters* (Munich, 1933), quoted in Maser, W., *Die Frühgeschichte der N.S.D.A.P.: Hitlers Weg bis 1924* (Frankfurt-on-Main and Bonn, 1965), p. 383
[2] The whole incident was closely examined in the libel suits between Dr Luppe and Streicher. See verdict of *III. Strafkammer des Landgerichts Nürnberg*, March 14, 1924. Also Luppe, *Memoirs*, MS., p. 381ff

was dismissed – and soon afterwards became an SA leader – those connected with the illicit weapons were let off with mild sentences. The Bavarian State of Emergency, declared on May 11th, was enforced entirely against the Left and did not prevent the right-wing organizations in at least one place[1] from practising with machine-guns and live ammunition. Dr Luppe was prosecuted for *Landesverrat*, on the grounds that he had got in touch with the Reich Government and sent for the 'Prussian' *Reichswehr* without having first informed a Bavarian official.

Worse than this, from Luppe's point of view, was that Streicher now launched a massive propaganda campaign against him and the City Government. Allegations of personal undesirability and administrative corruption were not enough: Streicher used events of May 1st to 'prove' the fantastic charge that the socialist defence organizations set up during the spring to counter the growth of the SA were intended to conquer the city for a Jewish-Bolshevik dictatorship; and that the Mayor and his supporters were planning to detach Franconia from the rest of Bavaria and throw in their lot with the left-wing extremists in Saxony and Thuringia. All this was quite openly intended to drag Luppe into court, and by finally issuing a writ against Streicher later in the summer the Mayor did indeed entangle himself in a series of law suits which were to last for almost the entire Republican period.[2]

In the meantime, the Nuremberg Nazis were beset by a new wave of internal quarrels. By the end of May, a virtual state of war existed between Streicher and the leaders of the local SA, who supported Kellerbauer.[3] An attempt by Göring to intervene in

[1] The *Reichsflagge* in Feucht. See Gärtner, G., *Mit uns zieht die neue Zeit. Geschichte der Nürnberger Arbeiterbewegung von ihren Anfängen bis zum Jahre 1928* (Nuremberg, 1928). When the SPD held a meeting to protest against this, the *Reichsflagge* and the State Police broke it up and in the scuffle a Nuremberg Socialist was shot dead.

[2] Luppe, *Memoirs*, MS., p. 401. The verdicts of the trials were collected together in a bound volume in *NS* 10; there are also numerous reports in *NL* 45

[3] Rohlfs (commander of the Nuremberg SA) to SA Command, Munich, May 28, 1923, *HAF* Reel 16

their favour simply provoked a mutiny by the storm troopers
loyal to Streicher and by June the entire branch seemed to be on
the verge of an irreparable split.

This time a solution was reached which permitted the reorganization of the SA in such a way as to give adequate control
to the Munich Headquarters and to lay the foundation for the
serious preparations of the late summer and autumn. At first,
however, Hitler moved with great caution. Early in June the
ex-naval officer Dr Helmuth Klotz was sent to Nuremberg with
instructions to take over temporary command of the SA and
restore order. Yet it was not until mid-July, after a good deal
more scandal, that Klotz's suggestions were actually carried out.
The reason for this delay seems fairly clear; at this time the
Munich leadership evidently had very little detailed information
about the outside branches; in at least one case, the SA command
did not even know the name of the local storm troop leader.[1]
The decision to take really positive action or to attempt yet
another compromise in Nuremberg depended far less on the
innocence or guilt of the opposed groups than upon their relative
strengths. It seemed at first[2] that Kellerbauer could command
enough support to split the branch if he were not upheld. As
soon as Klotz was able to report that this was not so, that the
vast majority of the rank and file were either neutral or
supported Streicher, the SA command took decisive action the
very next day.[3]

This time a clean sweep was made. The SA leader who had
opposed Streicher was expelled from the party and Kellerbauer
himself, though he remained a party speaker, had to hand over
the newspaper to Klotz.[4] Yet the settlement was not simply
a capitulation to Streicher. This was shown not only by the

[1] SA Command to NSDAP Kitzingen, August 23, 1923, *HAF* Reel 16
[2] Kirschner to SA Command, June 26, 1923, *HAF* Reel 16
[3] Klotz to SA Command, July 13, 1923; SA Command to Klotz, Kirschner and Dörfler, July 14, 1923, *HAF* Reel 16
[4] Max Amann to Streicher, August 16, 1923, *NS* 105. The name of the paper was soon afterwards changed to *Die Weisse Fahne*. See typescript *Geschichte und Entwicklung der Parteipresse in Gau Franken* by the *Gau* archivist, M. Sauerteig, September 30, 1942, *NS* 114

GERMAN DEMOCRACY AND THE TRIUMPH OF HITLER

simultaneous expulsion of one of his own supporters[1] but also by a long letter from the head of the party organization, Max Amann, on August 16th. While generously praising Streicher's political achievements, Amann made no secret of the party leadership's exasperation and annoyance at the perpetual feuds of the last six months and also criticized Streicher's independence. Now that the newspaper had been taken over by Klotz, he concluded, there was no further need for *Der Stürmer* and in future all literature and propaganda material was to be produced under the direct auspices of the party, as in Munich.[2]

Although in fact *Der Stürmer* flourished prosperously until the end of the Third Reich and Streicher's activities continued much as before, control of the SA passed quite clearly into the hands of the Headquarters in Munich. This was perhaps the most important single step in the history of the NSDAP since Hitler's establishment of his own leadership in the Munich rally of January 1922. For it not only helped to bring other refractory branches to heel[3] but also made possible the two major developments of the autumn: the great intensification of semi-military activity and the deliberate strengthening of the SA at the expense of Hitler's ostensible right-wing allies in Bavaria.

The particular importance of Nuremberg in these plans was shown by Amann's description of it as 'the first great bulwark against the Bolshevik North'.[4] There is no doubt that the growth of extreme left-wing organizations in neighbouring Saxony and Thuringia during the summer was one major reason for the decision at that time to transform Nuremberg from an ordinary SA *Bezirk* into the centre of a new command covering the whole of Franconia.

This, too, affected the balance of power within the branch. For the strengthening and reorganization of the entire Franconian SA necessarily involved close co-operation with Headquarters in

---

[1] SA Command to *Reichsflagge, Oberland* etc., July 13, 1923, *HAF* Reel 16
[2] Max Amann to Streicher, August 16, 1923, *NS* 105
[3] For instance in Würzburg: SA Command to 1st Chairman of Würzburg NSDAP, August 25, 1923, *HAF* Reel 16
[4] Max Amann to Streicher, August 16, 1923, *NS* 105

Munich[1] and required a man of far greater experience and authority than the ex-NCOs who had previously commanded the Nuremberg storm troops. The new commander, the ex-regular officer
and judge's son Major Walther Buch, who arrived on August
21st, did in practice have much more to do with *Staatskommissar*
Gareis on the one hand and with Göring, Kriebel and Röhm on
the other than with Streicher, who clearly ceased to play any
significant part in the activities of the SA.[2]

Major Buch was an interesting figure. Experienced both as a
soldier and an administrator, he was typical of the many ex-military
condottieri in the early Nazi Party whose personal admiration for
Hitler outweighed the monarchism more usual among ex-
Imperial officers.[3] Buch had left the army in December 1918 rather
than swear allegiance to the Republic and he later declined to
join the police for the same reason. Having tried his hand unsuccessfully at small-scale farming and book-keeping, he became
a DNVP secretary in Baden for a time and had finally ended up
writing articles against the *Dolchstoss* for a small *völkisch* newspaper in Karlsruhe.[4] He had belonged to the NSDAP since 1922
and since the early summer of 1923 had been writing to Amann
with the urgent plea for any kind of military or administrative
employment.

In spite of the disputes, the Nuremberg SA was by no means
unserviceable by the time Buch took over. Klotz had reported
that the morale of the men was good, that they simply wanted a
leader they could trust.[5] The SA and the *Landsturm* together
seem to have numbered about 550 men and recruiting continued
successfully throughout the autumn.[6] A basic organizational
structure had been built up and ever since the SA's formation,

[1] See the extensive correspondence between the Nuremberg SA and the
SA Command in Munich in *HAF* Reel 16
[2] Streicher was apparently not informed of the preparations for the
Munich *Putsch* until the very last moment.
[3] He referred to Hitler as 'the man whom God has sent us', Buch to Max
Amann, May 11, 1923, *HAF* Reel 16
[4] Buch to Max Amann, May 25, 1923, *HAF* Reel 16
[5] Klotz to Göring, July 7, 1923, *HAF* Reel 16
[6] Klotz to SA Command, July 27, 1923(1), *HAF* Reel 16

frequent field exercises had been held, evidently with assistance from the local *Reichswehr*. 'So far' wrote Klotz at the end of July 'an oath to the Government has not been required'.[1]

A major obstacle to growth, however, was the fact that it was still quite usual for SA men to belong simultaneously to other 'patriotic organizations', since many of these, unlike the NSDAP, had developed from earlier *Freikorps* or local defence formations. Röhm himself at this time was still a member of Captain Heiss's *Reichsflagge*, which had its headquarters in Nuremberg. The whole problem of divided allegiance was complicated by the very mixed motives which led people to join para-military groups at all. Idealism and admiration for particular leaders did play some part, but many belonged simply through boredom or because they liked wearing uniform. From this point of view there was still no particular reason to prefer the SA to most of the other organizations. If his men did not get military caps without delay, complained Buch's predecessor to SA headquarters at the end of June, it would be impossible to keep order and many of them were already threatening to leave for *Frankenland* or the *Reichsflagge*.[2] One of Buch's most important long-term tasks was to loosen the bondage of competition on this level until the party was in a position to demand exclusive allegiance from its members.

After the establishment of the new Franconian command, events in Nuremberg became more and more closely linked to the general course of Bavarian politics. Buch's first major undertaking on his arrival was to prepare for the famous *Deutscher Tag*, the elaborate right-wing festival which took place in Nuremberg on September 1st-2nd, the anniversary of the battle of Sedan. This occasion has been described in great detail elsewhere;[3] it need only be said that from the point of view of its organizers it

[1] Klotz to SA Command, July 27, 1923(2), *HAF* Reel 16
[2] Kirschner to SA Command, June 26, 1923, *HAF* Reel 16
[3] Report of State Police Office Nuremberg-Fürth (*Staatskommissar* Gareis), September 18, 1923, in E. Deuerlein (Ed.): *Der Hitler-Putsch. Bayerische Dokumente zum 8/9. November 1923* (Stuttgart, 1962), pp. 167-76; also Maser, op. cit., pp. 419-21

was an unqualified success. About 100,000 people came from all over Germany, including Field-Marshal Ludendorff, Admiral Scheer and Prince Ludwig Ferdinand of Bavaria. Popular enthusiasm was overwhelming: in the midst of the flags and flowers and *Heilgrüsse*, reported Gareis, many were moved to tears; and anti-semitic slogans were shouted up at the Mayor and his son as they watched the march-past from the windows of the *Rathaus*.[1] Discipline, however, was good and the socialists, for their part, made no attempt at all to compete with this display and decided, responsibly enough, to withdraw their organizations from the city altogether for the weekend.

Even so, one serious incident did occur. On the final evening the return of the worker's organizations led to a number of clashes with the Right and in one of these a middle-aged trade unionist named Krämer was shot dead by a young *Reichsflagge* man. The resulting wave of violent left-wing riots and demonstrations which dominated the next few days faced Gareis with a real emergency, not least because the Nazis and the *Reichsflagge* threatened to take the law into their own hands if the victimization of their sympathizers in the factories were not effectively checked. The *Staatskommissar*, however, was determined to handle the situation himself. Although at one stage he called up the *Reichsflagge* as auxiliary police, he was able to prevent an armed clash between Right and Left and to claim the whole episode as a victory for the authorities.[2]

The *Deutscher Tag* and its aftermath were significant because, as Gareis reported with great satisfaction, they marked another major setback to the prestige of Nuremberg social democracy.[3] As so often in the Weimar Republic, the socialists were defeated by the paradoxical fact that sometimes the constitution could only be upheld by risking an open and unequal clash with the State. Many workers who had taken part in the disturbances were sacked, others were arrested and put on trial; socialist protests to

---

[1] Luppe, *Memoirs*, MS., p. 385. The city council had earlier decided to ignore any festival in which Republican flags were not included as part of the decoration.

[2] Deuerlein, op. cit., p. 176   [3] Ibid.

the Goverment and the Public Prosecutor uniformly failed. Gareis refused his consent for a Republican rally to counter the *Deutscher Tag*: this could definitely not be allowed, he wrote, as it might look like an internationalist demonstration against the German idea of freedom.[1]

On the other hand, Gareis's refusal to turn the para-military organizations loose on the Nuremberg workers was an omen for the future. It was a clear indication that, however much the Bavarian authorities were prepared to tolerate or encourage these militant groups for their own purposes, they were determined to keep a tight hold on the reins of power. Ex-Imperial officials like Gareis and von Kahr might exploit National Socialism as an ally against 'Bolshevism' or the Republic, but only in the strictest subordination to themselves. There was certainly little prospect that the conservative, monarchist and particularist Bavarian regime would ever allow Munich to become simply a stepping-stone for the conquest of the Reich by a fundamentally radical, anti-Catholic and lower-middle-class movement.

External events continued to favour the Right in the autumn of 1923. From August onwards, the City Council began to issue *Notgeld*, food was scarce and unemployment was increasing. Although the inflation was playing havoc with their already shaky finances, the Nuremberg Nazis had little difficulty in exploiting the crisis for their own purposes. A police officer commented on September 8th, that while other political meetings were only sparsely attended, owing to the increased price of beer and admission, the National Socialists were able to rely increasingly on packed halls.[2] A week later, even the gangways were filled when Streicher spoke in the Bicycle Stadium on 'The Guilt of the Internal Enemies' and promised that the fall of Stresemann's government would be followed by the dictatorship of all really German-thinking people.[3] In general, Streicher caught up every likely theme with his usual inexhaustible energy, demanding the execution of food speculators and persistently representing the

[1] Gärtner, op. cit., pp. 352-3
[2] Police report of September 8, 1923, *HAF* Reel 85
[3] Police report of September 13, 1923, *HAF* Reel 86

JULIUS STREICHER AND THE ORIGINS OF NSDAP

'*völkisch* standpoint' at meetings of officials and white-collar workers.[1] As for the SA, some of its formidable financial and organizational problems at this time stemmed not from the inflation but from its steady growth in numbers and complexity after the success of the *Deutscher Tag*. Less than a week afterwards, Buch anticipated that his existing strength would double before very long.[2] On October 3rd, he wrote that SA units were forming 'in every little town' and added that 'our army is increasing so greatly that further decentralization is absolutely necessary'.[3]

The really significant thing about this increase in strength was that not all the new recruits were converts pure and simple or Nazi refugees from other parts of Germany: many were in fact ex-members of other para-military organizations who had decided to follow Hitler. This was an important symptom of the shift in Hitler's relations with his allies and with the Bavarian Government which was to dominate the last few weeks before the Munich *Putsch*.

Superficially, the relationship between the NSDAP and the 'patriotic leagues' is easy to trace. At the end of February 1923, an *Arbeitsgemeinschaft* was formed (and confirmed in July), consisting of the SA, Weber's *Freikorps Oberland* and *Unterland* and Captain Heiss's *Reichsflagge*, aligned with varying degrees of hostility against Ehrhardt's *Wikingbund, Bayern und Reich* and the *Blücherbund*. Then, during the *Deutscher Tag*, Hitler, Heiss and Weber formed a closer alliance or *Kampfbund* which was reorganized at the end of September with Hitler as political leader and Heiss in command of a new *Befehlsstelle Nord*, which included Franconia. On October 7th, however, Heiss suddenly broke with Hitler and split the *Reichsflagge*[4] by declaring his unconditional allegiance to von Kahr.

This split, which appreciably altered the balance of forces in

---

[1] *Nürnberger Zeitung*, September 25, 1923
[2] Buch to SA Command, September 6, 1923, *HAF* Reel 16
[3] Buch to SA Command, October 3, 1923, *HAF* Reel 16
[4] The branches north of the Danube followed Heiss, the rest turned to Hitler.

Nuremberg, did not result simply from the numerous local and personal disputes within the *Arbeitsgemeinschaft* and the *Kampfbund*, nor even solely from Hitler's characteristic impatience for leadership and independence, but from fundamental differences of aim between the various parties and organizations in Bavaria. If one leaves aside the fantastic projects for a revanchist campaign against the French, three main courses presented themselves to the Bavarian Right in the autumn of 1923. The first was simply self-defence against a possible Communist invasion from Saxony and Thuringia, combined with the forcible suppression of Bavarian Socialism. In principle, this found favour with almost all shades of right-wing opinion. The second course was an actual invasion of Saxony and Thuringia as the first stage of a march on Berlin to overthrow the Republic. This was favoured by some governmental and military circles, at least for a time, and it was of course what Hitler wanted, though he had no intention of being simply the expendable tool of a Directory of conservative generals and industrialists. The third possibility was a more or less complete isolation of Bavaria from the Reich, possibly combined with the prospect of restoring the Wittelsbachs. This was anathema to Hitler: for whatever he might say for tactical reasons, he was certainly not a monarchist and Point 1 of the Party Programme demanded the unity of all Germans within a single Greater Germany. Yet this was the solution favoured essentially not only by *Bayern und Reich* and the *Blücherbund* but also by Heiss, the *Reichsflagge*, the BVP and the Bavarian Government, particularly as the chances of a successful march on Berlin began to fade towards the end of October.

The unity achieved at the *Deutscher Tag* was therefore an illusion. A report of a conference on August 25th, at which Heiss had refused to accept Hitler's leadership, indicated that Hitler was now trying hard to increase his influence in the *Reichsflagge*. And it was hoped that Buch's personality and position in Nuremberg would gradually increase Nazi strength at Heiss's expense. Although an appearance of outward unity was to be maintained, the report continued, the SA's already-planned expenditure for the *Deutscher Tag* was to be doubled so as to outdo the turn-out

JULIUS STREICHER AND THE ORIGINS OF NSDAP

of Heiss's supporters.[1] The same day, the Würzburg SA was instructed gradually to recover its members from both the *Reichsflagge* and the *Bund Oberland*.[2] Given the widening gulf between radicals and conservatives on the Bavarian Right and the monarchist and federalist features of the *Kampfbund's* programme, the eventual breach was hardly a surprise. For Kahr's decision to defy the Reich while at the same time curbing the Nazis was a shrewd move which was bound to rally all those who hoped primarily for a Bavarian solution and to rob Hitler of much of his support. With Heiss, this succeeded admirably; he had always been a monarchist and the *Staatskommissar's* refusal to allow his arrest by the Reich Court was doubtless responsible now for his decision to commit himself totally to von Kahr and the BVP.

But although it led to a substantial increase in the strength of the Nuremberg Nazis,[3] the quarrel with Heiss – and all that it implied for relations with the Bavarian Government and the army – simply made nonsense of the preparations being made by Buch and his assistants. It was totally unrealistic for Hitler, in his speech in Nuremberg on October 14th, to denounce von Kahr and declare that he would rely on himself alone, for almost all Buch's plans involved a considerable amount of co-operation with the authorities. This applied especially to Gareis, with whom Buch had developed a particularly close relationship, and as late as October 27th, Buch was asking the SA Command how far he could take the *Staatskommissar* into his confidence, since this made matters so much easier.[4]

And whatever Hitler might say about relying on himself alone, there was no question of undertaking anything in opposition to the army, or even independently of it. On October 27th, Buch was still using the *Reichswehr* cypher for his instructions[5] and the

---

[1] Conference report of August 25, 1923, *HAF* Reel 16
[2] SA Command to 1st Chairman of Würzburg NSDAP, August 25, 1923, *HAF* Reel 16
[3] On October 12th alone, about 200 *Reichsflagge* men offered their allegiance to Hitler. Police report in *HAF* Reel 84
[4] Buch to SA Command, October 27, 1923, *HAF* Reel 16   [5] Ibid.

plans for mobilization envisaged the *Kampfbund* simply as a reinforcement for the army, subject to regular military discipline. Above all, the *Reichswehr* was to remain responsible for the issue of all weapons and the para-military reinforcements were to report for duty unarmed.[1] This is an appropriate point at which to end this essay. The surviving correspondence between Nuremberg and Munich closes at the end of October and the Nuremberg SA, in spite of its feverish preparations, had no influence on the events of November 9th. As for Streicher, called to Munich at the last moment and put in charge of propaganda by Hitler, he did play quite a prominent part in the *Putsch*.[2] Emerging unscathed from the fusillade at the *Feldherrnhalle*, he made his way back to Nuremberg and spent the next few weeks there and in Erlangen in a state of nervous exhaustion. Although several times interrogated by the police, it was not until the end of the year that he was finally arrested for 'national communist' activities – a very significant phrase – and sent to Landsberg, where he spent two uncomfortable months. Finally, after his release in the spring, he returned to Nuremberg to gather up the disordered remnants of the party's organisation and to prepare for his successful candidature for the Bavarian *Landtag*.

Several conclusions can be drawn from this study. First of all, it is clear that in post-war conditions, extremism was at a premium. The early *völkisch* groups were no match for the NSDAP because they shrank from the combination of right-wing ideology and mass political methods which was the secret of Nazi success. In spite of internal disputes, therefore, Hitler's movement was bound to remain the ideal base for natural fanatics like Streicher who had soon become impatient with the limitations of mere *völkisch* debating societies. But internal quarrels were nevertheless of the greatest importance. For they showed that, what-

[1] Memorandum by Kriebel, October 26, 1923, *HAF* Reel 16
[2] See the statements made to the police by Streicher, December 4, 1923 (*NS* 94), and November 24, 1924 (*NS* 78); by Kellerbauer, December 4, 1923 (*NS* 94); by Karl Strassmeier, December 5, 1923 (*NS* 94); by *Oberlehrer* Heinrich Krauss, November 25, 1924 (*NS* 98)

ever power he had in Munich, Hitler's authority in other places was still extremely limited. He was clearly unable to settle local conflicts either by decree or persuasion and the establishment of control via the SA was a gradual process dependent on a very cautious assessment of the strength of rival factions. It may have been that the Nuremberg branch was exceptional: it had been created by an unusually active and independent individual, while its strategic importance discouraged any over-hasty interference from Munich. But there is no doubt that it posed in an acute form the problem of relations with the branches which had to be solved before any major political enterprise could be undertaken.

Finally, and perhaps most important of all, events in Nuremberg underlined the hare-brained inconsistency of Hitler's plans in the autumn of 1923. For, even when he had established adequate control within his own party, the basic question of his position in Bavarian politics remained unanswered. While the SA and its leaders were tied by personal inclination and practical necessity to the Bavarian authorities, the fundamental division between Hitler and the Munich Government was plain for all to see. In their attempt to overturn the Republic, the Nazis were forced to depend on organizations from which their own character and aims had already isolated them. It was this insoluble contradiction which resulted in the fiasco of the Munich *Putsch*.

CHAPTER 8

THE WESTERN POWERS IN
HITLER'S WORLD OF IDEAS

ERICH MATTHIAS

The subject of this essay is not the foreign policy of Hitler at the time of his dictatorship, but some of the political concepts which he developed when he was not yet in a position to influence German foreign policy. When, in 1933, Hitler took over the conduct of German foreign policy, his first steps in this field did not seem to tally at all with the ideas on foreign policy which he had expounded in *Mein Kampf* and later reiterated in his innumerable *Kampfzeit* speeches. Nevertheless, even at the time when Hitler put the utmost emphasis on appearing to the world as a man of peace, he continued to adhere stubbornly to his basic views on foreign affairs, views which he had developed long before 1933. He never abandoned ambitions to realize his old aims. His early ideas are consequently of decisive importance when assessing his later behaviour in the field of foreign policy. This means that Germany started on her road into the catastrophe of the Second World War not in 1938 or 1939 but in 1933, with Hitler's seizure of power.

If we now turn to the question as to what Hitler's opinion was of the Western powers and what role they played in his foreign political ideas, *Mein Kampf* is and remains the most important source, even after the publication of his so-called *Second Book*.[1] I should like to argue this point regardless of the fact that his *Second Book*, unlike *Mein Kampf*, deals primarily with a future

[1] Gerhard L. Weinberg (ed.), *Hitlers Zweites Buch* (Stuttgart, 1961)

'National Socialist German foreign policy'. In fact the tedious passages, full of repetitions, which make the reading of the *Second Book* so tiresome contain little that is new compared with *Mein Kampf.*

Certainly, we should not underestimate the value of the *Second Book.* It shows, to quote Hans Rothfels in his introduction to the 1961 edition, 'the continuity of Hitler's foreign political axioms . . . which, when put into practice, may have allowed for opportunist deviations, but ultimately remained fixed in a neo-Darwinist conception with all its consequences, rigid to the point of fanaticism and invalidating the view of those who have drawn attention to the sheer opportunism, to the nihilist revolution for its own sake. In short, the view of those who tend to underestimate the actual contents of his programme.'[1]

This continuity of Hitler's foreign political axioms can be shown no less impressively for the later years of his dictatorship. Thus, his *Table Talk* in 1941-2 yields very interesting illustrations of how stereotyped his ideas on this point remained.[2]

Hitler developed his foreign political concepts in the last three chapters of the second volume of *Mein Kampf* under the headings 'German Alliance Policy After the War', 'Orientation Towards the East or *Ostpolitik*?', and 'The Right of Self-Defence'. But the essential elements of Hitler's ideas can be found already in his discussion of German alliance policies before the First World War in Chapter Four of the first volume. This means that one may start from the assumption that his ideas had taken a definite shape as early as 1924 when he wrote this first volume in Landsberg prison.

It is true that Hitler maintained in his *Second Book* in 1928 that he tried 'tenaciously to accustom the National Socialist movement by all means to the idea of an alliance between Germany, Italy, and England ever since 1920'; this, he added, was very difficult 'especially during the early post-war years' because 'the God-punish-England view at first robbed our people

[1] Gerhard L. Weinberg (ed.), *Hitlers Zweites Buch* (Stuttgart, 1961), p. 10
[2] Henry Picker (ed.), *Hitlers Tischgespräche im Führerhauptquartier* (third ed., Stuttgart, 1965)

of the capacity to think clearly and soberly in matters of foreign policy'.

However, this statement contains at best a half-truth, as an examination of the evidence about Hitler's early political activity up to the beer-hall *Putsch* of 1923 will show. Hitler, to be sure, did not fail to differentiate between Germany's various First World War enemies at a very early point in his career. Thus, he counted England, together with France and the United States, among the 'absolute opponents' of the Reich because they were all predestined to oppose Germany on account of their power-political and economic interests. Italy and Russia, on the other hand, had had in his view no reason to enter a war against Germany. Hitler offers two explanations for the entry of these two countries into the First World War which are very characteristic, yet by no means free from contradictions: on the one hand, both countries, he maintains, became Germany's enemies as a result of Jewish intrigues; on the other hand, Germany was bound to clash with Italy and Russia because of her adherence to the alliance with Austria-Hungary, a policy which Hitler considered to have been a 'crime'.

If to Hitler – for whom Bismarck, vulgarly misunderstood, always remained the example of a cold-bloodedly calculating power politician – Imperial Germany had been obliged to make Tsarist Russia her main ally, the Bolshevik Soviet Union could never be included in his plans as a potential ally because he saw in her the embodiment of Jewish domination. 'An alliance between Germany and Russia', Hitler declared as early as the summer of 1920, 'can only come about if Jewry is ousted.'

In view of the scarcity of sources it is very difficult to know whether Hitler hoped that Bolshevism would not last in Russia. This is also unfortunately true when considering the entire problem of an eastern orientation in the early history of the NSDAP. But there is no doubt that Hitler, quite unlike some nationalists in Germany or probably even some National Socialists with national-Bolshevik inclinations, did *not* consider the Soviet Union a potential ally. This meant that basically there was only one potential partner, namely Italy, whose interests in the

Mediterranean clashed with those of France. We know for certain that Hitler advocated a German-Italian alliance as early as August 1, 1920, in a speech which he made at Nuremberg. There is little doubt, though, that this idea gained much more importance in his foreign political concepts after Mussolini's March on Rome. Hitler had at first joined the general public condemnation of Italy's policy towards South Tyrol, but then, in January 1923, he declared in a meeting before an invited audience that 'a clear-cut renunciation by Germany of the Germans in South Tyrol' would be necessary in order to guarantee the co-operation between Italy and Germany 'which now witnesses her national revival and is looking forward to a great future'.[1] 'The clap-trap about South Tyrol', Hitler is reported to have continued, 'the empty protests against the Fascists will only be damaging to us in so far as they alienate Italy from us. What counts in politics is not sentiments but toughness.' Nobody should 'get emotional about the closing of a dozen German schools in South Tyrol'. 'In return for a renunciation of South Tyrol' Germany would 'obtain Italy's support for an *Anschluss* of Austria and the reintroduction of universal military service.'

The *Bayerischer Kurier* was not exactly a paper friendly to Hitler. Nevertheless, there is no reason to question the authenticity of this report. For in October 1923 the *Corriere d'Italia* published an interview with Hitler, in which he confirmed his renunciation of South Tyrol. He repeated his arguments in *Mein Kampf* and in his *Second Book* to which he then added endless polemics against the narrow-minded 'bourgeois-national' politicians who showed no understanding of such a sober approach to power politics as Hitler's.

As far as the 'absolute opponents' of Germany, i.e. the great Western powers, are concerned, the United States is hardly ever mentioned in Hitler's early speeches and recedes into the background. The French, 'the hereditary enemy', on the other hand, were destined to play the main role in his foreign political agitation. Again Hitler uses a double-track argument: on the one hand, he says the power-political goals of France, whose history

[1] Cited in *Bayerischer Kurier*, January 15, 1923

to him is the history of blind hatred against Germany, envisage the complete demolition of the Reich because Germany prevented France from realizing her hegemonical aspirations. And even the French claim to a frontier on the Rhine was, in Hitler's view, an objective the French would never give up. On the other hand, he believed that it was due to the machinations of World Jewry that France had been incited against Germany after 1870-1. As Hitler stressed in a speech on France and international Jewry made in January 1923, there were, in the main, two forces responsible for the Treaty of Versailles and its intolerable reparations demands: France with her 'perennial greed for German soil and money' and the 'German hereditary enemy . . . the international stock market'.

It appears that during the early post-war years Hitler also considered the conflicts of interest between Germany and Britain to be unbridgeable. Germany's recrudescence as a Great Power was in his mind inseparably connected with a renewal of her worldwide rivalry with England.

But whereas his attitudes towards France were clearly defined by deep feelings of hatred, his views of England were influenced more by a love-hate relationship, as Günter Schubert has stated in his study of the early phase of National Socialist foreign policy.[1]

Up to the end of 1922, hatred was unmistakably the dominant factor, although in a speech of October 1921 in which Hitler criticized Germany's pre-war alliance policy he mentioned an Anglo-German alliance as a possible alternative to a Russo-German alignment. But this is his only statement of this sort, contradicting all his other pronouncements on Britain during this period. Nevertheless it is important to realize that, from the very beginning, Hitler's hatred of England is always accompanied by an admiration for this 'absolute enemy'. He concedes that the British have a strong feeling of patriotism, preserved their racial purity even in the colonies and possessed a political ingenuity with which they had managed to use their economic power for their political aims and to make vanquished enemies their allies.

[1] Günter Schubert, *Anfänge nationalsozialistische Aussenpolitik* (Cologne, 1963)

The historical successes of British imperialism and of Britain's colonial policies he considers to be the fruits of a reckless policy of power which, not surprisingly, he does not find morally repulsive but rather worthy of imitation. Britain, in his view, has shown a power-political unscrupulousness which alone makes a nation strong and able to survive in the struggle for existence. It is with the example of England that he thinks it possible to prove 'that right is always only where there is might and that ultimately right without might does not constitute right'.[1]

Hitler's attitude towards England as we know it from *Mein Kampf*, from his *Second Book*, and last but not least from his *Table Talk* thus bore all the essential features long before Hitler made the idea of an alliance with England the hub of the alliance system of a future National Socialist Germany.

This reorientation of Hitler's position which we find in the first part of *Mein Kampf* and which is offered as the most obvious solution to the alliance problem in the second part, had taken place from early 1923 onwards after the occupation of the Ruhr area by French and Belgian troops against the British vote in the Reparations Commission.

If Hitler subsequently concentrated all his hopes increasingly on Britain, his ideas were quite in line with the so-called 'English illusion' which was widespread in German public opinion throughout 1923.[2]

After April 1923 Hitler began to discover historical Anglo-French rivalry. If Britain wanted to preserve the balance of power on the Continent, she had, in his view, to strengthen Germany's position. In his final speech before the People's Court on March 27, 1924, Hitler developed this line of thought: of the two powers which would be decisive for the future development of Europe, so he elaborated, England, unlike France, would not be 'an

---

[1] Hitler in a speech on September 20, 1920 in R. H. Phelps: 'Hitler als Parteiredner im Jahre 1920': Dokumentation, *Vierteljahreshefte für Zeitgeschichte*, 11 (1963), p. 318. Cf. Günter Schubert, *Anfänge Nationalsozialistische Aussenpolitik* (Cologne, 1963), p. 86ff

[2] Evidence produced in Chapter Six suggests that his attitude may have altered in 1922 as the result of Anglo-French differences. See p. 123 above.

enemy of Germany on principle'. Rather she would have to turn against that power 'which is trying to gain the leading position in Europe' simply because it would be the 'never-changing aim' of Britain to 'balkanize Europe and to create a balance of power so that her position as a world power remained unthreatened'. And whereas this continental opponent had been Germany up to the First World War, France had now become the rival. Yet France needed the 'balkanization of Germany to achieve her hegemony in Europe', just as England was dependent on the balkanization of Europe. There is a more detailed discussion of this argument in an article by Hitler, entitled 'Why the 8th of November had to come' which was published in a Pan-German periodical entitled *Deutschlands Erneüerung* in April 1924. For some curious reason this article had been disregarded by all historians until Wolfgang Horn rediscovered it recently.[1] It was written at the time when Hitler was in detention awaiting the verdict of his trial – probably during the very days of his final speech to the court. As these are most probably Hitler's last written deliberations on foreign policy prior to his drafting of *Mein Kampf* and thus throw some light on the origins of his book, it is permissible to quote some of the most significant passages:

'England desires the backing of the European continent for its world colonial policy by means of a maintenance of a European Balance of Power: that is with the help of European nations of about equal size and power-political status which, as a result of their rivalries, so severely impede one another that there is a general paralysis of forces. This also explains England's careful vigilance to ensure that this system of mutual checks and balances shall not be damaged because of an excessive growth of one of the individual powers. . . .

'If England fought Germany in conjunction with France in 1914, she did so to destroy the imminent German hegemony in

[1] Wolfgang Horn, 'Ein unbekannter Aufsatz Hitlers aus dem Frühjahr 1924', *Vierteljahrshefte für Zeitgeschichte*, 16 (1968), pp. 280ff

Europe; France, however [fought Germany] in order to become the first power in Europe herself by destroying the unity of Germany. In short: these are two war aims, which are not quite identical. The fact that France gained her ends almost totally, whereas England gained a French *Macht – und Militärstaat* with Napoleonic tendencies is, to be sure, not so much England's fault. Rather it is the fault of the truly unpredictable wretchedness and the unprecedented cowardice of those forces which wrested the rifle from the fists of the German Reich. . . . If England, after the end of four and a half years of struggle, therefore, had to yield to France's plans rather than be able to serve British interests, this was due to the difficult military situation of the British Isles, quite apart from the difficulty of redirecting the mentality of a nation which (to save itself from doom) had been inflamed with hatred to the boiling point, and [quite apart from the difficulty] of presenting their previous ally as an enemy, and conversely, of suddenly making their hated enemy an ally. England was exhausted and was incapable of opposing France, the more so because the power (Germany) on which the entire question depended, remained as tame as a sheep, accepted slap after slap in the face, humiliated itself and even craved for a "just" punishment.'[1]

What we must bear in mind is that this article, like the sources available for 1923 and like Hitler's final speech before the Bavarian People's Court, claims Britain as an ally against the French.

As has been seen above, Hitler was also not insensitive to the opportunity presented by Anglo-German collaboration in exploiting the land mass of Russia.[2] Doubtless his ideas on this subject were still of a vague character. Nevertheless, it is no longer possible to claim that Hitler's concept of living space in the East appeared in his world of ideas only during his months of imprisonment at Landsberg. Certainly, he may have been influenced there by the concepts of Professor Haushofer, but it

[1] Wolfgang Horn, 'Ein unbekannter Aufsatz Hitlers aus dem Frühjahr 1924', *Vierteljahrshefte für Zeitgeschichte*, 16 (1968), p. 280ff
[2] See above, p. 124

is impossible to say how far such influences were of any importance to Hitler. On the whole it would seem to be simultaneously unfair and over-generous to the unfortunate professor to credit him and his geopolitical ideas with the responsibility for creating Hitler's policy of *Lebensraum* in the East.

It is important to draw attention to the fact that in his first volume of *Mein Kampf* Hitler sees the programme for the conquest of living space in the East still in historical perspective and projects it back into the period before the First World War. Yet there is little doubt that, when developing his ideas, Hitler was thinking less of the past than he was of the future.

Prior to the First World War, so Hitler argued, Germany had four means of producing a more favourable balance between her population on the one hand, and her geographical space, on the other: birth control, internal colonization, *Bodenpolitik* (territorial expansion), and colonial and commercial policies.

For all practical purposes, however, there had been only two effective ways to 'secure work and bread to a rising population' – *Bodenpolitik* and colonial policy. Of these two, *Bodenpolitik* he said, was the 'healthier' solution which had the better prospects for the future. Germany would 'find its fulfilment not in the Cameroons, but exclusively in Europe'. However, such a 'renewed Teutonic migration' to the East, Hitler continued, would have been possible only with the backing of Britain. To win her over, no sacrifice should have been great enough. Germany should have renounced her colonies and her naval claims and should have spared British industry the competition of a powerful Germany on the world market. The ultimate result would have been, so Hitler believed, a business deal on a reciprocal basis. What Hitler called 'a clever German foreign policy' should have led Germany to assume 'the role of Japan' in 1904 and she should have waged war on Russia in Japan's place. Once again Hitler points to a Russo-German alliance as representing a possible alternative to an Anglo-German coalition: 'If a European *Bodenpolitik* is to be made against Russia it could be made only in co-operation with England; a colonial and commercial policy, on the other hand, could be conceived of only against England in combination with Russia.' Yet what is all too noticeable in Hitler's thought on this point is that he applied the idea of Russia as an ideal ally only to the pre-war period. In the intervening years she had become for him an ideological enemy.

In the second volume of *Mein Kampf* Hitler finally displays his foreign political design in its entirety: Italy and France retain their roles, with Italy, apart from England, being the desirable ally, and, what is more, the only obtainable one in Europe, whereas France remains 'the deadly enemy of our people'.

A coalition with Italy has the immediate purpose of isolating France and of giving Germany an opportunity 'to make, calmly and deliberately, those preparations which, within the framework of such a coalition, will have to be made anyway for the final reckoning with France'.

However, 'the destruction of France' – and this is Hitler's ulterior motive – gains its real importance only, 'when it frees our back for an expansion of the living-space of our people in Europe'. Or, to put it bluntly, if it offered the basis for an expansionist war against Russia.

It goes without saying that this plan was couched in the language of violent anti-semitism and anti-Bolshevism. It was based on the idea of a division of labour between England, the European sea power, and Germany, the European continental power, which in Hitler's view suited Britain's interests better than the old-fashioned Balance of Power.

The realization of this programme depended on whether 'a superior indigenous statecraft' will be victorious over the influence of the Jews. France, on the other hand, deserved destruction, if only because she had allowed herself to become dominated by Jews and Negroes to the point of no return. Of course, this was also true of Jewish-Bolshevik Russia whose Germanic upper class was exterminated in the Revolution and whose masses Hitler rated as belonging to 'an inferior race'.

Hitler does not touch upon the United States more than very briefly. However, he *does* emphasize the rising power of America, which would inevitably bring her into conflict with England and would threaten Britain's leading position as a sea power.

'The former colony', he says 'the child of the Great Mother, appears to become the new master of the world.' Under these circumstances it would be all too understandable that Britain was looking forward with some anxiety to the time when the slogan 'Britannia rules the waves' would be replaced by a blunt 'The Oceans of the Union'.

It was only in his *Second Book* that Hitler devotes more space to the power factor across the Atlantic which, he maintains, was about to revolutionize the traditional power relations in the international world on account of its vast dimensions. Again he foresees the emergence of a conflict between Britain and the United States which England would not be able to avoid if she wanted 'to remain loyal to her great world political aims'.

But a National Socialist Germany as the dominant factor on the European Continent would have to be no less prepared to show the Americans her teeth one day. His ideas are not particularly clear on this point and contain a number of inconsistencies. But the gist of his argument is that Germany and Britain would have to fulfil this task together.

It may be worth mentioning in this connection that he reiterated this same idea in his 'Table Talk' on September 8, 1941, when he was expecting a quick conclusion of the Eastern campaign and when he had not yet abandoned the hope of breaking the resistance of England and of persuading her to join hands with National Socialist Germany.

'I shall not live to see it,' he pontificated in this circle, 'but I am glad that the German people will witness the day when Britain and Germany will unite to combat America. Germany and England will know what they can expect from each other. And then we shall have found the right ally: They – the British – possess an impudence which is without precedent. And yet I admire them; there is much that we shall have to learn.'

This quotation shows once again how tenaciously Hitler stuck to his basic ideas on foreign policy. The picture which he draws of the American people in his *Second Book*, however, marks a clear deviation from his statements about the United States and their inhabitants which we find in other sources.

Without mentioning – as one would expect of him – the Negro problem or Jewish influence – usually his favourite topics – he characterizes the Americans as a 'young and racially selected people' composed of 'elements which are racially equal or at least related' to the Germanic race. This he thought was due to the fact that emigration had brought the cream of the European races to the United States. Ability and efficiency, he argues, had again been conditioned by 'Nordic ingredients' and 'scattered Nordic elements' to be found among all European nations. And they had now, to a large degree, become concentrated in America.

This rather curious line of reasoning is used by Hitler to underline the necessity of a 'racial policy which is consciously *Völkisch*', of a Nazi-dominated Europe, and to reject any plan for a united Europe 'consisting of Mongolians, Slavs, Germans etc. because it would be dominated by everybody else except by the Germans'. Only a Europe which is racially pure would be able to hold its own against a racially pure America 'which considered herself a Nordic-Germanic state and by no means an international hotchpotch of peoples'.

It has been the purpose of this survey to draw the outlines of the picture Hitler had of the Western powers and of the role which, he thought they were to play in his foreign political programme.

If one analyses the premises of Hitler's foreign political ideas, it emerges immediately that there exists an almost complete congruity between them and the ideological and pragmatic premises of his views on domestic politics.

In his view, domestic and foreign policies were governed by the same laws of biological vitality which had their roots in a vulgarized Darwinism and in which only one thing counted, namely success.

'Nature', he said, 'does not know political limitations. Rather she puts animals into this world and then observes the free interplay of forces. He who is the most audacious and diligent emerges as her favourite child and obtains the right of being the master.'

This view, which had dominated Hitler's world of ideas ever

since his emergence into political life, that is to say since *before* 1923, does not differentiate between domestic and foreign policy. Similarly, he uses anti-semitic racial ideology to demonstrate that Germany's internal and external enemies are in fact identical with one another. It is a technique, which is apparent in his earliest political statements and demonstrates that in the eyes of National Socialists all opponents were the same. Only the field of conflict was subject to change.

Inside Germany this identification of internal and external enemies, of Jewish democracy and Jewish Bolshevism, enabled Hitler to redirect all nationalist passions, which he mobilized as a result of his agitation, against the so-called Weimar 'system'. And it helped him to create the notion that victory over the enemy within would re-establish Germany's external power position.

Even on January 12, 1923, on the day of the French occupation of the Ruhr–at a time when the German nation was more united than at any other point since August 1914 – Hitler did not refrain from declaring that the slogan should be 'down with the traitors, down with the November criminals' rather than 'down with France'.

And again in his final speech before the Munich Court in March 1924 he proclaimed that the liberation of Germany was not a matter of foreign policy. Rather the struggle would have to be fought inside Germany, as 'Germany will be free only after Marxism has been destroyed'.

This sort of unreal logic, which identified domestic and foreign political successes, made it natural that the celebrations on the occasion of the Nazi seizure of power created the impression that the lost victories of the First World War had now finally been won with the help of the Brownshirts.

'Heaven shall be my witness', Hitler exclaimed in August 1933 when he celebrated his victory at Nuremberg, 'the guilt of our people has been extinguished, the crime has received its punishment, the shame has been rectified.'

Seen from this angle, it seems justifiable to characterize the nationalism which Hitler preached up to 1933 as an introverted nationalism.

This, of course, does not mean that his ideas on foreign policy, as developed during the *Kampfzeit*, were not to be taken seriously. In fact, he used his domestic power in exactly the same way as he elaborated it in *Mein Kampf* and in his *Second Book*: to prepare for the realization of his foreign political plans by means of war.

CHAPTER 9

WOMEN AND THE PROFESSIONS IN GERMANY, 1930-1940

JILL McINTYRE

Relatively little has been written about professional opportunities for women in Germany, and what has been written deals almost exclusively with the years of the Nazi regime. Dr Clifford Kirkpatrick, a contemporary observer, devotes a few pages in his *Nazi Germany: Its Women and Family Life* (Indianapolis and New York, 1938) to a narrative account of developments in the first years after the *Machtübernahme*, which provides a valuable basis for a deeper analysis. More recently, Dr David Schoenbaum has touched on the subject in his short chapter on women in *Hitler's Social Revolution* (London, 1967). As yet, however, there has been no comprehensive treatment of women's role in the professions in Germany in the years between the economic crisis and the war economy.

The professions, as they will be considered here, are those occupations for whose exercise a special qualification, such as a degree or a diploma from an institution of higher learning, is required. Therefore, even where all other things are equal, admission to a profession depends in the first place on the availability of opportunities for higher education. Speaking of the Federal Republic in the 1960s, Dahrendorf says: 'Inequalities of educational opportunity become starkly evident in institutions of higher education'.[1] In the 1920s, the promise in Article 146 of the Weimar Constitution that 'for the

[1] Ralf Dahrendorf, *Society and Democracy in Germany* (London, 1967), p. 76

admission of a child to a certain type of school its own gifts and inclinations, and not the economic and social position nor the religion of its parents, are decisive' remained unfulfilled. Most students at universities came from homes where the bread-winner was engaged in commercial or professional pursuits, or was employed by the State as an official of the higher or middle rank. The children of workers were greatly under-represented, constituting about 2 per cent of the students at universities. This disproportion was even more extreme in the case of female students: it was far more difficult for a working-class girl to obtain a university education than for a boy from a similar background.[1] Well-to-do girls had, however, been able to attend German universities on the same terms as their brothers shortly before the outbreak of the First World War, after a long campaign led by Helene Lange for the admission of women to the universities and the securing of secondary education to give them adequate preparation.

The war experience had shown that women could perform the duties of a responsible position with efficiency and conscientiousness. An outstanding example of this was Dr Marie-Elisabeth Lüders, who had served as leader of a section of the civil government in Brussels, and then as head of the Women's Central Employment Office in the Ministry of War.[2] Accordingly, in 1919 the Weimar Constitution did more for women than merely grant them the franchise. Article 109 stated that 'All Germans are equal before the law. Men and women have fundamentally the same rights and duties.' And Article 128 laid down that 'All citizens without distinction are eligible for public office in accordance with the laws and according to their abilities and services. All discriminations against women in the civil service are abolished.' Since, in Germany, the majority of teachers at every level as well as many lawyers are classed as civil servants, these clauses applied

[1] Conclusions drawn from statistical information relating to summer semester 1928 and winter semester 1928-9 in *Deutsche Hochschulstatistik*, Berlin, 1928, p. 20, and 1928-9, p. 9

[2] Cuno Horkenbach, (ed.), *Das Deutsche Reich von 1918 bis heute* (Berlin, 1930), p. 709

to a far wider range of people than those employed merely in administration.

Throughout the 1920s and 1930s there was no woman cabinet minister in Germany, but the same was true of the other western countries except for Britain and, at the end of the period, the United States. As early as 1920, however, Dr Gertrud Bäumer, who was active in the women's movement, was appointed to the high-ranking official post of *Ministerialrätin* in the Reich Ministry of the Interior.[1] Dr Helene Weber was appointed to a similar position in the Prussian Ministry of Welfare in the same year,[2] while Marie Baum held a post in the Baden Ministry of Labour before becoming a lecturer at Heidelberg University in 1928. Many women served as minor officials in state and local institutions, while women also sat in the *Reichstag* as representatives of the different political parties, but also as representatives of the interests of women in the community.[3] Germany had a far higher proportion of women legislators than had other western countries in the 1920s, although their numbers decreased fairly steadily throughout these years.[4]

The right of women doctors to practise ceased to be in contention after 1918, and they became active in all spheres of medicine in ever-increasing numbers.[5] By May 1927, there were 1,757 female doctors, who constituted 4 per cent of the total number.[6] At the same time, women teachers at all levels increased both in

[1] Ibid., p. 635   [2] Ibid., p. 766

[3] Women deputies from all parties (except the National Socialists and the *Wirtschaftspartei*, who had no female representatives) in the 1930 *Reichstag* formed a study group for the discussion of matters of special concern to women. Political bitterness prevented the forming of such a group after the election of July 31, 1932. This was reported in *Die Bayerische Frau*, October 1932, p. 6

[4] Conclusion drawn from information in Regine Deutsch, *Zwei Jahre parlamentarischer Frauenarbeit.* (Stuttgart-Gotha, 1923), p. 1.; Lida Gustava Heymann, 'Deutsches Debacle', *Die Frau im Staat*, November 1930, p. 2; a report in *Die Bayerische Frau*, January 1933, p. 5

[5] Mathilde Kelchner, *Die Frau und der weibliche Arzt* (Leipzig, 1934), p. 14

[6] *Statistisches Jahrbuch für das Deutsche Reich* (hereafter cited as *St. J.*) (Berlin, 1928), p. 486

M

number and also in proportion to their male colleagues. In the primary schools they rose to 25 per cent of the total, as compared with their pre-war share of 21 per cent; in the middle schools the rise was from 32 per cent to 50 per cent; and in the senior schools for girls they continued to constitute about three-quarters of the total number.[1] Women were also admitted to the staff of universities and colleges, and by summer 1927, thirty-one women formed o·6 per cent of the total number of university lecturers.[2] Perhaps the biggest breakthrough came in October 1922, however, when three women were employed as junior barristers in a Berlin court, thus entering one of the most sacrosanct of male preserves. But although their numbers had increased to twenty-five by September 1930, women made little progress beyond the lower levels of the legal profession. There was still, in 1930, no female public prosecutor in the whole of Prussia.[3]

Like their male colleagues, professional women joined together in organizations. Some of them joined organizations which had male members, such as the *Institut für Soziale Arbeit*, but the large number of professional organizations purely for women testifies to an alignment on the basis of sex. The women's professional organizations were associated with other women's clubs in the annual Women's Congress.[4]

The strongest of the women's professional organizations was the women teachers' association, *der Allgemeine Deutsche Lehrerinnenverein*, which had been founded in 1890. By 1930 it had more than 40,000 members, from a variety of localities, denominations and grades of school.[5] Just as various feminist groups had become corporate members of the national League of German Women's Associations, *der Bund deutscher Frauenvereine*, so the organizations of women teachers, lawyers, lecturers, doctors and

[1] *St. J.*, 1914, pp. 322-4; 1924-5, pp. 355-7 (percentages calculated from figures given)
[2] *St. J.*, 1928, p. 512
[3] '10 Jahre weibliche Richter', a report in *Die Frau*, January 1933, p. 249
[4] Bundesarchiv, *Nachlass Katharina von Kardorff*, No. 28, p. 9, 'Der XI. Frauenkongress in Berlin, 17.-22.6.1929, Ehrenbeirat der Verbände'
[5] H. W. Puckett, *Germany's Women Go Forward* (New York, 1930), p. 178

students were incorporated in an association of academically trained women, the *Deutscher Akademikerinnenbund.*[1] There were also separate denominational groups, like that for Protestant women teachers, the *Verein deutscher evangelischer Lehrerinnen*[2] and the Roman Catholic *Verein katholischer Lehrerinnen*[3]. The union of women doctors had its own monthly magazine, *Die Ärztin*,[4] to parallel the men's *Der Arzt*.

How far the advance of women in the various branches of the professions in the 1920s was due to a genuinely enlightened official policy must remain a matter for conjecture. A powerful influence in favour of women was the fact that many men had not returned from the war, and a large number of those who had returned were disabled. Therefore, in a number of cases, there were not enough men to replace the women who had taken over during the war years. Coincident with this was the appearance on the employment market in the early years of peace of the increased numbers of women who had been admitted to institutions of further education during the war.[5] In spite of the assertions of the Weimar Constitution, however, financial exigencies in the early 1920s led to the continuation of discrimination against married women in the civil service.[6] In 1929 the Reich Ministry of the Interior was still considering the introduction of new regulations concerning married women officials. Severing, the minister responsible, decided that no change was then possible since there was no prospect of achieving the necessary majority in the *Reichstag*.[7] More promising, however, was the fact that Hilferding, the Finance Minister, had been asked at a ministerial

---

[1] Clifford Kirkpatrick, *Woman in Nazi Germany* (London, 1939), p. 50

[2] Bundesarchiv R2/1291, letter of June 7, 1923

[3] Rolf Eilers, *Die nationalsozialistische Schulpolitik* (Cologne and Opladen, 1963), p. 76n

[4] Report in *Die Frau im Staat*, May 1929, p. 4

[5] For the figures relating to attendance at universities and technical universities in the First World War, see *St. J.* 1923, p. 318, and 1919, p. 191, respectively

[6] Bundesarchiv R2/1291, memorandum of March 31, 1923, and letter of May 1923 (exact date not given)

[7] Ibid., letter of July 12, 1929

conference at the end of 1928 to make provision in his budget for 1929 for the possibility of promoting some women employees in the ministries to high official status.[1] In the rare moments when they were not harassed by financial or political crises, the governments of the 1920s seem to have been prepared to consider measures for the implementing of the Constitution. But what was actually achieved was patently much more due to the ability of the women themselves, and to the support of sympathetic individual men.

By 1930 there were far more applicants for professional positions than there were jobs available.[2] Competition, already made severe by the steady rise throughout the 1920s in the number of students at institutions of further education, was greatly intensified in the shrunken market of the Depression years. The majority of those in the liberal professions could make only a meagre living while the large numbers of civil servants fared only slightly better.[3] Nevertheless the summer semester of 1931 saw a record number of students in the universities, with a total of 103,912, of whom 19,394, or 18·7 per cent, were female. A slight rise in their share of places in the following semester brought women to the strongest point of their representation in the years before the Second World War. They were most numerous in Arts subjects, which would lead many into teaching; but they also enjoyed above-average representation in medicine, dentistry and the sciences. Their lowest averages were to be found in theology, law, and agricultural and veterinary subjects.[4]

Of considerable concern was the ever-increasing flow of students of both sexes into training courses for the already oversupplied teaching profession. In Prussia alone, in summer 1931, there were altogether 15,000 potential male candidates for jobs already held by 13,600 permanent teachers. The position was

[1] Bundesarchiv R2/1291, letter of November 19, 1928
[2] Georg Gothein, 'Die wirtschaftlichen Aussichten für Industrie und Mittelstand', *Deutsche Handels-Warte*, 1929, No. 4, p. 90, found in Bundesarchiv, *Nachlass Gothein*, No. 79
[3] Dr Käthe Gaebel, reported in *Die Bayerische Frau*, October 1931, p. 4
[4] *St. J.* 1932, pp. 426-7

even worse for women: 7,500 candidates waited for vacancies among the 1,900 permanent members of school staffs.[1] A speaker at the general assembly of the Bavarian Union of Women's Associations, Frau *Regierungsrat* Fitting, observed that, while academic study by women was increasing, the professional opportunities for these women were becoming more limited, and the economic crisis was affecting women particularly severely. She estimated that in 1934 there would be 104,300 persons qualified for professional positions in excess of demand.[2]

One response to the increase in unemployment in general, and in particular to the overcrowding of the professions, was the attack on the *Doppelverdiener*, the second earner in a family. This in fact meant an attack on the position of the married woman engaged in paid employment outside the home. As early as April 1929, the writer of a letter to the Ministry of Finance argued that, while the dismissal of the 'small' *Doppelverdiener* often caused great hardship, there was a real need for a reduction of those women in the legal profession who were married to wealthy professional men. He claimed that he had found widespread support for his point of view throughout the country, especially among women. In his opinion, women were being made more equal than men since they were performing two full-time occupations, their professional one and that of housewife and mother.[3] As an active member of the Centre Party, the writer may well have represented a considerable body of opinion. Certainly, in Roman Catholic Bavaria the woman lawyer was still, in 1932, completely excluded from the administration and the judiciary.[4] In his encyclical 'Quadragesimo Anno' in 1931, Pius XI made explicit the opposition of the Roman Catholic Church to the employment of housewives and mothers, and demanded that this be stopped at all costs.[5]

---

[1] Report in *Die Bayerische Frau*, February 1932, p. 6
[2] Ibid., July/August 1932, p. 2
[3] Bundesarchiv, R2/1291, letter of April 24, 1929
[4] *Die Bayerische Frau*, July/August 1932, p. 2
[5] Found in Leo Zodrow, 'Die Doppelbelastung der Frau in Familie und Erwerbsberuf', *Stimmen der Zeit*, Vol. 171 (1962/3), p. 376

But while Catholic opposition dwelt on the harm done to the family by the *Doppelverdiener*, opposition from other sources was based more on economic considerations. As early as 1923, the *Verein Deutscher Evangelischer Lehrerinnen* had objected to the employment of married women teachers on the grounds that there were unemployed single women who had teaching qualifications.[1] As the effects of the economic crisis became harsher, the Government deliberated at length on the question of the *Doppelverdiener*, but in May 1931 pronounced that exhortation, and not legislation, was the answer.[2] This decision was bound to be unpopular in many circles, and was an easy target for the propaganda of the increasingly powerful National Socialists, whose slogan 'jobs first for the fathers of families' had direct popular appeal.[3]

The worsening of the economic crisis and the open attack on the position of the married woman in professional life, particularly as a teacher or a civil servant,[4] encouraged those who opposed the employment of any woman in a responsible position to make their voices heard. A student magazine called for the restriction of women to their 'characteristic occupations' and for the suspension of the right of full matriculation for women.[5] Conservative attitudes towards the status and capabilities of women were far from dead. Ernst Erich Schwabach, who in 1928 wrote a book describing, and sympathizing with, the emancipation of women from their condition in the nineteenth century, spoke for many when he said: 'Apart from a very few exceptions, women will never be able to do intellectual work in the creative sense because of their psychical make-up. . . .'[6]

The failure of successive governments in the 1920s to translate

[1] Bundesarchiv, R2/1291, letter of June 7, 1923
[2] The Reich Minister of Labour, reported in *Reichsarbeitsblatt* 1931, I, No. 15, May 25, 1931, p. 101
[3] *Völkischer Beobachter* (*VB*), April 4, 1934
[4] Grete Stoffel, 'Die Arbeitslosigkeit und die Frauenarbeit', *Die Frau im Staat*, August/September 1931, p. 5
[5] Report, 'Die Lage der Frau in den geistigen Berufen', *Die Bayerische Frau*, July/August 1932, p. 2
[6] E. E. Schwabach, *Revolutionierung der Frau* (Leipzig, 1928), p. 97

the high-sounding phrases of the Weimar Constitution into legislation led to impatience and disillusionment on the part of women active in organizations and in the press.[1] Under the editorship of Lida Gustava Heymann, *Die Frau im Staat*, a monthly magazine for educated women of left-wing tendencies, fulminated against the male desire to keep the Constitution a dead letter.[2] It also accused professional men of working to push women out of responsible jobs and even out of the universities.[3] The Government was criticized for taking a negative, if not a hostile, attitude towards the employment of intellectual women;[4] and in late summer 1931 it was reported with foreboding that 'There is still no law which entitles or obliges the State or the private employer to dismiss female civil servants or employees just because they are married'.[5] The Catholic Church was attacked as being reactionary, and of leading the struggle to send women back to the home. Part of the reason for all the animosity towards professional women was said to be that these women were regarded as a menace to the preservation of the family and a healthy rate of population growth.[6]

There was concern of varying degrees among people of most political complexions at the post-war decline in the birth-rate.[7] Probably the most obsessed by this problem, however, was Hitler's National Socialist German Workers' Party. Accordingly, the Nazis, as their speeches and publications testify *ad nauseam*,

[1] Bundesarchiv, *Nachlass Katharina von Kardorff*, No. 38, pp. 56-62, January 22, 1930, 'Brauchen wir eine Frauenpartei?' Bundesarchiv, *Kleine Erwerbungen*, No. 267-(1), p. 27, letter from Frau E. Maass to Gertrud Bäumer, June 24, 1930

[2] Lida Gustava Heymann, 'Frauen heraus', *Die Frau im Staat*, March 1930, p. 3

[3] Lida Gustava Heymann, 'Frauenbefreiung', *Die Frau im Staat*, September/October, 1932, p. 6. E. Knowles, 'Ketzerische Gedanken über die Invasion der studierenden Frau', *Die Frau im Staat*, April 1930, p. 9

[4] *Die Bayerische Frau*, loc. cit.

[5] Grete Stoffel, op. cit., p. 6   [6] Ibid.

[7] 'Reichsausschuss für Bevölkerungsfragen', *Archiv für Bevölkerungspolitik, Sexualethik und Familienkunde*, 1931, Vol. 1, pp. 62-5. Glass, D. V., *Population Policies and Movements* (London, 1940), pp. 270-6

regarded women primarily as child-bearers and rearers.[1] Any other function which women might take upon themselves, or have imposed upon them, had to be viewed in this context.

The Nazis had loudly publicized their theories at every opportunity, but had not been regarded as a serious political force until they emerged from the elections of September 1930 as the second strongest party in the *Reichstag*. As the Depression, which had been a considerable factor in boosting their share of the vote, grew worse, alarm at the prospect of their accession to power increased among those already apprehensive about women's standing in political and professional life. Lida Gustava Heymann warned that in the Third Reich women would revert to their role of imperial days, as child-bearing machines and maidservants of men, with all their political rights revoked.[2] Somewhat prematurely, she announced in autumn 1932 that the danger was receding, since the Nazis were in decline and the women's movement was going from strength to strength.[3] The editors of *Die Bayerische Frau*, however, felt no such optimism, and warned that a victory for National Socialism would mean the loss of professional opportunities, as well as political rights, for all women, married or single.[4]

Nazi propaganda may very well have justified fears of this magnitude, but it did not reflect Nazi ideas entirely correctly. In

[1] P. J. Goebbels, *Michael: ein deutsches Schicksal in Tagebuchblättern* (Munich, 1933), pp. 40-2. Wilhelm Frick, 'Die deutsche Frau im national-sozialistischen Staat', speech reported in *VB*, June 13, 1934. Adolf Hitler's speech to the *NS-Frauenschaft* at Nuremberg, September 8, 1934, found in M. Domarus, *Hitler: Reden und Proklamationen* (Würzburg, 1962), Vol. 1, pp. 449-52. Rudolf Hess, 'Die Aufgaben der deutschen Frau', speech reported in *VB*, May 27, 1936. Gertrud Scholtz-Klink, 'Unsere Sendung', *Nachrichtendienst der Reichsfrauenführerin* (Berlin, 1937), p. 146. These are only a few examples of the kind of speeches and publications typical of the utterances of Nazi leaders on the role of women.

[2] Lida Gustava Heymann, 'Nachkriegspsychose', *Die Frau im Staat*, March 1931, pp. 1-2

[3] Lida Gustava Heymann, 'Frauenbefreiung', *Die Frau im Staat*, September/October 1932, p. 6

[4] 'Die Stellung des Nationalsozialismus zur Frau', Report in *Die Bayerische Frau*, October 1932, pp. 2-3

fact, the Nazis recognized that many women were obliged to undertake employment out of economic necessity, often against their will.[1] These at least could be lured back into the home by family allowances and the marriage-loan scheme, which was announced only three months after the *Machtübernahme*.[2] But it would be more difficult to persuade the 100,000 or so professional women[3], who looked on a job as a career, that their true vocation lay within the sphere of the home and children. They would therefore have to be coerced into accepting their 'natural calling', in which they would find true happiness.[4] So ran the theory. In fact, throughout the inter-war period Germany had a surplus of two million women who could not be wives and mothers, many of them with dependants to support. These women were obliged to earn a living.[5] Their place in the Nazi scheme of things was, ideally, in occupations concerned with women, children and domestic matters, so that they might fulfil their innate maternal instincts – albeit at second hand.[6] The *Volk* could then benefit from the best use of their womanly talents. '*Helfen, Heilen, Erziehen*' (to help, heal, educate) were woman's functions, allotted to her by nature.[7] The Nazis, therefore, perhaps unintentionally,

[1] Alice Rilke, 'Die erwerbstätige Frau im Dritten Reich', *NS-Frauenbuch* (Munich, 1934), p. 65. Angela Meister, 'Die deutsche Industriearbeiterin', Munich dissertation, 1938, pp. 26-7

[2] 'Gesetz zur Verminderung der Arbeitslosigkeit', *Reichsgesetzblatt* (*RGB*), 1933, I, pp. 326-9

[3] Estimated from figures in *St. J.*, 1938, pp. 32-3

[4] 'Die Geschlechter im Dritten Reich', Report in the *Fränkische Tageszeitung*, April 17, 1934

[5] G. Vogel, *Die deutsche Frau, III: im Weltkrieg und im Dritten Reich* (Breslau, 1936), p. 6. Elfriede Eggener, 'Die organische Eingliederung der Frau in den nationalsozialistischen Staat', Leipzig dissertation, 1938, pp. 37 and 47

[6] Paula Siber, *Die Frauenfrage und ihre Lösung durch den Nationalsozialismus* (Berlin, 1933), pp. 26-7. Lydia Gotteschewski, *Männerbund und Frauenfrage* (Munich, 1934), p. 71. Both Paula Siber and Lydia Gotteschewski were active in the Nazi women's leadership for a short time after the *Machtübernahme*. For a brief account of this, see Kirkpatrick, op. cit., pp. 55 and 59-60

[7] *VB*, March 17, 1934

implicitly recognized the need for women in the medical and teaching professions and also in social work of all kinds.[1]

It was, however, before the Nazis came to power that the first legislative measure against the *Doppelverdiener* was taken. This had been foreseen in March 1931 by the German Branch of the Open Door International for the Emancipation of the Woman Worker, which had registered a sharp protest with the Ministers of the Interior and of Labour against 'a planned reduction of married women officials.'[2] Nevertheless, on May 30, 1932, the Brüning government issued a law concerning the 'legitimate position of female civil servants', which permitted national and local authorities, as well as public corporations, to dismiss married women whose financial circumstances 'seemed constantly secure'. The banks and the railway companies were empowered to adopt a similar regulation. Three months' notice had to be given and reasonable compensation paid, while re-employment was possible if the woman's financial circumstances changed for the worse.[3] But no amount of cushioning could disguise the stark fact that the Constitution was, in the context of equal rights for women, a dead letter.

A stinging attack on the measure came from Dr Kläre Schoedon in *Die Frau im Staat*, in an article entitled 'Sic transit gloria . . .'. She observed that the law was being introduced by the Centre Party and faithfully reflected Roman Catholic thinking on the employment of married women. The DNVP strongly supported the measure, and only the Communist Party came out against it, because it was a denial of equal rights for women. This argument did not inhibit the Social Democrats, including their female deputies, from voting in favour of the law, as, inevitably, did the Nazis. The *Staatspartei* – formerly the DDP – abstained, although Gertrud Bäumer, one of its deputies, prophetically called the law a 'dangerous precedent'. What disgusted Dr Schoedon most of all was the way in which the women *Reichstag* deputies meekly followed their party line, so much so that Dr Helene Weber of

[1] Vogel, op. cit., p. 6. Eggener, op. cit., pp. 39-40
[2] Report in *Die Frau im Staat*, March 1931, p. 9
[3] *RGB*, 1932, I, pp. 245-6

the Centre Party even spoke in favour of the measure. Since, Dr Schoedon estimated, a mere eight or nine hundred women would be affected by the law, the passing of it would do more to damage the rights of women than to benefit the employment situation.[1] Dr Marie-Elisabeth Lüders, who was a *Staatspartei* deputy at the time, has since written that a hard campaign was fought in the *Reichstag* against the law, but that some of the women's professional organizations approved of 'this arbitrary measure.'[2]

Kläre Schoedon and Marie-Elisabeth Lüders were not alone in regretting the lack of solidarity on the part of women in general when some aspect of women's rights was under fire. Lida Gustava Heymann had complained bitterly about it,[3] and, more surprisingly there was a similar reaction from a female supporter of Adolf Hitler. In a letter which she sent to the Nazi leader in March 1932, Irmgard Reichenau deplored the fact that there seemed no longer to be a place in Germany for the academically gifted woman, and that not only men but also other women were contesting her right to a professional position.[4] Certainly, conflicting aims and mutual jealousy on the part of the various branches of the women's movement prevented co-ordinated action on an effective scale.[5] It is doubtful, however, whether such action could have changed the course of events to any significant extent under the circumstances of economic crisis and growing political authoritarianism.

The climax of these circumstances was reached on January 30, 1933, with the appointment of Adolf Hitler as Reich Chancellor. A strong anti-intellectualism formed part of the Nazi reaction

[1] Kläre Schoedon, 'Sic transit gloria . . .', *Die Frau im Staat*, July 1932, pp. 5-7

[2] Marie-Elisabeth Lüders, 'Aus der Frauenarbeit des Reichstags, 1919-1933' in Ernst Deuerlein, (ed.), *Der Reichstag. Aufsätze, Protokolle und Darstellungen zur Geschichte der parlamentarischen Vertretung des deutschen Volkes, 1871-1933* (Bonn, 1963), p 122

[3] Lida Gustava Heymann, 'Frauen heraus', *Die Frau im Staat*, March 1930, p. 4

[4] Irmgard Reichenau, 'Die begabte Frau', in Irmgard Reichenau (ed.), *Deutsche Frauen an Adolf Hitler* (Leipzig, 1934,) p. 13

[5] Kirkpatrick, op. cit., p. 51

against all things associated with the Weimar Republic.[1] The party accused highly educated men and women of an individualism which was antithetical to its principle of *Gemeinnutz vor Eigennutz*, the subordination of self-interest to the general good.[2] The party's suspicion of intellectuals is illustrated by the tight control which it maintained over the professions. Of the eighteen 'works communities' of the German Labour Front, to which all workers of hand and brain belonged, only number 13, which the liberal professions constituted, was under the direct supervision of Dr Ley, the Party Organization Chief and Leader of the Labour Front.[3] In addition, the individual groups of doctors, engineers, teachers, civil servants, lawyers, lecturers and students became associated with the party itself, subordinate to Dr Ley's authority;[4] in this the professional groups were unique among all occupational groups.[5] The compulsory labour service for all school-leavers who sought admission to a university from 1934[6] was partly in order to bring students of both sexes – the future professional people – into the mainstream of the *Volk*, and to prevent their isolation as an intellectual elite.[7]

The Nazis claimed that their *Weltanschauung* demanded not the subordination of women to men but rather a true separation of the sexes, since men and women were, both physically and mentally, completely different.[8] For this reason co-education had

[1] Hitler's speech at the first congress of the Labour Front, May 10, 1933, found in Domarus, op. cit., p. 268. Hitler's secret speech to the press, November 10, 1938, found in Domarus, op. cit., pp. 975-6. P. W. Van den Nieuwenhuysen, *De Nationaalsocialistische Arbeidsdienst* (Louvain,1939), p. 44

[2] Point 24 of the Nazi Party programme, found in Walther Hofer (ed.), *Der Nationalsozialismus. Dokumente 1933-1945* (Frankfurt-am-Main, 1957), pp. 30-1

[3] Taylor Cole, 'The Evolution of the German Labour Front', *Political Science Quarterly* (1937), pp. 540-1

[4] *Organisationsbuch der NSDAP* (Munich, 1938), p. 154

[5] Wolfgang Schäfer, *NSDAP. Entwicklung und Struktur der Staatspartei des Dritten Reiches* (Hanover, 1956), p. 57

[6] *Wirtschaft und Statistik* (Berlin, 1935), Vol. 15, No. 9, p. 334

[7] *Reichsarbeitsdeinstgesetz*, June 26, 1935, *RGB*, 1935, I, pp. 769-71

[8] Anna Zühlke, *Frauenaufgabe – Frauenarbeit im Dritten Reich* (Leipzig, 1934), p. 32. Eggener, op. cit., p. 22-4

no place in Nazi policy.[1] The 'Jewish-intellectual' concept of the highly educated woman was violently attacked,[2] while it was claimed that the 'liberal-democratic-marxist' practice of encouraging women to achieve the same aims as men when their beings were different and complementary led only to a ridiculous caricature.[3] More than that, the intellectual pretensions of women under the Weimar regime, said the Nazis, had resulted in a devaluation of woman's natural calling as a wife and mother.[4] The female nature was more suited to practical occupations, while the male sex was essentially creative.[5] Even when it was conceded that some women could make a considerable success of opportunities for higher education, there was always the reservation that mathematics and physics were beyond the scope of female ability,[6] although this prejudice had no backing in university statistics.[7]

The accession of the Nazis to power encouraged a number of their female admirers to produce books and pamphlets dealing with the 'woman question'. Both militants and moderates favoured opportunities for women in higher education and the professions, but attacked the existing women's movement for its intellectual

[1] Ibid., p. 40
[2] Hitler's speech to the *Frauenschaft* at the Nuremberg Congress of 1934, found in Domarus, op. cit., p. 451
[3] Rudolf Hess, 'Die Aufgaben der deutschen Frau', speech reported in *VB*, May 27, 1936
[4] 'Die Geschlechter im Dritten Reich', *Fränkische Tageszeitung*, April 17, 1934. A. Mayer, *Deutsche Mutter und deutscher Aufstieg* (Munich, 1938), pp. 30-2
[5] Eggener, op. cit., p. 22
[6] 'Die Geschlechter im Dritten Reich', *Fränkische Tageszeitung*, April 17, 1934. Anna Kottenhoff, 'Vom Wesen und von der Verantwortung des geistigen Frauenschaffens', *Frauenkultur im Deutschen Frauenwerk*, January 1939, p. 4
[7] Girl students in mathematics and physics constituted 30·5 per cent of all university students in these subjects in 1930, 31·1 per cent in 1932, and 22·3 per cent in 1934. In these years their share in the total number of university students was, respectively, 17·5 per cent, 18·5 per cent and 16·3 per cent (*St. J.*, 1931, pp. 430-1; 1933, pp.522-3; 1935, pp. 523-4). The proportion of girls in mathematics and physics courses was, therefore, well above that of their general representation in the universities.

exclusiveness.[1] A curious exception was Gertrud Baumgart, who in *Frauenbewegung Gestern und Heute* defended the women's movement against this charge, while also rejecting the charges that the women's movement made against the Nazis.[2] The Nazis had their own feminists, however. Their leader, Sophie Rogge-Börner, wrote an impassioned plea to Adolf Hitler on February 18, 1933, for the inclusion of the best people in the leadership of the country, regardless of sex. She claimed that the State and various official bodies were denying women their rightful place in the professions.[3] But Paula Siber, the Nazi women's leader after the *Machtübernahme* (Nazi assumption of power), was at pains to point out that the universities were open to women, as were professional positions in medicine, teaching and the sciences. The idea that the Nazis would deprive women of their rights was, she said, 'nothing other than the last big lie of an age that is past.'[4]

But the desperate situation in the professions still obtained. The minister responsible for the labour exchanges wrote in February 1933 that many school-leavers with university entrance qualifications would in future have to find their niche in a position which did not require academic study.[5] The number of candidates for professional positions was out of all proportion to the number of jobs available, and it was therefore decided to persuade school-leavers individually not to apply for university education.[6]

The first legislative step was taken on April 7, 1933, with a law designed to remove from the public service those whom the Nazis felt to be politically undesirable, and their replacement by

[1] Siber, op. cit., pp. 16 and 30. Gertrud Baumgart, *Frauenbewegung Gestern und Heute* (Heidelberg, 1933), pp. 20-1. Lydia Gotteschewski, 'Zur Einführung!', *Die Deutsche Frauenfront*, August 1933, No. 1, p. 1
[2] Baumgart, op. cit., pp. 17-21
[3] Sophie Rogge-Börner, 'Deutsche Frauen an Adolf Hitler', in Irmgard Reichenau (ed.), *Deutsche Frauen an Adolf Hitler* (Leipzig, 1934), p. 8
[4] Siber, op. cit., pp. 30-1
[5] Bundesarchiv, R36/1929, letter of February 16, 1933
[6] Bundesarchiv, R43II/936, cutting from *Vossische Zeitung*, February 18, 1933

those faithful to the *Weltanschauung* of the new regime.[1] This to some extent merely legalized a practice already current, since a purge had begun almost immediately after the *Machtübernahme*. On February 27th, Gertrud Bäumer received a message, without previous warning, that she was being 'granted leave of absence until further notice'. Her policies relating to women and youth were in opposition to those of the new government, which felt that co-operation between her and the new Minister of the Interior Frick, would be impossible.[2] To add insult to injury, her pension was made as small as possible, with her service as a school-teacher left out of the reckoning.[3]

There were protests against the dismissal of both men and women on political grounds, but these tended to result in the dismissal of the person making the protest. It was for this reason that Professor Anna Siemsen lost her job at Jena University.[4] There could be little surprise that the Berlin lawyer, Hilde Benjamin, was banned from the practice of law: in addition to having been a member of the defence team in the trial of the murderer of the Nazi hero, Horst Wessel, she was a card-carrying Communist.[5] There was a strong element of pacifism among women prominent in politics and the professions, which immediately brought them into disfavour with the new government.[6] But all the measures taken did not receive unqualified approval from some of the Nazis' own supporters. The *Ring Nationaler Frauen*, for example, recognized the need to eliminate dissidents from prominent positions. Its leadership, however, wrote to Hitler himself to protest that women dismissed in this way were

[1] 'Gesetz zur Wiederherstellung des Berufsbeamtentums', *RGB*, 1933, I, April 7, 1933, pp. 175-7
[2] Bundesarchiv, *Kleine Erwerbungen*, No. 296-(1), p. 16, letter of March 7, 1933, from Gertrud Bäumer to Dorothee von Velsen
[3] Emmy Beckmann (ed.), *Des Lebens wie der Liebe Band* (letters of Gertrud Bäumer) (Tübingen, 1956), p. 53, letter of June 30, 1933
[4] Kurt Grossmann, 'Der Fall Anna Siemsen', *Die Frau im Staat*, March 1933, pp. 7-8
[5] Erich Stockhorst, *Fünftausend Köpfe* (Baden, 1967), p. 51
[6] 'Die Welt wird schöner mit jedem Tag', *Die Frau im Staat*, May 1929, p. 4, on the pacifism of women doctors. Baumgart, op. cit., pp. 27-8

often being replaced, not by women of the right political persuasion, but by men.[1] They should perhaps have been aware that, from the earliest days of the party's existence, the Nazis had insisted that women could have no share in the leadership.[2] It was a logical step to apply this rule to the leadership of the State also, after the *Machtübernahme*.

As Gertrud Bäumer had feared, the law of May 30, 1932, formed a convenient precedent for measures directed against professional women. On June 30, 1933, a law was published which stipulated that only women of thirty-five and over could be given permanent appointments in the public service. The prohibition of employment of married women was made unconditional for those whose husbands were in the service of the State. It was this same law which decreed that 'non-Aryans' and those married to 'non-Aryans' were not to be employed by the State, and that in addition to the special qualifications for particular positions, guaranteed support of the 'national state' was required.[3] The *Frankfurter Zeitung*, which had managed to retain some of its character and independence after the *Machtübernahme*,[4] pointed out that the Nazis had converted the possibility of dismissal on marriage into a mandatory rule, and had extended the scope of the 1932 law far beyond the intentions of its creators.[5] Some authorities acted promptly to implement the new law. The zealous educational officials of Hamburg dismissed 103 permanent and sixty-eight temporary married women teachers only a month after the passage of the law.[6]

The law of June 30th applied specifically only to married women, but nevertheless gave rise to fears regarding the position of women in general in the professions. In October 1933 Frick

[1] Bundesarchiv, R43II/427, letter of April 1933 (exact date not given)
[2] G. Franz-Willing, *Die Hitlerbewegung* (Hamburg, 1962), p. 82
[3] 'Gesetz zur Änderung von Vorschriften auf dem Gebiet des allgemeinen Beamten-, des Besoldungs- und des Versorgungsrechts', *RGB*, 1933, I, pp. 434-5
[4] F. B. Aikin-Sneath, 'The Press in Modern Germany', *German Life and Letters* (London, 1937), p. 58
[5] *Frankfurter Zeitung (FZ)*, July 18, 1933
[6] Report in *FZ*, July 4. 1933

felt it necessary to allay these fears, at least partially, in a note sent to the local authorities. He explained that the law was not intended to justify a general attack on women civil servants and teachers, and that the practice of transferring officials to a lower grade or retiring them prematurely was not being used against women particularly, but came more within the scope of the law of April 7th, which was directed against those regarded as politically unreliable. Frick did admit, however, that of two candidates for a post, the male would be given preference over the female if they were of equal ability. But he did emphasize that women were needed as public servants in particular spheres, predictably in the care of youth and to some extent also in education.[1]

While women were not to be hounded out of the professions altogether, it soon became apparent that they were no longer to be found in the highest grades, where formerly they had at least been represented. Most women industrial superintendents were in the middle grades even before 1933, with only four in the higher grades. After the *Machtübernahme* three of these were retained, while the medical adviser in Magdeburg was retired.[2] There were women employed as higher officials in the appropriate ministries of the national and *Länder* governments before 1933, to advise on questions concerning female and child labour, but these were dismissed by the new regime.[3] Gertrud Bäumer's dismissal meant that there was no longer a woman in a high position in the State, but it was, surprisingly, she who later defended the Nazi record against the criticisms of foreign news-papers. She pointed out that, although a considerable number of women were dismissed from lecturing appointments in the univer-sities, this had mainly been on 'racial-political' grounds, and that a number of women had been appointed to university staffs for the first time after 1933.[4]

---

[1] Bundesarchiv, R43II/427, letter of October 5, 1933
[2] Else Lüders, 'Weibliche Aufsicht in Fabriken', *Die deutsche Kämpferin*, August 1935, p. 182
[3] Ibid., p. 183
[4] Gertrud Bäumer, 'Zur Berufsgeschichte der deutschen Akademikerin', *Die Frau*, June 1939, p. 453

It was claimed, however, that women teachers were being driven out of their jobs in favour of men, especially in the senior schools. Hamburg was regarded as a particular offender, since in addition to dismissing its married women teachers it was also forcing unmarried women into premature retirement at fifty-two years of age.[1] In April 1934 the Prussian Minister of Education announced that in future the ratio of male to female teachers in the senior schools for girls would be 3 : 2, where it had previously been 3 : 5·3. Vacant places were to be offered first to war-wounded men teachers, except in subjects like biology and gymnastics, which should be taught by women.[2] There had, however, been some difficulty for women in obtaining the better positions in the senior schools in the years before the Nazis came to power,[3] so that the contrast between opportunities before and after 1933 is not as great as it might appear. Nor did Nazi policy in this sphere conform to the party's much-publicized theory of the separation of the sexes and the insistence on reversing the previous era's policy of co-education.

Effective protests against the actions of the new government were hardly possible, since the Nazis had taken the astute step of 'reforming' the professional organizations before proceeding against the professions. The *Allgemeine Deutsche Lehrerinnenverein* had seen no alternative to dissolution in May 1933, as the result of official pressure on its members. Its last act was to recommend that its members join the *NS-Lehrerbund* (Nazi teachers' association), which included both men and women.[4] The constituent groups of the old Union were thus left isolated. The control of the party over the teaching profession seemed undisputed when in January 1934 the Bavarian Education Minister, Hans Schemm, announced that 90 per cent of all German teachers were members of the Nazi organization.[5] The *Deutscher*

---

[1] 'Mädchenbildungs- und Lehrerinnenfragen in der Pädagogischen Presse', report in *Die Frau*, June 1934, p. 571
[2] Report in *FZ*, April 9, 1934
[3] Puckett, *Germany's Women Go Forward*, p. 197
[4] Gertrud Bäumer, Das Haus ist zerfallen', *Die Frau*, June 1933, p. 513
[5] Ibid., June 1934, p. 570

Akademikerinnenbund, which encouraged the intellectual elitism which the Nazis were determined to destroy, was surprisingly allowed to continue in existence, on condition that its president, the renowned liberal social worker and former *Reichstag* member, Dr Marie-Elisabeth Lüders, resigned.[1] The Nazis, however, formed a rival organization, the *Reichsbund deutscher Akademikerinnen*, which was both influenced and supported by the Reich Women's Leadership. Eventually, in December 1935, the *Deutscher Akademikerinnenbund* was forced to dissolve itself.[2]

The old multiplicity of organizations within the individual professions was superseded by monolithic bodies under strict party control.[3] There was the *Reichsbund deutscher Beamten* for civil servants, the *NS-Rechtswahrerbund* for members of the legal profession, the *NS-Ärztebund* for doctors, the *NS-Dozentenbund* for university lecturers, and the *NS-Studentenbund* for students, in addition to the *NS-Lehrerbund* for teachers.[4] The lines were now firmly drawn between the individual professions, with men and women belonging to the same organizations. This contrasted noticeably with previous practice, and was out of step with the policy of keeping the sexes in separate groups because of the essential differences between them. Since women were in a minority in all professions, and in a small minority in the legal profession and the civil service,[5] their chances of having a say in the running of their organization – in so far as this was possible under the Nazis – were minimal. The *NS-Lehrerbund*, however, recognized that this was a problem, and early in 1934 Frau Dr Auguste Reber-Gruber was appointed the 'national representative of women teachers' within the

[1] Kirkpatrick, op. cit., pp. 50 and 55
[2] 'Fünf Jahre Reichsfrauenführung', report in *Frauenkultur*, February 1939, p. 4
[3] Hermann Neef, *Das Beamtenorganisationswesen im nationalsozialistischen Staat* (Berlin, 1935), pp. 4-5, 11-12, describes the merging of the large number of organizations for civil servants into one enormous group.
[4] *Organisationsbuch*, p. 154
[5] Statistics relating to women in the various professions are found in *St. J.*, 1938, pp. 32-3

organization. Frau Hedwig Förster was, for the same reason, appointed 'leader of the section for girls' education' in the *Lehrerbund*.[1]

Professional groups were only a small fraction of those to be reorganized in accordance with the Nazi policy of *Gleichschaltung*. From 1933 onwards there took place the dissolution of all non-Nazi women's groups including those of neither a political nor a professional character.[2] All organizations were required to be affiliated to *Das Deutsche Frauenwerk*, founded in 1933 as the successor to the original Nazi *Frauenorden*. The *Frauenwerk* accepted either group or individual members, and its policy was controlled by an elite called the *NS-Frauenschaft*. By December 1936 the *Frauenwerk* claimed to have eleven million members.[3] The large and independent *Bund deutscher Frauen vereine*, which prided itself on its non-party and non-denominational character, dissolved itself in May 1933 rather than conform to the Nazi pattern.[4] After some initial confusion, a Nazi directorate of women's activities, the *Reichsfrauenführung*, was created as an administrative department of the party on February 24, 1934.[5] Its leader was Gertrud Scholtz-Klink, who had served for some months in the Baden Ministry of the Interior and was also the *Frauenschaft* leader in Baden. She was, in addition, appointed leader of both the *Frauenwerk* and the *Frauenschaft* at the national level, as well as of the Red Cross and the Women's Labour Service. In June 1934 she became the leader of the newly founded Women's Section of the German Labour Front.[6] She was thus at least the nominal head of all activities concerning women in the Nazi scheme of things, although at the top level of the party organization the office of the *NS-Frauenschaft* was directed by a

[1] *Die Frau*, June 1934, p. 571
[2] *NS-Frauenschaft* (*Reichsfrauenführung* publication) (Berlin, 1937), p. 15. There seemed surprisingly little urgency about completing this task. The Union of Catholic Women Teachers, for example, was not dissolved until October 1937 (report in *FZ*, October 20, 1937)
[3] Eggener, op. cit., pp. 57-8
[4] *Die Frau*, June 1933, p. 513. Report in *FZ*, May 17, 1933
[5] *Frauenkultur*, February 1939, p. 4
[6] Ibid.

man called Hilgenfeldt.[1] He, in turn, was responsible to Dr Ley, while in the last resort political control of women's affairs lay in the hands of Rudolf Hess, Hitler's Deputy.[2] The day-to-day running of the vast organization was, however, in the hands of women, and soon it was found that enthusiasm and party loyalty, while essential attributes, were no substitute for professional training.[3] The Nazis' own elitist system of leaders and followers demanded a sufficient degree of education to equip women for leadership and management.

The Government soon realized that any ideas it might have had of removing women from professional and responsible positions were not at all practicable. At the beginning of 1934, Göring, as Prussian Minister of the Interior, expressed concern at the reduction in the number of women welfare workers. Naturally, he said, 'this profession too must be purged of those elements whose personality prevents their performing service to the national state. But it is not the intention of the National Socialist state to remove all female civil servants and employees from the service of the state on account of their sex as a matter of principle. . . . Often the decrease in the number of women welfare workers is the result of a false application of the principles concerning the *Doppelverdiener*.'[4]

It was in 1934 that a women's section of the *Reichsbund deutscher Beamten* was created to deal with matters specifically concerning female civil servants, under the leadership of Dora Hein, an office-holder in the *Frauenwerk*.[5] Once again, as with the appointment of Frau Scholtz-Klink to a number of positions, the Nazi policy of co-ordination is visible: if women were to be accepted

---

[1] Kirkpatrick, op. cit., p. 61. 'Eine neue Hochschule der nationalsozialistischen Idee', *VB*, May 31, 1934

[2] *Organisationsbuch*, p. 154

[3] Report in *Die Frau*, April 1935, pp. 437-8. Auguste Reber-Gruber in *Die deutsche höhere Schule*, 1935, No. 14, pp. 483-4. 'Die "typisch fraulichen Berufe" ', *Die Frau*, April 1937, p. 402

[4] ' "Weibliche Beamte in der Wohlfahrtspflege teilweise unentbehrlich" ', *Der Deutsche*, January 5, 1934

[5] 'Eine Frauenabteilung beim Reichsbund der Deutschen Beamten', *Die Frau*, November 1934, p. 120

in the professions, they should be reminded, by their association with the *Frauenwerk*, that they were first women and then civil servants or teachers or doctors. More than merely tolerating the presence of women in these fields, the Nazi leaders actually appointed married women to high representative positions, in direct contrast to their objections to and measures against the *Doppelverdiener*. The fundamental objection seems to have been to politically unreliable women, while docile party members were not denied advancement within the limits of Nazi organizations purely because of their sex. Nevertheless, even these women were not admitted to the top echelons of the party or government. In keeping with the theory of the separation of the sexes, they could hold key positions only in the women's section of a national organization which was firmly under male leadership.[1]

Concern at the high numbers of students in the universities had not abated by the close of 1933. Accordingly, the Minister of the Interior decided to place a limit of 15,000 on the number of new students in 1934, stipulating also that the proportion of girls in this number must not exceed 10 per cent.[2] The number of new entrants to all colleges of further education had in fact been falling after reaching the abnormally high point of 29,708 in 1931. After a figure of 20,829 in 1933, there was a dramatic drop in 1934, when there were only 13,678 new students. Girls constituted 12·5 per cent of these, although their share in 1933 had been 16·7 per cent.[3] This meant, however, that the aim of restricting girls to a share of 10 per cent was not enforced, and that girls were still being allowed to prepare themselves for a professional career. Even in April 1936 it was felt that the continuing surplus of teachers must be arrested, and so Rust, the Education Minister, ordered that girls leaving school in that year should not be

---

[1] *Hitler's Table-Talk, 1941-4* (London, 1953), p. 252, discussion in the evening of January 26, 1942. Hitler pointed out that 'In no local section of the Party has a woman ever had the right to hold even the smallest post'

[2] Bundesarchiv, R43II/936, p. 275, 'Zahlenmässige Begrenzung des Zuganges zu den Hochschulen', report from *Wolff's Telegraphisches Büro*, December 28, 1933   [3] *Deutsche Hochschulstatistik*, 1934/35, p. *5

admitted to teacher-training courses for either primary or secondary schools. The possibility of admission in 1937 remained, and in the intervening year the girls were advised to join the Labour Service or engage in domestic work of some kind.[1] In spite of the measures designed to reduce the number of women in the teaching profession, the proportion of women teachers remained fairly stable throughout the 1930s. As might be expected, their numbers increased, although only marginally, in primary schools, while in the middle schools their share fell by almost 5 per cent. But, most surprisingly, in spite of the setting of a 3 : 2 ratio in favour of male teachers in Prussian schools of the senior grades, the percentage of women teachers in these schools declined by a mere 2 per cent between 1931 and 1939, remaining very much in the majority with a share of 68 per cent.[2]

The Nazis were well aware that teachers were in a very influential position with regard to the youth of Germany. It was therefore urged that all women teachers should be members of the *Frauenschaft*, and that they should help in the other activities of the women's organizations in their spare time. They should also accept and welcome the work of the *Bund deutscher Mädel*, which had great educational value from the point of view of character development. Those teachers who could not see this had no right to be teachers in the Third Reich.[3] Lip service to these Nazi demands was not sufficient. A party official in Trier reported in 1935 that one woman teacher in the area 'has been a member of the *NS-Frauenschaft* since July 1, 1934. She does not buy our newspapers and has a very close association with the clergy. . . . Her entire attitude to us at present can only be considered as a façade in order to maintain her position.'[4] On the

---

[1] 'Die Laufbahn der Studienrätinnen', report in *FZ*, April 16, 1936. 'Einschränkung des pädagogischen Studiums', report in *Die Frau*, May 1936, p. 501

[2] *St. J.*, 1932, pp. 424-5; 1937, pp. 574-6; 1939/40, pp. 611-14

[3] Auguste Reber-Gruber in *Die deutsche höhere Schule*, 1935, No. 14, pp. 480-4

[4] F. J. Heyen, *Nationalsozialismus im Alltag* (Boppard, 1967), p. 256, document No. 130, 'Beurteilung einer Lehrerin durch einen Ortsgruppenleiter in Trier vom 7. January 1935'

other hand, zealous party workers were noticed and praised, and sometimes rewarded. Party member Matthias was given a senior position in the educational administration of the city of Kiel in 1935 because she had dissolved a teachers' organization and enrolled its members in the Nazi Teachers' League, and had won for the *Reichsbund deutscher Akademikerinnen* a respected position among international professional women, without departing from Nazi principles.[1]

The number of women doctors, and their share in the total number of doctors, increased steadily throughout the 1930s. From 2,455 (5 per cent) at the beginning of 1930, they increased to 2,814 (6 per cent) at the beginning of 1934, and to 3,650 (7·6 per cent) at the beginning of 1939.[2] In spite of the threats of the leader of the Nazi doctors' organization, and contrary to the fears of some women doctors,[3] the Nazis did not ban women from panel practice. In fact, by early 1936, almost half of all practising women doctors were engaged in panel practice. In addition, 42·4 per cent of all women doctors were married, and 70 per cent of these were mothers.[4] At least in the medical profession, then, Nazi fears that women would selfishly sacrifice motherhood for a career were not confirmed. Women doctors came to be very important in the network of organizations built up by the Nazis to involve women directly in the life of the *Volksgemeinschaft*. The women's section of the Labour Service, the *Bund deutscher Mädel* and educational and welfare services needed expert medical advice,[5] and the theory of the separation of the sexes meant that it would have to be provided by women. The Nazi leadership accepted women in this field without feeling their campaign against intellectual women to be compromised since they argued that medicine was essentially a practical occupation.[6]

[1] 'Aus dem NSLB', report in *Die deutsche höhere Schule*, 1935, No. 10, p. 10
[2] *St. J.*, 1932, p. 404; 1936, p. 510; 1939/40, p. 586
[3] Mathilde, Kelchner, *Die Frau und der weibliche Arzt* (Leipzig, 1934), p. 42
[4] 'Zahl und Familienstand der Ärztinnen', report in *Die Frau*, January 1936, pp. 238-9
[5] *Die Frau*, April 1937, p. 402. 'Was Zahlen lehren', *VB* September 4, 1936   [6] Ibid.

WOMEN AND THE PROFESSIONS, 1930-1940

The favourable position of women in the teaching and medical professions was not maintained in academic life itself, although, as Gertrud Bäumer pointed out, women continued to be admitted to university staffs after 1933.[1] Women had never constituted more than about 1 per cent of this profession, a level which they reached in the winter of 1930-1. But by the winter semester of 1934-5 their numbers had been reduced from the high point of 74, reached in 1932-3, to 28, or 0·5 per cent. They managed to make good part of this loss in the following year, however, by increasing their numbers to 46, almost 0·8 per cent of the total. Technical universities had even fewer women lecturers, with the same pattern of an initial and severe drop followed, in the winter semester of 1935-6, by a slight rise to a grand total of 8, who constituted 0·5 per cent of the whole. The teacher-training colleges, however, experienced the most spectacular drop in both the number and the percentage of women lecturers. The highest point of women's representation here had been 20 per cent in 1931, this declining to 14 per cent in the following year. But by the winter semester of 1934-5, numbers which had once nearly reached a round 100 were reduced to a bare 9, which was less than 4 per cent of the whole. The slight revival of women's fortunes in the other higher institutions was not paralleled here, since there was a further drop to below 2 per cent the following year.[2] This trend can be explained by the measures designed to restrict and delay the entry of girls to teacher-training colleges, as a result of the Nazis' anxiety about the surplus of women teachers in the early 1930s.

Even in the years before 1933 women had not been well represented in the legal profession, although the battle for admission had been won in 1922.[3] The 1933 census showed that out of a total of 10,441 judges and public prosecutors only 36 were women.[4] Hitler's deep antagonism towards the judiciary led

[1] See above, p. 193
[2] *St. J.*, 1932, p. 431; 1933, pp. 524-7; 1935, p. 525; 1936, pp. 548-9
[3] Lüders, op. cit., p. 123
[4] *St. J.*, 1938, p. 32

201

to a purge of it after the *Machtübernahme*, and also to a restriction of its sphere of competence.[1] It was not until 1936, however, that a definite move was made against women in this field. After a conference held in the Ministry of Justice in August 1936, Hitler's view on the admission of women to the practice of law was sought. He decided that women should be neither judges nor lawyers, but added that women law graduates could be employed in administrative positions.[2] This decision caused some concern in the Ministry of Justice, since it was felt that the women lawyers had been responsible and hard-working, and that a number of them had to support not only themselves but also dependants. Freisler, acting on behalf of Frank, came to an agreement with Frau Scholtz-Klink that a number of the women who would be forced to give up their practice, and for whom there might not be places in the administration, should be employed in the women's organizations in positions suitable to their legal training.[3] Accordingly, in the same month, January 1937, the official newsletter of the *Reichsfrauenführerin* contained an article which explained in detail the opportunities which remained open for women with legal training in the women's organizations, the welfare service, in all cases in which women or children might need legal guidance, in all matters of marriage and family law, and in party educational courses. The article was written by Dr Ilse Eben-Servaes, Frau Scholtz-Klink's adviser on legal matters.[4] She was used as a showpiece of the professional opportunities open to women in the Third Reich, and was even admitted to the Academy of German Law, a distinction also conferred on Frau Scholtz-Klink in December 1936.[5] At least women were not barred from the study of law, and their proficiency was proved in 1935 when female law

[1] Hubert, Schorn, *Der Richter im Dritten Reich* (Frankfurt, 1959), pp. 11-14, 83-4

[2] Bundesarchiv R43II/427, letter of August 24, 1936, from Bormann to Frank

[3] Ibid., letter of January 16, 1937

[4] Ilse Eben-Servaes, 'Die Frau als Rechtswahrerin', *Nachrichtendienst der Reichsfrauenführerin*, January 1937, pp. 6-7

[5] Kirkpatrick, op. cit., p. 219. *Frauenkultur*, February 1939, p. 4

students acquitted themselves favourably in the final examinations.[1] Frau Eben-Servaes was anxious to point out that the female lawyer's ability was not in doubt, but that she would nevertheless be of greatest service to the community by working in those fields especially concerned with women's affairs, and leaving the areas of less immediate relevance to women to her male colleagues.[2]

The professional occupations to which women were most suited were, in the Nazi view, those which had a direct practical application. This justified the large numbers of women in teaching and medicine. In 1935, a contributor to the official magazine of the *Frauenwerk*, *NS-Frauenwarte*, pointed out the connection between architecture and daily life, and claimed that woman's knowledge of household demands made her particularly suited to be an architect.[3] It was, however, social work of every kind that the Nazis regarded as the ideal occupation for women. This was partly because it was compatible with their theories about the nature and abilities of women. But it was perhaps more because the vast network of party and governmental organizations, particularly those involving women and children, really needed the advice and practical assistance of social workers.[4] The operation of the women's section of the Labour Front for example, required a considerable number of factory social workers and inspectors, as well as experts in its numerous advisory centres throughout the country. In spite of reports of increasing numbers of women both in these positions and in training courses,[5] there was nevertheless a shortage

[1] 'Die Prüfungsergebnisse in der Justiz', report in *Die Frau*, May 1936, p. 501

[2] Eben-Servaes, loc. cit.

[3] Irmgard Depres, reported in 'Frau und Beruf', *Die Frau*, March 1935, p. 382

[4] Lydia Gotteschewski, *Männerbund und Frauenfrage* (Munich, 1934), p. 64. For an account of the place of women in social work, see Hildegard Villnov, 'Die Frau in der sozialen Arbeit', *NS-Frauenbuch* (Munich, 1934), pp. 70-3

[5] 'Aus der Arbeit des Frauenamtes der Deutschen Arbeitsfront', report in *Die Frau*, May 1939, p. 442

reported in 1940, which was a source of concern to the Minister of Labour.[1]

As the economic situation changed, so did Nazi policy with regard to women. By 1936, unemployment had virtually disappeared, and there was, on the contrary, a shortage of labour, especially of skilled labour. This was the result of the intensive build-up of the heavy and chemical industries for rearmament and the drive towards national self-sufficiency which gathered momentum after the announcement of the Four Year Plan in September 1936, which was to give Germany a form of war economy even before the outbreak of war in 1939.[2] Both the Labour Service for both sexes and military service for young men removed a number of workers from the labour market, and also students from the universities. As early as February 1935, the order which had limited the number of new students at the end of 1933 was rescinded because of its success.[3] At the beginning of 1937, the Minister of Education, Rust, announced that school-leavers should be encouraged to enter universities in greater numbers, particularly for the study of scientific and technical subjects. The Four Year Plan required a large supply of chemists and engineers, and the general expansion which would result would mean a need also for experts in other disciplines. Better job prospects had already led to an increase in the number of entrants to universities, and this trend could be expected to continue. But in view of the urgency of the matter, senior schooling was to be cut by a year.[4]

It became abundantly clear that the new policies were not to be restricted to men. Only days before the Four Year Plan was announced, the Thursday women's section of the official party newspaper, the *Völkischer Beobachter*, was devoted entirely to the

[1] 'Vermittlung von Volkspflegerinnen in soziale Betriebsarbeit', *Reichsarbeitsblatt*, 1940, I, March 15, 1940, p. 101

[2] Franz Borkenau, *The Totalitarian Enemy* (London, 1940), pp. 41-2. David Schoenbaum, *Hitler's Social Revolution* (London, 1967), p. 134

[3] Report in *Wirtschaft und Statistik*, 1935, No. 9, p. 334

[4] Bundesarchiv R43II/938b, 'Die Inflation auf den Hochschulen beendet', *Deutsches Nachrichtenbüro*, No. 74, January 18, 1937

justification of both an academic education and professional employment for women, in so far, it was emphasized, as these would benefit the community. 'Today', it was categorically stated, 'we can no longer do without the woman doctor, lawyer, economist and teacher in our professional life.' Parents were urged to make sacrifices, if necessary, to give a talented daughter the chance of higher education, in order that the community might benefit from her particular abilities. The idea of studying for one's own satisfaction was obviously still regarded as egoistic and decadent. The value of women doctors in the girls' and women's organizations, in child welfare, and in industrial society was stressed – doubtless in view of the recognition that women formed an indispensable share of factory labour. Emphasis was also laid on the value of women as economists, both as teachers of their subject and as employees in government service. There was some caution, however, with regard to the legal profession, probably in view of the decision taken by Hitler against the employment of women judges and lawyers only ten days earlier. But it was conceded that women had a special contribution to make in all matters concerning marriage, the family, or the legal problems of women and children. The final judgment was: 'It is wrong if today a gifted and capable girl takes the attitude that there is no point in studying since she will not find employment.'[1] Clearly, expediency was a more powerful part of the Nazi scheme of things than principle.

The new trend was duly reiterated by the representatives of the women's organizations, just as the old ideas had been. Trude Bürkner, the national spokeswoman for the *Bund deutscher Mädel*, expressed the view that girls of ability who wanted to enter a profession ought to attend a university, since antagonism to the universities was 'not in accordance with the intentions of the BDM'.[2] The *Reichsfrauenführung* took every opportunity to increase contacts with professional women. In June 1936 it reached an agreement with the *Lehrerbund* for close co-operation

[1] 'Die Akademikerin von heute', report in *VB*, September 4, 1936. 'Was Zahlen lehren', Report in *VB*, September 4, 1936
[2] *Die Frau*, April 1937, p. 402

between the two organizations, while a section dealing with 'academic problems' was set up in the *Reichsfrauenführung* on July 1, 1936. Frau Scholtz-Klink also made a point of addressing meetings of girl students and women lecturers.[1] The danger of academic elitism was thus avoided, since close links between the leadership and professional women involved the latter in the Nazi women's movement as a whole, and gave force to the claim that all German women, from every class and occupation, were united in harmony, each making her best contribution for the benefit of the community.[2]

By the end of 1937 even the concern about the surplus of women teachers seems to have abated. Not eighteen months after his measure designed to delay the entry of girls to teacher-training colleges, Rust himself opened a new college exclusively for the training of women teachers in Koblenz, with words about the 'special mission of women teachers'.[3] At the end of 1939, the number of special courses designed to prepare girls with only an elementary school education for entry to teacher-training colleges was doubled.[4] This was, of course, at a time when the outbreak of the Second World War would suddenly have removed a large number of men from every occupation and profession, leaving gaps which could only be filled by women. But even before the war broke out, there had been forecasts of a shortage for the years from 1942 onwards, since by then male teachers of the years of birth around 1880 (when the birth-rate had been at its highest) would be due to retire. Greater use of female teachers in the girls' senior schools and also in the junior classes of boys' schools was therefore recommended.[5]

[1] *Frauenkultur*, February 1939, pp. 4-5
[2] Gertrud Scholtz-Klink, 'Die Berufung der schaffenden Frau im Arbeitsleben unseres Volkes', *Die Frau am Werk*, No. 1., January 1936, p. 5
[3] Bundesarchiv R43II/938b, 'Rust eröffnet Hochschule für Lehrerinnenbildung Koblenz', *Deutsches Nachrichtenbüro*, November 10, 1937
[4] 'Aufbaulehrgänge für Mädchen von der Volksschule zur Akademie für Lehrerinnenbildung', Report in *Die Frau*, December 1939, p. 84
[5] 'Studienräte und Studienrätinnen an höheren Schulen', report in *Die Frau*, November 1938, p. 94

But even as the demands made by the Four Year Plan became clear, influential members of the party and the government continued to be exercised by the question of the place of women in professional life. Those who may have thought that Frick's ruling in 1933 that there was not to be a general campaign against women in the professions had settled the matter, may only have begun to have doubts after Hitler's order in 1936 that women were to be barred from actual legal practice.

In May 1937, a letter from the office of Rudolf Hess asked Lammers at the Chancellery to find out whether Hitler felt that women were still to be permitted to be members of the higher ranks of the civil service.[1] This category covered a number of posts, such as those in the universities, that were not purely administrative. It appears that at this time there were still women employed as responsible civil servants in Lammers's own department.[2] His reply was that as a matter of principle Hitler wanted only men to be appointed to positions in the higher civil service. An exception was made in an addendum that in individual cases, particularly in welfare work, the appointment of a woman should not be ruled out as a possibility.[3] Frick made the request that positions in education and health should be considered as relevant also,[4] and Lammers incorporated these fields in a statement of the final decision.[5]

After this ruling had been communicated to the Reich Ministries, Frick felt it necessary to ask Lammers if there were any objections to its being intimated to Frau Scholtz-Klink, as *Reichsfrauenführerin*.[6] Although Lammers replied that there were no objections to this,[7] it is obvious that, in spite of her title, Frau Scholtz-Klink was given no real say in decision-making which affected women. After years of meekly following the line laid down by male leaders in party and government, in January 1938

[1] Bundesarchiv R43II/427, letter of May 4, 1937
[2] Ibid., Women officials were numbered among those to whom departmental documents were to be shown, e.g. on July 19, 1935; September 18, 1937; March 17, 1938; January 3, 1940   [3] Ibid., letter of June 8, 1937
[4] Ibid., letter of June 18, 1937   [5] Ibid., letter of July 25, 1937
[6] Ibid., letter of December 17, 1937   [7] Ibid., letter of January 31, 1938

she felt moved to protest against 'the tendency not to allow
talented women to realize their potential simply because they are
women [which] has increased recently'. The occasion for this
protest was the refusal of the Minister of Education to allow the
promotion of Dr Margarete Güssow, a talented astronomer with
an international reputation, to a senior post in the Berlin Observatory, in spite of a recommendation by her male superior. The
reason given was Hitler's ruling against the appointment of
women to high official positions. Frau Scholtz-Klink put in a
very strong plea on Dr Güssow's behalf to Bormann in Hess's
office in Munich. She also asked that a basic clarification of the
position of women in high posts might be given, with special
reference to women as lecturers; and, most surprisingly, she asked
Bormann to try to arrange a meeting between her and Hitler to
consider the matter, since 'I have not yet once been admitted to
discuss personally with the *Führer* the sphere of activity of
women'.[1] Bormann passed the matter on to Lammers, who replied
simply and without clarification that there was no objection to
Dr Güssow's appointment.[2] Frau Scholtz-Klink succeeded on
this occasion, but she was to fail in a similar attempt in 1942,
when the appointment of Professor Ilse Esdorn as a scientific
adviser in a forestry institute was rejected.[3]

Nevertheless, women were still being appointed to high
positions in the academic world. Dr Maria Lipp, who had begun
her lecturing career in the 1920s and had continued it throughout
the Nazi period, became the first woman Professor of Engineering
at a German technical university, in 1938.[4] In the following year,
Dr Maria Kösters became a professor in the medical faculty of
Munich University.[5] The census returns showed that in 1939, in
comparison with 1933, the number of women involved in
education of one kind or another had risen slightly, by 1 per cent
to 35 per cent of the total of those in this field. At the same time

[1] Bundesarchiv R43II/427, letter of January 24, 1938
[2] Ibid., letters of January 29, and February 21, 1938
[3] Ibid., letter of February 5, 1942
[4] 'Zur Lage der deutschen Frau', *Die Frau*, November 1938, p. 98
[5] Ibid., February 1939, p. 271

there was a rise of over 4 per cent in the proportion of women employed in administration at the national and local level and in the administration of justice, bringing their share to as much as 15·5 per cent.[1] In 1938-9 the Government awoke to the fact that there was a shortage of highly skilled and qualified men. The result was that careers advisers began to encourage women to enter occupations which had been considered suitable only for men in 1933. They took posts as engineers, veterinary experts and as scientists of all kinds in industry or in research institutes. Women doctors were now acceptable not only in areas of medicine concerned with women and children but also as medical officers of health and as medical advisers in administrative posts. Although women were not allowed to be appointed to public positions in the legal profession, there were still women who had been appointed to such posts before the order of 1936, and who had not been forced out. Experience in law was useful for women in employment exchanges, as trustees of labour and also in the service of corporations, as well, of course, as in the women's organizations. The function of women as economists was similarly regarded.[2] In keeping with this trend, and doubtless also as a result of the withdrawal of manpower from employment after the outbreak of war in September 1939, a national agency for advising women graduates on vacancies in economic, administrative and social service positions throughout Germany was opened in Berlin on October 1, 1939.[3]

Female civil servants continued to receive considerable official attention. Orders of October 1938 and April 1940 still assured the woman who resigned from the State service in the event of her marriage of monetary compensation.[4] But on May 3, 1940,

---

[1] Calculated from figures in *St. J.*, 1941-2, p. 38

[2] *Die Frau*, November 1938, p. 94. Report in *FZ*, February 4, 1938. Report in *FZ*, March 19, 1939

[3] Report in *Die Frau*, December 1939, p. 85

[4] '2. Durchführungsverordnung des Deutschen Beamtengesetzes', *RGB*, 1938, I, p. 1423, October 13, 1938. '2. Änderung der Allgemeinen Dienstordnung', *RGB*, 1940, I, p. 650, April 13, 1940

an order was passed which stated that 'a married woman civil servant does not have to be dismissed because her economic circumstances seem from the size of the family income to be secure', and added that women who had previously been dismissed for this reason could apply to be reinstated.[1] The growing lack of civil servants which gave rise to this measure also led Frick to issue a memorandum modifying Hitler's ruling against the appointment of women to high positions, except in special cases. He advised his fellow ministers to appoint the most suitable applicant for a position, whether male or female. Women lawyers, he said, might be appointed to permanent positions of a high rank if these positions were regarded as being particularly suitable for women.[2]

The question of employing unmarried mothers in the service of the State, which had been under discussion since August 1936,[3] was finally settled in the summer of 1939. A memorandum from the Ministry of the Interior advised that the bearing of an illegitimate child should not of itself ever be made the reason for dismissing a woman, although the circumstances of the conception and the general conduct of such a woman might well lead to dismissal if they impaired the image of the public service.[4]

In conclusion, the reduction of the number of women in professions under the Nazi regime has been exaggerated, not only by foreigners and by opponents of National Socialism but first of all by the Nazis themselves. Their loud demands for the reinstatement of woman in her true occupation, in the home, and for the release of women from academic pursuits which were in conflict with their basic nature, were publicized at home and abroad,[5] and were – and indeed still are – accepted at face value.

[1] '2. Verordnung über Massnahmen auf dem Gebiet des Beamtenrechts',
RGB, 1940, I, p. 732, May 3, 1940
[2] Bundesarchiv R43II/427, memorandum of May 20, 1940
[3] Ibid., R43II/443, letter of August 12, 1936 from Pfundtner to Lammers
[4] Ibid., R43/427, memorandum of July 14, 1939
[5] Many foreign journalists wrote articles about the new situation with regard to women in Germany after 1933, e.g. Alice Hamilton, 'Woman's Place in Germany', *Survey Graphic*, January 1934, pp. 26-7, 46-7; K. Woodsall, 'Women in the new Germany', *Forum*, 1935, Vol. 93, pp. 299-303

Less publicity was given to the exceptions attached to many of their measures.[1] There were protests against individual local acts of discrimination against professional women, but little was said of the number of women who continued in professional or academic positions unaffected by the new measures, although their presence is evidenced in official statistics.[2] Early in 1938, the *Frankfurter Zeitung* baldly stated that the original expectation – that after 1933 women would sooner or later be completely removed from professional life – had not been, and was not likely to be, fulfilled.[3]

Thus the Nazi theory that the happiness of women, and their best service to the *Volk*, lay in the home was compromised by economic necessity, as the shortage of manpower at all levels became increasingly acute. The theory had to be abandoned completely, in the end, as the outbreak of war made the utilization of all available skills the first priority. But Nazi theory in this field would not have been altogether viable, even had there been no war. The turning-point in the economic crisis came even before the *Machtübernahme*, and the depression had receded considerably before rearmament and conscription were begun. Opposition to women in employment varied in direct proportion to the degree of unemployment, so that it was less marked in 1934 than it had been in 1930 or 1932. The party organizations needed women of ability and education in the years of peace, particularly in view of Nazi ideas about the separate functions of the sexes. Women in professions were accepted as long as they allowed themselves to be drawn into the women's work of the nation and did not cut themselves off from members of their own sex who were in other occupations. Thus a division was created between men

[1] E.g. 'Drittes Gesetz zur Änderung des Gesetzes zur Wiederherstellung des Berufsbeamtentums', *RGB*, 1933, I, p. 655, September 22, 1933. This allowed for exceptions to be made to the law of April 7, 1933, by which politically undesirable and non-Aryan persons were unconditionally barred from the service of the State.

[2] Census reports in *St. J.*: 1933 census in 1938, pp. 32-3; 1939 census in 1941-2, p. 38. *St. J.* also gives annual figures relating to the professions until about 1936.

[3] *FZ*, February 4, 1938

and women in the same profession. But this can be seen as a return to the pre-Nazi system, in which a strong element of feminism led to the creation of separate organizations for men and women in the same profession. The appointment of women's representatives in the general professional organizations as early as 1934 shows acceptance of the *de facto* situation, that women were quite firmly entrenched in the professions, even if they were not actively welcomed in them until autumn 1936. However meagre the gains of the 1920s may have seemed to progressive women at the time, they were the result of long years of campaigning, and were not to be eradicated on the whim of a governing elite whose ideology bore little relation to economic or social reality.

The 1930s, then, started with a growing antagonism towards women, especially married women, in the professions, since it was felt that preference should be given to men with family responsibilities. In the deepening crisis, the ideals of 1919 were forgotten, and the Government passed a measure discriminating against women in its own service. The first concern of the Nazi Government was to remove from any position of power, influence or prestige those whom it regarded as its political enemies, regardless of sex. It then proceeded specifically against women in professional positions, less, however, as a matter of principle than as a means of providing opportunities for men with families to support and for men who had fought for their country in war-time. Steps were only taken against women as a matter of principle when Hitler made known his opposition to their appointment to the higher grades of the civil service, and especially to positions in the legal profession. But by this time – late 1936 and 1937 – it was too late, for the employment of women with professional training in institutions of party and State had been found to be both necessary and desirable, and became even more so with every month that passed. By 1938, in fact, official encouragement was being given to women to engage in professional training of every kind, and in 1940 the last remaining barriers came down. In spite of the fluctuations, the fears and the propaganda, the net result of the decade was one favourable to women in professional occupations, since the vicissitudes of depression and Nazi ideology regarding women's basic nature had been withstood, and woman's place in professional life had been proved to be not only a right of the individual but also a necessity for the community.

CHAPTER 10

THE LEGACY OF 1918
FOR NATIONAL SOCIALISM[1]

TIM MASON

'The total war of the future will make demands on the people
on a scale which we can hardly imagine. The moral and physical
efforts of the First World War, which did place really heavy
burdens on our German people, will be exceeded by far in a
future war.'

Colonel Thomas

Thomas made this dark prophecy before the assembled functionaries of the German Labour Front at a meeting of the Reich
Chamber of Labour in November 1936. He went on tactfully to
praise the efforts of the Labour Front to overcome class conflict
and to guarantee the social harmony essential to economic recovery and rearmament, but he made no bones about the need
for continued discipline in matters of wage and social policy in
order to ensure that the high level of economic activity already
attained by late 1936 should remain compatible with the ex-
panded arms procurement programme, for which he was himself
partly responsible. If there were shortages of raw materials,
'Strength through Joy' recreational facilities would have to take
second place behind the military in the allocation of priorities;
the labour shortage must not be permitted to result in wage

[1] Revised version of a lecture given at the University of Mannheim in
October 1968. Detailed evidence on some of the themes in the following
essay are presented in the author's forthcoming book, *Arbeiterklasse und
Volksgemeinschaft* (Köln, 1971). The author is grateful to the *Stiftung
Volkswagenwerk* for its generous financial support of this work.

215

GERMAN DEMOCRACY AND THE TRIUMPH OF HITLER

increases and consequent increases in consumer purchasing power; similarly, profits must be restricted; but above all the leadership must establish a basis of public confidence in itself and in its great aims, which would enable it to tell the people the truth about all economic problems at all times. Thomas laid great stress upon this last point. Education and enlightenment on these subjects, not only by the Propaganda Ministry but by all political and economic leadership groups, was the most important precondition of success, of avoiding a repetition of the strikes and uprisings of 1917-18. Honesty and consistency in public utterances would assist the people to carry hardship lightly, borne up by the knowledge of its necessity and its purpose, and it would permit anticipatory measures to be taken *before* bottle-necks arose, measures such as had long been necessary in both the question of the production of synthetic raw materials and that of foodstuffs. Chances here had been lost and Thomas implied (not without reason!) that the Four Year Plan, which had just been announced, was remedial rather than prophylactic. Domestic propaganda on these issues should not be left until war had begun, but must be firmly initiated in peace-time. Rearmament and war meant hardship and economic sacrifice, long hours, low wages and modest living standards.

Much of what Thomas said in this vein was directed straight at his audience, Labour Front officials who had of late been pressing with ever greater confidence and deliberateness for improved wages, living standards and social amenities for the industrial working class.[1] Robert Ley, leader of the Labour Front, understood his words in this sense and replied to Thomas in an impromptu speech at the close of the proceedings. The partners in this semi-public debate showed a good deal of skill and finesse in minimizing their differences, emphasizing the points which they had in common. Thus Ley for his part agreed on the need for massive efforts and sacrifice by the working population in order to secure adequate living space for the nation. But he brought a quite new perspective into the argument when he

[1] See T. W. Mason, 'Labour in the Third Reich, 1933-1939', *Past and Present*, No. 33 (April 1966)

insisted that it was the task of the Labour Front 'to make the German people happy and strong, powerful in body and mind, to build up and awaken their energies'. It was no use just demanding sacrifice after sacrifice; something had to be offered in return:

'. . . the World War showed us that with all possible clarity: endure, endure, hold out, hold out! – that's all well and good; but there is a limit to the endurance of every individual, and naturally of every people also. It's just as with an iron girder or any construction which has to bear a burden. There is a limit and if it is reached everything just breaks. And for us, that was exactly 1918, then on 9 November. We may be sad about it and embittered, we may curse and swear; but the fact is, that the men in power then forgot to compensate the people for the fantastic strain of those four-and-a-half years, forgot on the other hand to inject new sources of strength, to pump in new strength again and again.'

And Ley went on to defend 'Strength through Joy' in particular as a pioneering achievement in social policy, 'which will show us the way for all time'.[1]

It was a significant debate – not because it resolved anything, for decisions of this order were taken elsewhere, if at all; but because it was one of the few occasions on record when the views of the Nazi leadership on the November Revolution were made explicit in the period after 1933, in the period when it was forced to face up to the real implications of these events. A brief discussion of these views in the context of Nazi policy towards the working class may perhaps do something to clarify the expansionist dynamic of National Socialism and may perhaps also contribute a little to the growing discussion of the theme of the continuity or otherwise of modern German history.[2]

[1] All quotations from the protocol of this meeting, Deutsches Zentralarchiv Potsdam (hereafter: DZA), Reichswirtschaftsministerium (hereafter: RWM), file 10314, pp. 114-71
[2] Cf. Andreas Hillgruber, *Kontinuität und Diskontinuität in der deutschen Aussenpolitik von Bismarck zu Hitler* (Düsseldorf, 1969) and refs. therein; Hans-Ulrich Wehler, 'Bismarck's Imperialism 1862-1890', *Past and Present*, No. 48 (August 1970)

In this latter context, National Socialism appears as a radically new variant of the social imperialism of Bismarck and Wilhelm II. Whereas pre-1914 governments had attempted to use imperialism to integrate the nation, to use aggressive and expansionist foreign policies to discredit internal opposition and to reinforce or to legitimize the domestic social and political structure, Hitler's procedure was based precisely on the lessons drawn from the failure of this strategy. The weakening of internal democratic opposition was no longer a hoped-for function of expansionist policy, but its precondition; successful foreign expansion would legitimize not an inherited political and social system but an entirely new one, in which there would be no room for organized opposition groups but in which the leadership would continue to need constant popular support. November 1918 was the turning-point in this transition, the touchstone of any new approach towards expansionist policies.

The stab-in-the-back legend was a legend. It was a grotesquely untrue version of the end of the war, which was in part deliberately prepared at the time by the German Army High Command.[1] But it was a potential truth — it expressed in distorted and exaggerated form the real fact of the high tension which existed between working-class traditions and interests on the one hand, the prosecution of aggressive war on the other.

Much has been made of Hitler's diagnosis of the foreign policy errors of the Imperial regime, errors which in his view necessarily produced a war on two fronts and a fundamental uncertainty within Germany as to what the First World War was being fought about, and were thus responsible for the defeat. On the other hand, however, the legend of the stab-in-the-back has been seen primarily within the context of the weakness of the Weimar Republic, the heavy domestic mortgage with which it started out and the unscrupulousness of right-wing propagandists, who fabricated a supposedly national myth to advance their own sectional interests.

[1] Cf. Gerald Feldman, *Army, Industry and Labour in Germany 1914-1918* (Princeton U.P., 1966), Ch. ix

But, as Robert Ley recognized in the discussion quoted above, the November Revolution was of much more general import to the political Right in Germany. The success of the Bolsheviks in Russia and the alleged success of the 'Jewish Marxist conspiracy' in Germany in bringing the First World War to a conclusion, posed fundamental problems to any regime in the capitalist industrialized countries which embarked upon a course of aggrandizement through war. October 1917 and November 1918 pointed to the greatest danger for such policies – that they could be brought to defeat *from within* by the action of those who bore the brunt of the suffering caused by war. The November Revolution and the defeat not only raised the issues of the legitimacy of the republican order and of Germany's best future alliance and war-aims policy; it also raised the issue of the domestic circumstances under which military expansion would be possible at all in future.

Hitler's own attitude to the First World War and its outcome was complex. On the one side he considered Germany's defeat to have been an inevitable result of the racial and political degeneration of the Reich, which had its own deep seated causes. This relative detachment, which gave a pseudo-historical dimension to his thinking, was politically necessary in that it alone could justify his claim that something approaching a total renewal of German political life under National Socialist leadership was necessary in order to ensure the success of a second bid for world power. Only the existence of profound causes for the defeat could make the need for a profound regeneration appear plausible. On the other hand, Hitler's writings are full of bitter criticisms of specific policy errors, actions and attitudes of the rulers of Wilhelmine Germany which suggest that another outcome might have been possible in 1918 had certain mistakes not been made. These passages had a similar tactical function for the National Socialist movement, in that they served to differentiate the party clearly from those responsible for these errors, the conservative right, whose exponents were among Hitler's contemporary rivals for power in the 1920s. But they also have a programmatic quality: National Socialism would succeed where the Empire had failed precisely because it avoided making the same errors. The passages critical of the foreign policy of the pre-war leadership have rightly attracted considerable attention in this context, since they outlined important aspects of Hitler's subsequent policies. Hitler's utterances on the revolution itself, however, belong in the same category and it is worth looking at them more closely.

He saw no contradiction between his long-range analysis of the degeneration of German politics and a rigid insistence on a conspiracy theory of November 1918. Responsibility for the 'collapse' was laid firmly at the door of 'these hoary . . . perjured criminals . . ., this viper . . ., this political rabble . . ., the whole gang of miserable party politicians who had betrayed the people . . ., a gang of thieves . . ., a gang of despicable and depraved criminals . . ., the *canaille* which more or less shunned the light . . ., the Jew wire-pullers', as Hitler termed the leaders of Social Democracy and of the revolutionary movement. The 'treasonous machinations' of these groups had brought defeat and dishonour to Germany; they had mobilized 'rioters, thieves and robbers' and by subterfuge and insinuation gained the confidence of the basically patriotic German worker.[1] The programmatic conclusion of this part of the analysis was simple and ruthless: the elimination of the leaders of the working-class movement and the destruction of their organizations. This omission of August 1914, for which Hitler bitterly blamed the Kaiser – given that the workers themselves had shown how shallow was the internationalism of Social Democracy on the outbreak of war and had thus presented him with the opportunity for repressive action – was promptly made good in the spring of 1933. The Nazi leadership had at this time little idea of what, if anything, should take the place of the working-class parties and trade unions; it was in the first instance sufficient that the enemy within had been exterminated. The first condition of avoiding a repetition of November 1918 had been swiftly realized. It is perhaps worth noting that Hitler did actually speak of the liquida-

[1] Adolf Hitler, *Mein Kampf* (London, 1939), pp. 151, 173f, 178, 431f

THE LEGACY OF 1918 FOR NATIONAL SOCIALISM

tion and extermination of these groups in his early writings.[1] His dogmatic adherence to the stab-in-the-back legend was thus much more than a propagandist stance to discredit the Weimar Republic; it reflected one aspect of his real understanding of the events of November 1918, an understanding upon which subsequent Nazi policies were based.

The second part of Hitler's diagnosis of the causes of the November Revolution was closely related to the above, but was at once less clear-cut and yet of more central importance to the character of National Socialism. It turned upon his assessment of the role of political ideas:

'*Only by a fanatically extreme nationalism with the highest social ethic and morality will marxist internationalism be broken.* One cannot take the false idol of Marxism from the people without giving it a better god. For this reason the socialist laws of Bismarck could only fail if that vacuum was not successfully filled, which must make itself felt for millions after Marxism had been broken. Dear God, only a political child could believe that the workers, once freed from Marxism and thus from the proletarian attitude of class conflict, would have nothing better to do than to hurry into the ranks of the bourgeois parties . . .'[2]

Marxism was for Hitler, however, only the extreme form of a general moral and ideological degeneration. The military collapse was the 'catastrophic consequence of a moral and ethical poisoning'.[3] Hitler went out of his way to insist that the collapse was *not* an economic breakdown, *not* a military defeat, but a crisis of purpose, will and morale which the old regime had not been able to bear.[4] It was general decadence in education, in the press, in attitudes to race, in religion, economic life, at the Kaiser's court, in sexual mores, art and town life, etc., which caused the collapse,

[1] See e.g. Ibid., p. 151; Adolf Hitler, 'Warum musste ein 8. November kommen?', *Deutschlands Erneuerung*, iv (1924), p. 207
[2] Ibid., p. 207. There are several similar passages in *Mein Kampf*.
[3] Author's translation from *Mein Kampf* (Munich, 1941), p. 252. The published English translation, op. cit., p. 198, is defective at this point.
[4] Ibid., Book I, Ch. 10

disorientation and cowardice of 1918-19: 'All these symptoms . . . must be attributed to the lack of a definite and uniformly accepted *Weltanschauung* and the general uncertainty of outlook consequent on that lack.[1] Thus the final cause of the collapse and the revolution lay in wrong thinking: in defeatist attitudes and democratic illusions, in misplaced loyalties and in suggestibility towards the skilled appeals of Jewish-Marxist demagogues. United public consciousness of the right issues and an unshakeable will to solve them thus formed the second precondition for a renewed attempt at imperial expansion.

This belief in the force of ideas and attitudes constituted a basic assumption about the nature of modern politics and ran like a red thread through the whole political culture of National Socialism. *Weltanschauung* was all-important. Hitler's statements, public and private, all bear witness to this style of thought. It was one of the characteristics which distinguished National Socialism quite fundamentally from other right-wing movements. This basic assumption is not easy to analyse briefly, for it was at once cynical and idealistic: cynical in postulating an almost limitless gullibility and consequently limitless malleability of 'the people',[2] idealistic both in its posture and vocabulary and in its belief that political actions are *finally determined* by people's political attitudes. This assumption too was both diagnostic with reference to 1918 and programmatic with respect to subsequent Nazi policies. The elimination of the working-class organizations in 1933 gave National Socialism the ideological monopoly necessary for the re-education of the social democratic and communist rank-and-file. Though there was no shortage of realistic voices, which insisted that this re-education would take a very long time, there is little evidence that the Nazi leadership thought during its first years in power that anything else (aside from the end of unemployment which it achieved by re-arming) was necessary to gain the active loyalty of the working class to the regime – a loyalty which was realized to be essential to its success.

[1] *Mein Kampf* (London, 1939), p. 224
[2] The notorious sections of *Mein Kampf* on this theme have been too often rehearsed to need quoting again in detail here; cf. Book I, Ch. 6 and 10

THE LEGACY OF 1918 FOR NATIONAL SOCIALISM

These were strange conclusions to draw from the experience of 1918; they clearly contained a great deal of wish-fulfilment, but Hitler basically stuck to them throughout his life. The same opinions recur with a remarkable constancy which borders on the monotonous in his war-time conversations. He continued to talk of the basically patriotic, decent industrial worker, misled in the past by a cynical Jewish-Marxist leadership:

'I'm full of understanding for a worker who was hurled into a hostile world, and, quite naturally, found himself exposed to the seductions of Marxism. But not for those swine of theoreticians like Hilferding and Kautsky.'[1]

He spoke as though the main effort of the party had been directed towards winning over the industrial working class,[2] despite the fact that the failure of the party in this respect before 1933 was notorious and despite the fact that this had been the substance of his quarrel with Gregor Strasser. He even indulged in conversion fantasies, according to which the regime now had no more loyal supporters than its erstwhile working-class enemies.[3] His attitude to the success of Nazi propaganda was wholly in accordance with these views. He saw himself in many roles, but he was especially proud of his and his party's achievements in political education and, in conformity with his verdict on the Second Empire and the World War, he attributed a great deal to the effect of laying so much stress on this factor. 'My whole life can be summed up as this ceaseless effort of mine to persuade other people', he insisted.[4] Some months later he added an original perspective to the historiography of his regime:

'For goodness' sake, don't let us rush to the police every time some small peccadillo raises its head. Let us rather stick to educative measures. Don't forget, after all, that it was not by using

[1] *Hitler's Secret Conversations 1941-1944* (*Tischgespräche*) (New York, 1961), February 1, 1942
[2] Ibid., April 8, 1942
[3] Ibid., August 2, 1941, November 30, 1941   [4] Ibid., January 18, 1942

223

fear inspired by police methods that we National Socialists won over the people, but rather by trying to show them the light and to educate them.'[1]

The accuracy of these statements will be considered below; here it is their consistency which must be stressed.

It is worth considering what is omitted from Hitler's version of the stab-in-the-back legend. There is firstly no indication that Germany's collapse might have been due to other causes, to the superior strength of the Allied and Associated powers, or to the inadequacy of Germany's economic and population resources to the goals of her policy. Such reflections were from the outset tabu in public, since they called into question the possibility of carrying out any second bid for world power. That Hitler none the less gave some weight to them is clear from his foreign policy and military strategies during 1938-41, which were designed in no small part to compensate for these weaknesses.[2] While it is secondly no cause for surprise that Hitler should have been unable to comprehend people rising in protest against a war which had become meaningless to them, about the progress of which they had been deceived and which they had come to abhor, it is remarkable that he gave little or no weight to the intense privations suffered by the working population and their dependents in Germany during the war, where the wages of only a small group of armaments workers rose sufficiently to keep pace with the rapid inflation. The only type of suffering for which Hitler showed any understanding was that of the man facing sudden death in the trenches. To this posture, *Mein Kampf* furnishes only a single fleeting exception: Hitler was wounded at the Somme and returned late in 1916 on sick-leave to Berlin – 'Bitter want was in evidence everywhere. The metropolis, with its teeming millions, was suffering from hunger. There

---

[1] *Hitler's Secret Conversations 1941-1944* (*Tischgespräche*) (New York, 1961), June 23, 1942

[2] See Alan S. Milward, *The German Economy at War* (London, 1965), Ch. I and II; Berenice A. Carroll, *Design for Total War* (The Hague, 1968), Ch. V

was great discontent.'[1] But the point was swiftly passed over and Hitler went on to dismiss the alleged social and economic causes of the revolution as superficial and unimportant. By the time of the *Second Book* he had reflected a little further on the relationship between the national unity of the kind which he had to create for expansion through war, and the economics of class conflict. He had come to the conclusion that an appeal to ideals would *not* suffice in order to keep down the living standards of a 'cultured people' for any great length of time (*auf die Dauer*):

'The broad masses especially will seldom show understanding for this. They experience the deprivation, curse those who are, in their opinion, responsible, which – at least in democratic states – is dangerous, since they thus become the reservoir for all attempts at revolt'.[2]

Hitler decided, however, that it *was* possible to distract the people from material things for a short period, by concentrating their attention on 'overwhelming spiritual ideals, . . . forceful ideals', provided that the sacrifices demanded were not too great, and provided that the realization of these ideals then helps 'to strengthen the people' (i.e. presumably, to alleviate their material want).[3]

In terms of social and economic policy, this was the basic gamble of the Third Reich. It was a gamble which failed completely. The repeated rhetorical invocation of a united and harmonious society, marching in step towards and through victorious wars, came, as the 1930s wore on, to bear more and more the character of a stern warning against growing dissension, competition and the ruthless prosecution of selfish interests. It was addressed to a public which had never existed and could not exist. Classes were not the less real for the term having been banned; and the interest of the working class in higher wages,

---

[1] *Mein Kampf* (London, 1939), p. 168. The last sentence is omitted from the English translation – cf. German ed. (Munich, 1941), p. 211. Hitler suffered a similar fleeting moment of comprehension in a discussion with Rauschning: Hermann Rauschning, *Hitler Speaks* (London, 1939), p. 201
[2] *Hitlers Zweites Buch* (Stuttgart, 1961), p. 121   [3] Ibid., p. 53

shorter hours and greater freedom had not been changed by the incessant but vacuous propaganda about the common good having priority over the sectional and about the over-riding need for achievement, production, efficiency.

There was no 'November Revolution' in 1945, no stab in the back by the working-class movement in the last phase of the Second World War. This was due above all to the police terror against organized resistance groups; the extent of unorganized, individual and discrete popular resistance in the years 1943-5[1] leaves little room for doubt that an effective stab in the back would have been possible but for the Gestapo's activities and the fear which they engendered. Police terror stood between the regime and collapse. The Nazi leadership, however, took no chances on this score; fear of working-class discontent over social and economic issues was a recurrent and dominating feature of government and party policy throughout the period 1936-45. Precisely those background reasons for the November Revolution, the relevance of which had been denied in the Nazi version of the stab-in-the-back legend, came to play a foremost role in the history of the Third Reich. If the terror was politically successful, 'education' was, despite Hitler's wishful thinking, a resounding failure. The durability of the great ideal as the factor governing social and economic affairs was limited by the labour market: it was possible effectively to repress wage-earner and consumer interests to the advantage of the military sector as long as there was widespread unemployment; full employment re-asserted the bargaining power of labour, whose economic interests were in the short run diametrically opposed to the requirements of Germany's armaments economy. Rather than risk discontent and unpopularity, the NSDAP and its affiliated organizations tended after 1936 to become the spokesmen of this pressure for higher living standards, and the government repeatedly capitulated to a combination of economic forces and political lobbying.[2]

Speer gives a succinct summary of the problem:

[1] Cf. Walter Ulbricht *et al.* (eds.), *Geschichte der deutschen Arbeiterbewegung*, Vol. V (Berlin, 1966)
[2] Cf. Mason, loc. cit., *Past and Present*, No 33

'It remains one of the astounding experiences of the war, that Hitler wished to spare his own people those burdens which Churchill or Roosevelt imposed upon their peoples without second thoughts. The discrepancy between the total mobilization of the labour force in democratic England and the sluggish treatment of this question in authoritarian Germany serves to characterize the regime's fear of a change in the people's loyalties. The elite wanted neither to make sacrifices itself or to require sacrifices of the people; it was concerned to keep the mood of the people as good as possible by making concessions. Hitler and the majority of his political followers belonged to the generation which in November 1918 had experienced the revolution as soldiers and they had never got over it. Hitler often made it clear in private conversations, that one could not be careful enough after the experience of 1918.'

Among the examples which he cites were the high level of consumer goods production until 1943, the very generous war pensions and allowances paid to soldiers' wives (allowances which were so generous as to make it very hard to persuade married women to take up industrial work), and a war-time propaganda which constantly stressed that final victory was just around the corner and thus made sacrifice and effort appear the less necessary. Though he is inclined himself to over-rate the importance of the unwillingness of the leadership to set an example by tightening their own belts, he concludes unambiguously that 'it was a confession of political weakness; it betrayed considerable anxiety that a loss of popularity could give rise to domestic crises'.[1] Speer's own notes on his war-time policy discussions with Hitler themselves provide ample evidence of this anxiety.[2]

The study of history is rarely tidy enough for generalizations such as that of Speer to be fully documented: the cases in which the leadership of the Third Reich can be clearly shown to have drawn upon their fears of a repetition of 1918 in making

[1] Albert Speer, *Erinnerungen* (Frankfurt-am-Main, 1969), Ch. 16, esp. p. 229

[2] Willi A. Boelcke (ed.), *Deutschlands Rüstung im Zweiten Weltkrieg* (Frankfurt-am-Main, 1969), pp. 65, 74, 86, 91, 98, 109, 142, 315, and *passim*

concessions to the working class are few and far between. On one occasion, however, the connection was explicitly made. Under the Auxiliary Service Law of 1916, employers had been permitted to restrict the mobility of their workers. Local and industrial agreements among employers bound the signatories not to poach labour from each other, to hire workers at present with one of the contracting parties only if they had been granted a leaving certificate by their employer. The purpose of the scheme was to secure a sufficient labour force to firms in the armaments sector and to keep wage levels down; the employers themselves were deemed the best judge of these problems. The system of leaving certificates was bitterly resented by the workers whom it affected and its abolition was among the first acts of the revolutionary government in November 1918. As labour became short in the armaments industries in the mid-1930s, employers in some areas resurrected on their own initiative the arrangements which had been in force during 1916-18, but the Government, mindful of the unpopularity of the system, declared against the leaving certificates and introduced instead a complex and relatively inefficient scheme under which job-changing by certain categories of workers was made subject to the approval of the labour exchanges. In justifying its policy, the Ministry of Labour referred directly to the experience of the First World War and it persisted with its prohibition in the face of criticism from industry and the army procurement agencies: given the importance of job-changing as a method whereby workers could better themselves materially, it would place too great a strain on class relations to leave the final decision in this matter in the hands of an interested party – the 'neutral' authority of the State must take the responsibility.[1]

The experience of 1918 also lurked in the background of other decisions and statements made by the leadership of the Third

[1] 'Anordnung über den Einsatz von Metallarbeitern', February 11, 1937, together with official commentary in *Reichsarbeitsblatt*, I, p. 38; DZA Potsdam, RWM, file 10410, pp. 43ff, 425-35; Bundesarchiv Koblenz (Hereafter: BA), R41, file 151, pp. 4-14; BA/Militärarchiv Freiburg (hereafter: MA), WiIF5, file 1215

Reich in questions of social policy. Fragmentary references often occur in improbable contexts or casual remarks. Thus the naval dockyard at Kiel pressed the supreme command of the German navy early in 1940 to give priority to the catastrophic housing conditions of the dockyard workers; in one of the very rare understatements in official German documents of this period, the Kiel authorities reminded their superiors that 'bad social conditions can be a hindrance to the military effort' as 1918 had shown![1] The police and the judiciary were also aware of the precedents of the First World War. The extensive official justification of the verdict against Georg Lechleiter and thirteen fellow resistance workers in Mannheim in May 1942 contained a detailed comparison between their efforts to enlighten fellow-citizens as to the criminal character of the regime and the war, and the activities of the 'November-criminals'. Lechleiter and his group had produced several editions of a resistance broadsheet, *Der Vorbote* (The Herald); all were condemned to death and executed.[2]

Explicit references to 1918 in the context of the major social policy issues of the years 1936-9 are few and far between, chiefly for the reason that the regime had no policy. This was apparent to the leading civil servants responsible for social and economic affairs, and perhaps also to a few industrialists, but it was a position of weakness, which the leadership was understandably reluctant to furnish with a systematic justification. And it is in the context of such a justification for sparing the working population as much hardship as possible that one may assume the example of the November Revolution to have had its effect. As Speer noted, Hitler's fears were expressed in private conversations: it was not a theme which lent itself well to publicity by a regime which prided itself upon its total power, and had in fact, whether it liked it or not, predicated its strategy of expansion precisely upon the success of a domestic policy of 'blood, sweat, toil and tears'. Germany's slender economic resources and unfavourable

---

[1] BA Koblenz, R41, file 92, pp. 26-9

[2] Max Oppenheimer, *Der Fall Vorbote* (Frankfurt-am-Main, 1969), pp. 96ff, 200-17

strategic position left no margin for wastage in the re-armament programme, but in effect the position taken by Ley in his debate with Thomas was adopted by the Government by default. In the face of rapidly increasing wages, the Government at first opted to do nothing, and, when controls were introduced in the shadow of the Czech crisis in the summer of 1938, they were very loosely implemented: average hourly wages rose faster in the first twelve months of controls than in the preceding twelve-month period.[1] A similar laxity characterized the measures of the Government to overcome the labour shortage, which was estimated late in 1938 by the Minister of Labour at over a million.[2] Civil conscription was a solution and one to which the regime had no objections in principle; it was introduced simultaneously with wage controls, but was not used systematically to achieve a redistribution of the labour force in favour of the armaments sector, such as was urgently necessary. The domestic policies of the regime swung inconsistently backwards and forwards between brutal attacks upon rights and interests and a fearful circumspection which was inspired by the need to gain or maintain popularity. Systematic policies were from the start ruled out by this constellation, and civil conscription was used almost exclusively in national emergencies: for the building of the Siegfried Line and for the replacement of workers in armaments industries who were called to the ranks in the first ten days of the war. In calmer intervals, the Labour Exchanges were repeatedly ordered to make most sparing use of their powers under the decree, the enforcement of which was greatly disliked by those affected.[3]

Before the outbreak of war, there was no concerted policy of

[1] Gerhard Bry, *Wages in Germany 1871-1945* (Princeton U.P., 1960), pp. 242f. Gross average hourly earnings increased by 10·9 per cent between December 1935 and June 1939, weekly earnings by 17·4 per cent.

[2] Minister of Labour to Head of the Reich Chancellery, December 17, 1938, BA Koblenz, R43II, file 533

[3] Decrees of June 22, 1938, and February 13, 1939, *Reichsgesetzblatt*, I, pp. 652, 206. *Reichsarbeitsblatt*, I, 1939, p. 345. BA Koblenz, R41, file 279, p. 96; file 285, pp. 98-107. Roughly 1 million of the total 1·3 million conscripts up to the end of September 1939 were conscripted in connection with these emergencies.

closing down firms in the consumer goods sector in order to free materials, capacities and labour for the armaments drive. Average consumption levels considerably outstripped the previous highest levels of 1928-30. On the outbreak of war, *per capita* consumption was lower than in 1930 only in the cases of certain dairy products, imported fruits and beer; these were all long-standing bottle-necks, resulting from Germany's agricultural policies and relative shortage of foreign exchange. Firms dealing in goods for which there was an elastic demand experienced unprecedented boom conditions – furniture, confectionery, spirits, shoes, etc. were all in high demand and the demand was being met.[1] It was not without good reason that Thomas was to point out in an address to the country's leading industrialists in November 1939 that 'We shall never defeat England with radio sets, vacuum cleaners and cooking utensils'.[2] Total consumer expenditure in 1939 was RM 7,000 millions higher than in 1929, prices on average some 12 per cent lower than before the economic crises.[3] The economy of Nazi Germany was neither a war nor a peace economy, but both at the same time. The resources were not sufficient to maintain this dualism indefinitely.

The dangers for the armaments programme and the war of expansion posed by this development were not the less serious for being indirect. The Gestapo saw to it that there was no real possibility of insurrection, but in order to make doubly sure and in order to combat a growing demoralization of the industrial labour force which took the form of declining productivity and discipline, the regime permitted improvements in the material conditions of life which drastically limited the resources available for war preparations. For example, the armaments sector was heavily dependent upon imported raw materials, especially iron

[1] *Statistisches Jahrbuch des deutschen Reiches, 1934,* pp. 332-5; *1936,* pp. 361f; *1939-40,* pp. 398-413. *Statistisches Handbuch von Deutschland* (Stuttgart, 1949), pp. 488f, 576f

[2] Georg Thomas, *Geschichte der deutschen Wehr-und Rüstungswirtschaft,* ed. W. Birkenfeld (Boppard-am-Rhein, 1966), p. 501

[3] Bry, op. cit., p. 264; Carroll, op. cit., p. 186. 12 per cent is an estimate, since the official cost-of-living index was wholly unreliable.

and other metal ores. Production was repeatedly held up through-out the 1930s by shortage of these materials; yet from 1935 onwards the volume of imported foodstuffs increased steadily and rose as a proportion of Germany's total imports from 34·5 per cent to 39·5 per cent in 1938. Imports of textile raw materials also began to rise again in these years, despite the Government's efforts to encourage the use of domestically produced synthetic products.[1] The mechanisms for control of foreign trade were full and potentially efficient; it was a case of the regime giving way to the forces of an effective demand, upon the satisfaction of which it believed its stability and popularity to rest.[2] Under these circumstances the effect of major increases in armaments ex-penditure in 1936, 1938 and 1939 was to produce an overburden-ing of economic capacities, bottle-necks in all sectors, a latent inflation and a competition among procurement agencies and interest groups which made all planning a labour of Sisyphus.[3] Industry was not able to produce as much or as quickly as the armed forces were willing – if not always able – to buy; on the outbreak of war, the contract books of many firms working for them were full for two years in advance. The achievements were considerable, but, as Thomas never wearied of reminding his superiors, they lagged far behind Hitler's strategic plans in the years 1938-40; and they were gained at the cost of producing growing economic instability. Thus on the one hand, at the end of the Polish campaign the German army had just enough munitions to allow one-third of its divisions to fight for a further four weeks; the *Luftwaffe* had no reserves of bombs and the army was extremely short of motorized transport, which was crucial to its aggressive tactics.[4] On the other hand, Hitler's conception of an optimal German strategy, which would have placed the

[1] *Stat. Handbuch*, op. cit., pp. 396, 402, 404, 406, 408

[2] This at least is the impression given by the bare facts. German foreign trade policy in the years 1936-40 still has to be investigated.

[3] Impressive new calculations of armaments expenditure in Carroll, op. cit., p. 184

[4] Hans-Adolf Jacobsen, *Fall Gelb* (Wiesbaden, 1957), pp. 19ff, 131-7, 187ff, 192-7

outbreak of major hostilities in Europe in 1942-3, was utterly unrealistic from the point of view of domestic social and economic policy. In order to postpone major gains of territory and resources until this date and to continue the re-armament drive at its 1938-9 pitch, draconian measures against wage-earners and consumers would have been necessary, measures which, in the event, the Government was not even able to impose in 1939, when the outbreak of European war gave it the best of pretexts for doing so.

The nearer war came, the more often was the experience of the First World War drawn upon for guide-lines. Contingency planning in the social and economic sphere began in 1935 in a leisurely fashion, but after the re-occupation of the Rhineland the pace accelerated and drafts of labour and tax legislation for the event of war were being considered in detail. August 1936 saw the beginning of a fundamental policy dispute on these issues which was to last until November 1939 and around which the contingency planning came to revolve almost entirely. All ministries concerned were agreed that the working class would have to bear heavy sacrifices: freedom of movement would be curtailed, limits on working hours made more flexible, bonus rates for overtime stopped and wages themselves would have to be reduced to the minimum legal rates. The Ministries of Economics and Finance, however, wished to go further and to introduce a 50 per cent increase in the income tax and impose in addition a further levy upon earnings which increased as a result of the war. The Ministry of Labour rejected these proposals on the grounds that the draft legislation did not foresee similarly increased taxes upon war profits:

'If the worker suspects that the burdens of war are not being equitably distributed, it will not only depress his mood but also reduce the effort which he puts into his work. Those dangers will thus be re-created, which proved to be so fatal during the last war.'[1]

[1] Minister of Labour to President of the Reichsbank, August 29, 1936, BA/MA Freiburg, WiIF5, file 420/1

The weight of the argument was not appreciated and the other ministries failed to produce draft tax legislation for the case of war which satisfied the demands of the Ministry of Labour for an equitable distribution of burdens; they insisted that tax legislation could only be introduced after the war had been in progress for some weeks and the needs could be accurately assessed. The Ministry of Labour insisted that all belts must be seen to be tightened at one and the same time. Stalemate on this issue persisted for three years, until on August 9, 1939, the Ministry of Labour refused to delay any longer and single-handedly redrafted the contingency plans, introducing a wage-stop in the place of the previously intended reductions. 'There can be no doubt', its spokeman wrote,

'that drastic measures in the field of wage policy are only possible and *psychologically bearable*, provided that the burdens to be laid upon incomes which are untouched by these measures are made known to the population the same day that the wage cuts are announced.'[1]

A hasty compromise was arranged, under which some wage cuts were pushed through in September 1939, though less than had originally been intended, but on the other hand a majority of industrial workers were exempted form the income tax increase, which was now extended to cover all higher incomes. Göring was evidently uneasy about the compromise, which still represented a drastic reduction in the working and living standards for the working class. In a speech to the armaments workers at a large Berlin firm on September 9, 1939, which was broadcast throughout the Reich, he warned against a repeat of the stab in the back:

'Here I must demand from all those who remain at home: those at home must stand just as the front stands – iron hard and inspired by duty; the home front must no more be shamed by the army; it must stiffen the army's backbone, not break it. When the

---

[1] Circular from the chairman of Sub-Committee I of the Reich Defence Council Committee on social policy, August 9, 1939, BA/MA Freiburg, WilF5, file 319

front holds it must know that behind it the home front is holding too, ready to give everything which it possibly can give in order to ease the dreadful lot of those who are away facing death in battle with the enemy. Thus there are today two soldiers, the soldier with his weapon and the soldier at his machine. All of you are on the front [*Ihr seid alle Frontkämpfer*].'[1]

The home front was not holding. Passive resistance and discontent among the working class as a result of the cuts in living standards and increased pressure of work were such that the regime had to give way on major points of the war legislation. The Research Institute of the Labour Front prepared the way with a memorandum on the social amenities of industry in wartime, which was circulated in September 1939. Although the memorandum paid lip-service to Hitler's interpretation of 1918 as above all a crisis of morale, one did not need to read between the lines to gather the force of the argument:

'It is generally accepted that the World War ended in Versailles not least because the social structure of the German people was not adequate to the pressure of the war and the blockade. The external preconditions of the collapse (shortages of materials and of foodstuffs, etc.) could only have such catastrophic effects in those years because the mental conditions [*seelische Verfassung*] of the people offered no more possibility of coping with the given circumstances.

'These are well-known and undisputed facts, from which the general lessons for our present position in many areas of public life have already long been drawn. The most general of these lessons is that the home front must be at least equal to the fighting front in its effectiveness and resilience'.[2]

The terms of the argument had changed completely. The leaders of the Third Reich had a monopoly of political 'education', but were utterly unable to raise enthusiasm for the war. They had

---

[1] *Völkischer Beobachter* (hereafter: *VB*), September 10, 1939
[2] Arbeitswissenschaftliches Institut der DAF, 'Betriebliche Sozialleistungen in der Kriegwirtschaft', msc., DZA Potsdam.

liquidated the working-class movement and its organizers, but were helpless in face of a residual class conflict over wages, working conditions and policy priorities, which, under conditions of full employment, had no need of organizational expression in order to make its impact felt. The language of debased political idealism was as inappropriate as that of conspiracy to the problems of the regime in 1939. These were almost exclusively defined by those aspects of the domestic history of the First World War, which Hitler had dismissed as superficial, external manifestations of a moral degeneration. The gamble that it would for a short time prove possible to distract a class society from material issues by inspiring it with a great political ideal had manifestly failed. It failed, above all, because the brutal assumption that it would be possible to exchange one ideology for another in the minds of the working class by sheer force and repetition was quite false; because the ideology of the working class was not just a contingent set of beliefs and attitudes, but was above all a social experience, which National Socialism had done nothing at all to alter.

In the months of October, November and December 1939 the hard line in wartime social policy was abandoned step by step. It was wholly appropriate that Ley, leader of the Labour Front, who had insisted upon the need 'to pump . . . new strength again and again' into the working population and who had never shown much concern for the level of military preparedness, should have taken it upon himself to provide a bizarre public justification of this dramatic change of face; for what appeared to him as confirmation of his policy of pumping new strength in, was to the rest of the regime a capitulation to the working class for which there was no possible military-economic justification. Something of the ambivalence of the situation crept into Ley's announcement of the return to peacetime conditions of work. 'National Socialist workers [*das nationalsozialistische Arbeitertum*] have nothing in common with that marxist rabble of the munitions strikes of the World War', he proclaimed hopefully. He praised the regime for having had the courage and foresight to have implemented (!) the hardest measures at the very outset of the war, in contrast to 1914-18, when the people were allowed to live in a fools' paradise to begin with and the situation gradually became worse and worse. But he was not wholly at ease with the new position; identifying himself with the workers on the home front, he said, 'with our small part in the war-time sacrifices of the nation we must almost be ashamed, above all when we think of the blood-sacrifice of the soldiers'. The contradictions, circumlocutions and untruths then multiplied:

'The World War has taught us that it is not enough to have brave soldiers and good weapons, but that a modern war is a total war, that everyone takes part in it and that therefore the whole people has to be in the best mental and physical condition and must be kept in that condition. Every war means a complete re-orientation of life. People's wishes and needs must take second place behind the one and only goal: *the strengthening of the military power of the nation*. But at the same time, all sources must be opened up, from which flow the maintenance and deployment of the total strength of the nation. This was not recognized in 1914.

'What strength for example lies in the fact that, in so hard a time as this, the inexhaustible spring of a people's wonderful culture has been made accessible to the people. In 1914 all joy was prohibited, today the temple of art is open . . .'[1]

Such implausible public rationalizations of the weakness and fear of the ruling elite were hardly calculated to improve morale, discipline and the spirit of sacrifice among the sullenly discontented working class; the regime slid from weakness into fantasy, announcing each year, in an attempt to placate a public opinion which could only be placated by peace and quiet, that war would be over by Christmas, it thereby further weakened the domestic war effort. The rhetoric of sacrifice only began to bite when it became clear to all, despite official propaganda, that the war had become a desperate war of defence. It may be suggested that this fact, rather than any supposed success of Nazi propaganda or real achievements in economic organization, explains why the enormous social and economic effort of 1942-4 was possible.

[1] *VB*, November 20, 1939

Not the pumping in of new strength, not the joyous opening of the temples of culture drove the German people on to make these efforts, but fear of invasion. Nor was it the case that a light-handed domestic policy in the years 1936-41 had left great reserves of energy to be called upon in the crisis: long working hours had been the price of material welfare in this period and already in 1939 there were widespread fears in government circles that the working population was overtired. It is true, however, that the German workers were spared the worst excesses of the full war economy; these were reserved for the foreign slave labourers. But the regime's domestic policy was most successful when it was parasitic upon the need for national defence – a situation which the imperial government had never allowed to come about in 1917-18. Even this success, however, was dependent upon the continued operations of the Gestapo.

There was no stab in the back against the National Socialist war, but the regime lived in fear that one could occur. The programmatic diagnosis of the November Revolution did little to remove this fear; indeed it is possible that the violence which they did to the working-class movement and to working-class interests in the first years of their rule made the Nazi leaders aware that they could expect little active support from this quarter. The outcome was a social and economic policy which placed such a strain on resources and capacities that it helped to push the Third Reich into war prematurely. In the domestic configuration of 1938-9, war had a dual function. General war alone offered the prospect of creating conditions under which the hardships which were in any case necessary for the maintenance, let alone intensification, of the armaments drive could be made acceptable to the working population. And if this tactic failed, as in fact it did, war then offered the possibility of making good the deficiencies in Germany's resources through plunder; the plunder of men and materials permitted the continuance of economic policies which were directed at fulfilling simultaneously the civilian and the military needs of the system. This war and peace economy was the foundation of a desperate but necessary gamble of securing the home front for wars of aggrandizement

THE LEGACY OF 1918 FOR NATIONAL SOCIALISM

by methods which weakened the military potential. Hitler was not operating with a finely calculated margin of free resources: the surprising thing is not that the gamble failed in 1942, but that it did not fail earlier, for Speer's technocratic stance leads him to mistake the nature of the problem when he writes that the level of armaments output in 1943 could have been achieved in 1940-1.[1] Fundamental domestic political contradictions stood in the way of this.

How deeply ingrained Hitler's scepticism about the solidarity of his regime was can be seen from an incident in the spring of 1945. All ministers were agreed that a drastic increase in taxation was necessary in order to combat inflation and to reduce civilian purchasing power. Hitler signed the order for this, but insisted that it should not be put into effect until the German forces had won a victory which would help to sweeten this bitter pill. The tax increase was never enacted.[2] In this novel form, the stab in the back was institutionalized in the structure of National Socialist political thought and in the social bases of its political power.

[1] Speer, op. cit., p. 546 n.1, quoting his final report of January 27, 1945
[2] Fritz Federau, *Der Zweite Weltkrieg. Seine Finanzierung in Deutschland* (Tübingen, 1962), p. 28

CHAPTER 11

GERMAN POLITICAL REFUGEES IN THE UNITED STATES DURING THE SECOND WORLD WAR

WERNER LINK[1]

Discussion of emigration and exile politics seems necessarily to become an essay on frustration, failure and despair, and this *leitmotiv* is indeed well known in western history.[2] However, there is also another, more positive aspect: political determination, hope and the anticipation of future victory over the sadness of present reality. As in the parliamentary system the dissenter often articulates the future truth,[3] so the exile is frequently the one who is in accord with the policy of a later period. He may at one and the same time be the vanquished of today and the victor of tomorrow. There is, however, an essential distinction: while the dissenter in a democracy can try to convince his compatriots in relatively free discussion, the exile is isolated from his countrymen living in a foreign country under more or less severe restrictions. In his very existence he is often the product of revolution or counter-revolution, and this implies that he is not merely dissenting against some aspects but against the fundamental principles

---

[1] I am indebted to Antony Nicholls and Dr Berghahn, who were kind enough to assist with the English text of this manuscript.

[2] Cf. the articles 'emigration' and 'exile' in the *Encyclopaedia of the Social Sciences* (New York, 1931), Vol. V, pp. 488ff and 686ff; and Helge Pross, *Die Deutsche Akademische Emigration nach den Vereinigten Staaten 1933-1941* (Berlin, 1955)

[3] See A. J. P. Taylor, *The Trouble Makers – Dissent over Foreign Policy 1792-1939* (London, 1957), p. 16ff

of the political regime that forced him to leave his country. Hence his radical opposition, hence his profound despair mixed simultaneously with desperate hope.

Those Germans who took refuge when Hitler and his party attained power realized that they were in a similar position to earlier political exiles. The socialists and communists, in particular remembered the waves of emigration after the revolution of 1848, during the period of Bismarck's Anti-Socialist Laws and the exodus from Russia before and after 1917. They were eager to learn from the lessons of history in order to avoid the mistakes of earlier exiles and to exploit their well-proven tactics. As Otto Bauer, the Austrian Marxist, put it:[1]

'. . . the political emigration has only one chance to escape the fate of becoming jetsam of history, namely to help the illegal underground movement and to undertake those functions which can only be carried out abroad'.

Research undertaken during the last decade has provided convincing evidence that the socialist exiles did their best to fulfil this task – on the one hand by using leaflets and illegal periodicals as a so-called *Kollektiver Organisator* (Lenin – an apparatus for collective organization) and on the other hand by starting an 'offensive of truth', appealing to the world, and denouncing Nazi war preparations. But thinking in analogies also involved some negative consequences: it rendered more difficult the recognition of differences between earlier illegal experiences and the conditions which prevailed under the Nazi regime. The terror and propaganda apparatus worked with scientific precision in handling the supervision and suppression of potential and actual opponents and in manipulating the indifferent masses of the people. The 'national successes' of Hitler and the rising standard of living (which was a by-product of the rapid armament boom) reconciled many groups of the population to the regime, whilst the resistance groups were atomized and brutally suppressed. By 1939, when Hitler began to wage war, many opponents (especially members of the labour movement) had been murdered. Accord-

[1] Otto Bauer, *Die illegale Partei* (Paris, 1939), p. 142

242

ding to the statistics of the Gestapo 168,000 Germans lived in the concentration camps, 112,500 were jailed and 27,500 were committed for trial.[1] The political exiles had become 'generals without an army'.[2]

Whereas in the concentration camps, under the terror of the ss, old political differences gradually disappeared and the unity of the anti-Nazis was brought about, the exiles failed to achieve similar unity or to construct a platform for all opposition groups. The majority of the political refugees belonged to the labour movement – ranging from the far left (the Communist Party, the Oppositional Communists and the Trotskyists)[3] to the Social Democrats and their splinter groups. The exiled Social Democratic Executive Committee (*Sopade*) had been weakened by the secession of many members as the result of bitter personal and ideological feuds. However, it had regained a good deal of influence when, in 1938, one dissentient faction, the Revolutionary Socialists, dissolved itself and the large majority of these Social Democrats living in France began to co-operate with the Executive Committee after it moved from Prague to Paris. The left-wing socialists were organized in three groups: the activist group 'New Beginning',[4] the Socialist Workers' Party,[5] and the Militant Socialist International (ISK; a small group of intellectuals and workers fostering an 'ethical socialism')[6]. In 1939, these three

[1] Cf. Wolfgang Abendroth, *Sozialgeschichte der europäischen Arbeiterbewegung* (Frankfurt, 1965), p. 145f

[2] Lewis J. Edinger, *German Exile Politics – The Social Democratic Executive in the Nazi Era* (Berkeley and Los Angeles, 1956), Ch. 6. The ideological development of the German Social Democrats in exile before the Second World War has been analysed by Erich Matthias, *Sozialdemokratie und Nation* (Stuttgart, 1952)

[3] See Karl Hermann Tjaden, *Struktur und Funktion der KPD-Opposition (KPO)* (Meisenheim, 1964)

[4] See Kurt Kliem, *Der sozialistische Widerstand gegen das Dritte Reich, dargestellt an der Gruppe 'Neu Beginnen'*, unpublished Ph.D. thesis (Marburg, 1957)

[5] See Hanno Drechsler, *Die Sozialistische Arbeiterpartei Deutschlands (SAPD)* (Meisenheim, 1965)

[6] See Werner Link, *Die Geschichte des Internationalen Jugend-Bundes (IJB) und des Internationalen Sozialistischen Kampfbundes (ISK)* (Meisenheim, 1964)

factions formed a working committee together with the Austrian socialists.[1]

Before the war political emigrants in the USA played only a minor role. To be sure, many Jewish refugees crossed the Atlantic and many professors, deprived of their chairs in Germany, found shelter in American universities and colleges.[2] But the number of those exiles who were politically active was relatively small; the activist part of the German emigration preferred to live in Czechoslavakia, France or Switzerland in order to maintain contact with the underground movement.

The Social Democratic Federation and the German Labour Delegation (GLD)[3]

The main centre for Social Democrats in the USA was the German Branch of the Social Democratic Federation (SDF), a right-wing group which had seceded from the Socialist Party. The SDF had been founded in 1936 in protest against the admission of the Trotskyists to the Socialist Party. Wilhelm Sollman, Gerhart Seger, Rudolf Katz, Hans Staudinger and others who had emigrated to the USA in the mid-thirties joined the German Branch. Katz and Seger became the editors of the *Neue Volks-Zeitung*, the most important German-language newspaper in the USA. It was quite natural that the Executive Committee of the German Social Democrats (*Sopade*) in Paris should realize that it might be advantageous for them to approach the Branch for financial assistance. In January/February 1939, when the funds of *Sopade* were nearly exhausted, the Executive Committee sent one of its members, the former editor of *Vorwärts*, Friedrich Stampfer, to the USA on a

[1] See Werner Link, *Die Geschichte des Internationalen Jugend-Bundes (IJB) und des Internationalen Sozialistischen Kampfbundes (ISK)* (Meisenheim, 1964) p. 257ff; cf. Joseph Buttinger, *Am Beispiel Österreichs* (Cologne, 1953), p. 555ff

[2] Donald Fleming and Bernard Bailyn (eds), *The Intellectual Migration, Europe and America 1930-1960* (Cambridge, Mass., 1969); cf. note 1, page 1

[3] The following is based on *Mit dem Gesicht nach Deutschland, Eine Dokumentation über die sozialdemokratische Emigration aus dem Nachlaß von Friedrich Stampfer*, edited by Erich Matthias; compiled, and introduced by Werner Link (Düsseldorf, 1968), Parts II and III, pp. 381ff

fund-raising mission. The German Branch arranged contacts with the American Federation of Labour (AFL) and the Jewish Labour Committee. The outcome was satisfying in that it revealed the existence of a friendly spirit and a basic preparedness to give support, but the German Social Democrats found that it would be necessary to foster these new connections if they wanted to turn verbal promises into actual financial assistance. So in March 1939 they formed the German Labour Delegation which *Sopade* henceforth used as its trustee.

The list of the American trade union leaders who functioned as sponsors of the GLD was impressive: William Green (President of the AFL), Adolph Held (Chairman of the Jewish Labour Committee), Abraham Cahan (editor of the *Jewish Daily Forward* George Meany (Treasurer of the AFL), Matthew Woll (Vice-President of the AFL) and others.

Katz and Staudinger were very skilful canvassing these persons and in attracting a number of other wealthy and influential people such as Morris Waldman of the American Jewish Committee; George Backer of the American Labour Party of New York; and Sir William Wiseman of Kuhn, Loeb & Co. From January to the end of April 1940 Stampfer paid a second visit to the USA and intensified the campaign, conferring with sponsors and addressing trade unions. After delivering a speech before the Executive Council of the AFL at Miami, Green was authorized by the AFL Executive Council to call upon its affiliates to give financial support. In addition to the contribution of these AFL affiliates, the *Sopade* and the GLD enjoyed continuous financial support from the Jewish Labour Committee, beginning with a first instalment of $10,000 in 1939/40. It enabled *Sopade* in Paris to continue the edition of the *Neue Vorwärts* and of *Germany Reports* until Hitler attacked France.

The American Friends of German Freedom

At the time when *Sopade* organized the GLD, the group 'New Beginning', the left-wing opposition to *Sopade*, established a similar centre in the USA, the Friends of German Freedom. This organization had the same political purpose as the GLD, namely 'to interpret the struggle for democracy in Fascist Germany to the American people by distribution of reports on actual conditions there and to gain friends for those who carry on the daily work for a free Germany';[1] in other words it was also trying to raise money by establishing permanent connections with socialist and trade union circles. Karl Frank, the leader of 'New Beginning' and Paul Hertz, a former member of *Sopade* who had become a strong supporter of 'New Beginning', succeeded in securing Reinhold Niebuhr as chairman and Adolph Held as treasurer of the Friends of German Freedom. In both the Executive and the Sponsoring Committee there were a number of well-known socialists and liberals, including Norman Thomas (Socialist Party), Paul Kellogg, Max Lerner, Paul Tillich, and Joseph Baskin, the President of the Workmen's Circle. Like the Social Democratic Federation this Circle (originally founded as an organization to assist those Russian emigrés who came to the USA after the revolution of 1905) had a German Branch which served as a centre for those German exiles who were in opposition to *Sopade*, namely the Socialist Workers' Party (SAP), the Militant Socialist International (ISK), etc. In short the Friends of German Freedom sponsored the left-wing German Socialists.

It is obvious that the GLD and *Sopade* were in a better position because they enjoyed the support of the AFL which, in view of its own ideological attitude, refused to co-operate with the extreme left-wing. The Jewish Labour Committee, however, hesitated to reserve its help completely for the GLD and so inevitably the old feud between *Sopade* and 'New Beginning' was reproduced in the United States, reflecting a bitter competition to gain the assistance of the same people. Backed by Abraham Cahan, the grand old man of the Jewish labour movement in the USA, and his *Jewish Daily Forward*, the German Labour Delegation questioned the moral integrity of Karl Frank, attacked him as being a crypto-communist and denied that 'New Beginning' had any connection with German underground groups.[2] This struggle did not end

[1] *Inside Germany Reports*, No. 7, November 10, 1939, p. 1
[2] *Mit dem Gesicht nach Deutschland*, Doc. 80, p. 428ff; see also '*Memorandum über die Anti-Hagen-Kampagne*', February 1, 1945 (mimeograph)

until the war was over and poisoned the atmosphere in a fashion most detrimental to the socialist cause.

Rescue activities
The struggle of one exile group against another was interrupted by a short truce when, after the German victory in the West, the German exiles in the USA co-operated in order to rescue their German and European comrades who had fled to the unoccupied zone in southern France. As is well known, this was not a safe refuge for them because Vichy France was obliged under Article XIX of the armistice 'to surrender on demand all Germans named by the German Government'. Spurred on by this emergency, the German exiles already living in the USA and their American friends carried out an extraordinary rescue operation.

William Green, President of the AFL, persuaded Roosevelt to give emergency visas to about 800 anti-Nazi refugees and their families who were on the emergency list of the AFL; and the GLD was entrusted with the task of naming the German contingent of about 160 families. Frank Bohn, a sponsor of the GLD, was sent to Marseilles in order to organize the transfer and to help overcome the difficulties in getting the French *visa de sortie*; the Jewish Labour Committee paid more than 60 per cent of the transatlantic fare (about $100,000) and the Joint Distribution Committee gave financial aid to the refugees as soon as they arrived in the United States.

The GLD was also a member of the Emergency Rescue Committee (Emerescue), a private and non-partisan organization to rescue anti-Nazi politicians, writers and artisans. Frank Kingdon (President of the University of Newark and one of the leaders of the Union for Democratic Action) was the chairman of this Committee, which was initiated by Paul Hagen and the American Friends of German Freedom. Having much more financial support than the GLD, it lacked on the other hand the assistance of the AFL and of the authorities in Washington. This meant that Emerescue had to undergo lengthy bureaucratic procedures in order to get the required affidavits and visas. Emerescue worked together with some other rescue committees, such as the American Friends Service Committee, the Unitarian Service Committee and *Hicem*.[1]

But not all refugees could be rescued; some – including the most brilliant leaders of the SPD, Hilferding and Breitscheid – were arrested, surrendered to the Gestapo, and were finally murdered; others lived underground until the liberation and joined the French resistance. When Nazi Germany declared war on the United States the total number of German and Austrian refugees in the USA amounted to about 105,000 persons. It is very difficult to say how many of them represented the political emigration and how many had had to flee for so-called 'racial 'reasons. Often both reasons were inseparably connected and a great number of Jewish socialists regarded themselves in the first place as political refugees. It is, however, quite clear that only a minority had a political background or were willing or able to continue their political activity in the United States.

Experiments in united German exile representation
During the war – cut off from the underground circles in Germany – the political refugees in the USA and in other countries recognized more clearly than ever before that unity was the *sine qua non* of any successful activity. In Great Britain the experience in the internment camps and the pressure of the Labour Party at least led the various social democratic and socialist factions and parties to bury their feuds by forming the so-called *Union deutscher sozialistischer Organisationen in Gross-Britannien* (Union of German Socialist Organisations in Great Britain) in March 1941.[2] Similar combinations emerged in other countries, for instance in Sweden. The GLD in the USA, however, was in opposition to this general trend and disapproved of the decision of its friends in London. Despite the fact that many former members of the Executive Committee (for instance Paul Hertz, Marie Juchacs, Georg Dietrich) did not belong to the GLD,

[1] Cf. *Mit dem Gesicht nach Deutschland*, Doc. 105, p. 470ff
[2] Cf. Werner Röder, *Die deutschen sozialistischen Exilgruppen in Grossbritannien 1940-1945* (Hanover, 1968)

Friedrich Stampfer claimed[1] 'that the Executive Committee in London and its affiliate in the US, the GLD, are the only legitimate representatives of the old German Labour movement'. Hence, the GLD firmly refused to unite with the other socialist groups on terms of equality. Instead it tried to maintain a special relationship with *Sopade*. Stampfer was enabled by the financial assistance of the Jewish Labour Committee to pay a visit to London in the winter of 1941-2 (formally as a representative of the American Labour Committee to Aid British Labour) and the idea was ventilated that regular correspondence should be arranged between the executive members in London and New York. Friedrich Stampfer's correspondence with Hans Vogel and Erich Ollenhauer[2] reveals a difference in their views on the left-wing socialists (such as 'New Beginning'), although there was substantial agreement between London and New York on other ideological and political questions.

Compared with their comrades in England, the Social Democratic refugees in the United States were unable to set up a unified socialist movement. They nevertheless proceeded to form a *non-partisan* representation of German exiles. Disregarding the stillborn peoples' front experiment in 1936-7, the first attempt to do this was made in the summer of 1939. Members of 'New Beginning', SAP, the Peoples' Front Group and Social Democrats of the GLD came together in a so-called *Informationsausschuss* (Information Committee) and the GLD representatives proposed to enlarge this circle by inviting into it refugees who had been active in the bourgeois-democratic parties of the Weimar Republic. Heinrich Brüning, the former Reich Chancellor and leader of the Catholic Centre Party, refused to participate in exile politics, but a few others – for instance Gustav Stolper (economist and member of the German Democratic Party), Götz Briefs (economist and member of the Centre Party) and Kurt Rietzler (German People's Party) – announced their agreement in principle. And officials in Washington showed sympathetic interest when the war began.

---

[1] Stampfer (New York) to *Sopade* (London), April 12, 1942, in *Mit dem Gesicht nach Deutschland*, Doc. 142, p. 587

[2] Published in *Mit dem Gesicht nach Deutschland*, Parts III-V

There was the suggestion that a German non-partisan committee might participate in certain diplomatic actions in the USA and in Europe.

This first attempt to form an all-embracing democratic representation failed, because the GLD refused to co-operate with persons who were supposed to be former communists or to be favouring the Communist Party. What the GLD wanted was nothing less than a 'peoples' front minus CP, (and it indulged extensively in labelling its opponents on the left as 'communist'). The Stalin-Hitler pact seemed to justify this line and so the GLD itself took the initiative in creating an alliance of liberal and Social Democratic refugees known as the 'German-American Council for the Liberation of Germany from Nazism' and the 'Association of Free Germans'. In addition to their main purpose (namely to organize the democratic, non-communist German refugees in the USA and to articulate their political convictions) these bodies were intended to counterbalance Nazi propaganda among Americans of German origin. Since their political base was too narrow they never attained any real importance, although some American politicians favoured their aims – for instance by incorporating the platform of the Association of Free Germans into the records of Congress on March 22, 1943.

However peripheral this latter gesture may have been, it indicated the increasing interest in the German exiles among politicians in the USA. The founding of the Soviet-sponsored Free German Movement, which spread from Moscow to western countries, induced even the authorities in Washington to give more positive attention to the German Labour exiles as a whole, and particularly to the Social Democrats, whose anti-communist record was well known. As Stampfer asked 'What will be the future of the blue-prints of Washington when the red-pencil of Moscow begins to scribble over them?'[1] So Washington was eager to strengthen contacts with German exiles and their representatives.

At the same time a number of leading German refugees took up the attempt to unite all German exiles (except for a few followers

[1] Stampfer (New York) to *Sopade* (London), August 7, 1943, *Mit dem Gesicht nach Deutschland*, Doc. 153, p. 61

of Vansittart and Morgenthau). The Council for a Democratic Germany (as it was finally called in April 1944) originated from a meeting held in New York on November 4, 1943, under the chairmanship of Thomas Mann. Its chief promoters were Paul Hagen (i.e. Karl Frank) and Paul Hertz of the 'New Beginning' group; Siegfried Aufhäuser, Horst Baerensprung and Hans Staudinger of the German Labour Delegation; Hermann Budzislawski (who had pro-communist leanings); Carl Zuckmayer and the religious socialist, Paul Tillich. They decided to exclude former Nazis but not former communists or communist sympathizers, provided they adhered to democratic principles. They did not pretend to have any mandate from anti-Nazi groups in Germany; they wanted to build up a well-balanced representation avoiding domination by one faction. To quote from an official letter to the State Department:[1]

'The Council does not act or speak for, or represent in any way any specific group or combination of persons in Germany or the German people as a whole. We do not even claim to represent the future democratic Germany. We believe only that we typify to some extent the various points of view on which the future democratic and peaceful Germany will be based. . . .'

Until the official records are open it is impossible to say why us Government officials did not favour the Council, but it can be assumed that the inclusion of communists was one reason. If the files of the Council are correct the coolness of the State Department induced Thoms Mann to leave the Council, and Paul Tillich became its undisputed chairman; the three other members of the Administrative Board were Siegfried Aufhäuser, Professor Bärwäld (as the representative of the Catholics) and Albert Schreiner (as the representative of the Communists).

The list of those who supported the 'Council'[2] proves that it was indeed correct in claiming a 'typifying' character. But from the beginning it was apparent that the left-wing 'Association

[1] Tillich to Department of State, June 26, 1944, copy (files of the Council for a Democratic Germany)
[2] *Mit dem Gesicht nach Deutschland*, Doc. 163, p. 652

for a Democratic Germany' (a new name for the former American Friends of German Freedom) and its Research Director Hagen were the 'dynamic element' in the Council.[1] So it was not at all fortuitous that the Association used a similar name and enthusiastically hailed the Council in the first edition of its *Bulletin*.

The hope that the German anti-Nazi forces in the USA had buried their factional differences by organizing the Council was, however, much too optimistic. K. O. Paetel has demonstrated[2] that the newspapers of the right-wing Social Democrats, of the Vansittartists, of the Ruth Fischer circle and of some Jewish groups (*Der Aufbau* and the *Jewish Way*) immediately started severe attacks on the Council. Their arguments were varied. The Vansittartists, or those who were close to the Rex Stout Group (the so-called Society for the Prevention of World War III), denied the existence of an operation against Hitler in Germany and imputed that the Council was propagating a 'soft peace'. Some Jewish writers and William Shirer (*New York Herald Tribune*) shared this opinion. On the other hand the *Neue Volks-Zeitung* – organ of the GLD – which maintained a radically anti-Vansittartist attitude – asserted that the Council was following a pro-Soviet policy, that it was inclined to justify the Soviet annexation of East Prussia and that it represented a disguised communist united front. The GLD revived its old feud with Paul Hagen, denouncing him as backstage manager.

Both arguments were obviously incompatible and so it was not surprising that the opposition to the Council remained split and was unable to destroy it. The fact that Siegfried Aufhäuser resigned as chairman of the GLD and joined the Council proved that the GLD had isolated itself.

The real menace did not come from external opponents but from internal dissension. The integration of a variety of groups and opinions had been a significant accomplishment of the Council, but was at the same time a cause of weakness and fragility.

[1] Karl O. Paetel, 'Zum Problem einer deutschen Exilregierung', *Vierteljahrshefte für Zeitgeschichte*, Vol. 4 (1956), p. 290

[2] Ibid., p. 293ff

Difficulties began when the Yalta Conference of February 1945 aroused widely different reactions. While some members of the Council, especially the Social Democrat Aufhäuser and the Communists, hailed the decisions of the Big Three, others, such as Paul Hagen and 'New Beginning', voiced strong criticism. Hagen made the point: 'If the leaders of the Big Powers have chosen to base their security plan on the imposition of a semi-colonial status for Germany for an indefinite period, including territorial and industrial dismemberment, of course we disagree. . . .'[1]

During the following months the fronts hardened and finally – in autumn 1945 – the non-communist members resigned from the Council, protesting against the communist defence of Allied policies towards Germany. Thus the work of the Council ended in frustration and failure. But this is only one side of the story. Its very existence had been a positive development and had opened the way for a useful programmatic discussion on the future of a democratic Germany. The Council's proposals for the political, economic and educational reconstruction of Germany which would form part of a Free European community were published in several pamphlets. They make worthwhile reading and would have offered an alternative to Allied conceptions about the future of Europe.[2]

Political concepts of the exiles and the Allied war aims
The Council for a Democratic Germany, and practically all other German exiles, agreed that the defeat of Hitler's Germany was the prerequisite for any 'creative solution' of the German question. There was also broad agreement between all groups represented in the Council and the German Labour Delegation that such a 'creative solution' could be brought about only by the anti-Nazi Germans themselves. The programme of the Council proclaimed:[3]

'If Germany is to develop a democracy it is necessary that the military and civil representatives of the United Nations give

---

[1] *Bulletin of the Council for a Democratic Germany*, Vol. I, No. 4, February 1945, p. 2
[2] Cf. Karl O. Paetel, op. cit., p. 296
[3] *Mit dem Gesicht nach Deutschland*, p. 651

political leeway from the beginning to those who might best be able to create a new democracy . . .

'. . . all those must be considered who resisted Nazism, for instance the presently nameless men and women now in Gestapo prisons and concentration camps, trade unions and workers of the labour movement, those who resisted in the churches and in intellectual circles, in the middle class, in the cities and in the country, and other qualified individuals. The German democracy of the future will depend on all these people. With their help, preparations must be made for the inauguration of an independent German government. . . . No obstacles should be placed in the way of the rebuilding of a labour movement. . . .'

The strong influence of the socialists within the Council was reflected in those parts of the declaration which dealt with the politico-economic requirements of a new democratic order in Germany. Recalling the failure of the revolution of 1918 and the Weimar Republic it urged not only that the Nazi organization and the military apparatus should be destroyed but also that

'those groups which were the bulwarks of German imperialism and which were responsible for the delivery of power into the hands of the Nazis must be deprived of their political, social and economic power. This applies particularly to the large land-holders, the big industrialists, and the military caste whose political concepts and influence have had repeatedly a disastrous effect on German history. If, therefore, the German people will decide to dissolve large landholdings, to control heavy industry, to eliminate militarism and to remove those civil servants, judges and teachers beholden to these groups, they ought not to be impeded from outside. . . .'[1]

The Council and the GLD repeatedly expressed their conviction that such a social revolution would give the only guarantee for a stable democracy and a lasting peace whereas it would be 'the greatest blunder in history to destroy such a revolution *in statu*

---

[1] *Mit dem Gesicht nach Deutschland* p. 650

nascendi by military force' (Stampfer).[1] A democratic revolution, 'secured by far-reaching social changes' (Hagen),[2] was recognized as the positive alternative to the destructive programme of Henry Morgenthau and his adherents. Using the same arguments as Henry Morgenthau's opponents within the US government, the Council stressed:[3] 'It would be disastrous for the future of Europe if Germany were to be dismembered and split up economically and politically. This would create fertile soil for new pan-German movements. . . . It is essential for the economic future of Europe and the world that Germany's productive power be conserved. If it were destroyed, the economic conditions would become hopelessly depressed in all countries of Europe, and trade between Europe and other continents would be heavily reduced. Moreover, millions of Germans would become permanently unemployed. . . . Thus a constant source of unrest would arise in the very centre of Europe.'[3]

In spite of numerous accusations, which culminated in the denunciation of leading members of the Council as agents of Hitler or Stalin,[4] the Council reiterated its fundamental thesis:[5] 'The victory of the United Nations will break the external hold of Nazis over the German people. But only the German people can free themselves spiritually'.

However, the majority of the socialist refugees (being the most important group among the political emigrants) doubted whether the progressive forces in Allied countries would be strong enough to determine the war aims of their governments along these lines. From the beginning left-wing socialists, especially, realized that (to quote an Austrian socialist) the fall of Hitler was in the common interest of the working class all over the world; but the fact that this could only be done by war did not represent a common

---

[1] Friedrich Stampfer, 'The German Problem', *New Europe*, July-August 1943, p. 16
[2] See note 1, p. 253
[3] *Mit dem Gesicht nach Deutschland*, Doc. 163, p. 650
[4] Cf. Karl O. Paetel, op. cit., p. 294ff
[5] See note 3, above; cf. Nos. 1-5 of the *Bulletin of the Council for a Democratic Germany*

interest but a common disaster (*nicht mehr ein gemeinsames Interesse, sondern ein gemeinsames Verhängnis*).[1] These socialists expressed their scepticism about the hopes of some Social Democrats that the end of the war would coincide with a German socialist revolution. On the contrary, the war against Hitler would – according to their expectations – integrate the working classes of the Allied countries into a united national front. The fact that the international working class was fighting for the downfall of Hitler would not necessarily transform the war policy of the Allies into a revolutionary, a socialist or even a democratic one. It would rather disguise the fact that the so-called 'democratic' policy of the Allies was not intended to prepare the German revolution but to prevent it.

In spite of this the left-wing German socialists and the more optimistic Social Democrats 'did not hesitate for a second to join in the war for freedom' (Hagen)[2] in 1939. They refused the Leninist concept of 'revolutionary defeatism' since they realized that thereby they would merely help Hitler.

In the beginning it seemed that the apprehensions of the German refugees were unfounded. As is well known, the Atlantic Charter contained the renunciation of territorial aggrandizement and a promise of the restoration of self-government to those deprived of it: the German exiles naturally hailed this statement of war aims. However, the more the Allies revised their policy the greater became the frustration of the German exiles. As mentioned above they proclaimed their disagreement–'hoping against hope'.[3] When the last year of the war opened, the chairman of the Council for a Democratic Germany expressed the general feeling of the majority of German political emigrants by saying:

'In spite of the proposed division of Europe we shall fight for a Europe which will be more than the colonial battlefield of the three world powers. In spite of the proposed disruption of

[1] See Joseph Buttinger, *Am Beispiel Österreichs*, p. 570
[2] See note 1, p. 253
[3] Paul Tillich, 'Outlook for 1945', *Bulletin of the Council for a Democratic Germany*, Vol. I, No. 3, January 1, 1945, p. 1

Germany we shall *fight for a meaningful future for the German people as a past section of the people of Europe and not a no-mans-land between them.* In spite of the tension between the East and the West we shall fight for a world-wide solution on the basis of the collaboration between East and West.'[1]

The German political refugees realized that their voice hardly reached the ear of the public – let alone that of the governments. So they turned to the anti-Nazis in Germany hoping 'that those who will finish off the monster will be influenced by the democratic action of the non-Nazis in Germany in and after the hour of Nazi defeat' (Paul Hagen).[2] With this in mind many refugees took the chance of co-operating with the Office of Strategic Services, mostly by giving advice and outlining their ideas on the organization of a new democratic Germany. A few others dared to assume a more active role. The oss had established a special department for dealing with the labour movement in the enemy countries, the so-called 'Labour Desk', which was directed by Major Arthur Goldberg (who had been the legal adviser of the AFL, Chicago). The Labour Desk enjoyed good connections with the International Trade Union Movement; it trained reliable socialist refugees from European countries and sent them back to their countries in order to contact anti-Nazi underground groups and to prepare for post-war reconstruction. As these men were not bound by the directives of the oss and were only responsible to the political group or party to which they belonged, some German socialists profited by this opportunity. Sometimes their missions failed because they were captured by the Gestapo. Others succeeded in reaching their underground comrades in Germany and did a remarkable job in co-ordinating separate groups and and in preparing the reconstuction of the labour movement after the liberation.[3]

On the whole, neither the representation of the German exiles nor these underground activities had any decisive impact on the general line of the US Government's policies in occupied Germany.

[1] Ibid.   [2] See note 1, 253
[3] See Werner Link, *Die Geschichte des Internationalen Jugend-Bundes (IJB) und des Internationalen Sozialistischen Kampfbundes (ISK)*, pp. 312ff

The American military authorities impeded the spontaneous development of political organizations and dissolved the numerous 'Anti-Fascist Committees', which combined resistance groups including social democrats and Liberals as well as communists.[1] This policy was determined by the fear that any revolutionary activity might impair the occupation and that the communist and left-wing groups might strengthen their influence as they had done in France.

Only when the Cold War began were the right-wing social democratic refugees in the USA given a chance to make a contribution to the reconstruction of West Germany – not by fostering the social revolution but by helping to strengthen the anti-communist forces there.[2]

Conclusion

So far as the organizational aspects are concerned, the socialist and social democratic refugees in the USA failed to form a union as did their comrades in Great Britain.

Apart from personal differences, the main reason for this failure was that, unlike the British labour movement, the American labour movement was not organized in a strong labour party. So it can be postulated that the disunited condition of domestic socialist forces in the country that provided them with a refuge hampered German émigré attempts to create unity among themselves.

The decisive anti-communist conviction of the right-wing Social Democrats who were united in the GLD helped the close co-operation between the GLD and AFL, and this contact with the AFL stimulated – in a form of feed-back process – the anti-communist policy of the GLD.

Compared with the German refugees in Great Britain the refugees in the USA were, however, more successful in establishing a broad representation of all anti-Nazi groups and tendencies.

[1] Cf. Albrecht Kaden, *Einheit oder Freiheit, Die Wiedergründung der SPD 1945/46* (Hanover, 1964)

[2] On the beginning of co-operation between AFL officials and the German trade unions see *Mit dem Gesicht nach Deutschland*, Docs. 181-5

The Council for a Democratic Germany set out valuable programmatic principles; it unanimously condemned the atrocities of the Nazis, speaking on behalf of the silenced underground opposition in Germany: it informed the American public about this resistance and protested against the identification of the entire German people with the Nazis and their crimes; it called for a 'creative solution' of the German problem on the basis of collaboration between the East and the West.

There never existed anything like a German Government in Exile but it seems unlikely that such a government would have increased the influence of the German refugees. As the comparison with other European refugees proves, the mere existance of an exile government did not guarantee political influence on Allied policy. Independent military forces and the possession of some colonial territory were the main reasons for de Gaulle's position. So, even if the German exiles had succeeded in establishing an exile government and even if the Allies had been ready to recognize it, it was obvious that it could not possibly have wielded a greater influence than the exiles already possessed.

The fact that no social and political revolution occurred in the hour of defeat cannot be attributed to any failure on the part of the German refugees. Many exiles did, of course, cling to illusions and false hopes, but most of them realized from the beginning that the revolutionary forces inside Germany would only have a chance of bringing about social changes if they were not impeded by the occupation powers. In the event, the Allies did obstruct any such revolutionary development.

Whereas Allied policy towards Germany split the Council for a Democratic Germany and destroyed the possibility of a 'creative solution', the beginning of the Cold War transformed the anti-communist groups of German exiles, particularly the GLD, into a valuable ally of the American officials. This co-operation, however, was combined with the renunciation of socialization and fundamental social change. It favoured, directly or indirectly, the restoration of the old social order. This development reflects the main tragedy of the German exiles: when the USA revised its destructive policy and accepted the opinion that it was incorrect to identify the entire German people with the Nazis (a thesis which the German exiles had stressed in vain during the war), they restored at the same time the political, social and economic power of those groups which the German democratic opposition (not only the socialist part of it) wanted to destroy in order to secure democracy and peace.

NOTE ON CONTRIBUTORS

Dr Lothar Albertin is Senior Lecturer for Political Science and Contemporary History and Dean of the Faculty for Social Sciences at the University of Mannheim. He has published work on the subject of Liberalism and Political Theory.

Dr Hans Boldt is a member of the Institute of Social Sciences at the University of Mannheim and is working mainly in the field of Government and Constitutional History. He has published a major study of Emergency Laws in the nineteenth century.

Robin Lenman is a lecturer in Modern History at Hull University. Formerly a student at St Antony's College, Oxford, he is working on a study of censorship in Munich before 1914.

Dr Werner Link is a *Privatdozent* and member of the Institute of Social Sciences at the University of Mannheim and teaches Political Science at the University of Marburg/Lahn. He has published books and articles on German exile politics and on relations between the United States and Germany.

Miss Jill McIntyre is a lecturer in Modern History at the University of Edinburgh. Her main field of interest is recent German history.

Tim Mason is a Research Fellow of St Antony's College, Oxford, working on the social and economic history of Nazi Germany, about which he has published several articles. He was an assistant editor of *Past and Present*, 1967-70.

Dr Erich Matthias, who is Professor of Contemporary History and Political Science and Director of the Institute of Social Sciences at the University of Mannheim, has published numerous works on constitutional history and the history of political parties.

Anthony Nicholls is a Fellow of St Antony's College, Oxford. He is working in the field of recent German history and international relations.

NOTE ON CONTRIBUTORS

Dr Michael Stürmer is a *Privatdozent* and teaches history at the *Technische Hochschule*, Darmstadt, working mainly in the field of German social and constitutional history in the nineteenth and twentieth century. He has spent the academic year 1970-71 as a lecturer at the University of Sussex.

INDEX

Bund deutscher Frauenvereine, 178, 196
Bund deutscher Mädel, 199-200, 205
Bürger, Ferdinand, 145, 146 fn.
Bürkner, Trude, 205
BVP (Bavarian People's Party), 101, 106, 113, 118, 156

Cahan, Abraham, 245-6
Centre Party, in elections of 1919, 39; and Peace Treaty, 44; in Weimar Coalition, 61; and Christian trade unions, 66; and DNVP, 70, 76; and Article 48, 76-7; and BVP, 101; and women, 181-2, 187; mentioned, 24, 34, 249
Christlicher Bauernverein, 106, 111
Churchill, Winston Spencer, 227
Clemenceau, Georges, 20, 43
Cohn, Dr Oskar, 88
Communist Opposition (*KPO*), 243
Communist Party of Germany, *see* KPD
Constantinople, 119
Corriere d'Italia, 164
Cossmann, Paul, 104
Council for a Democratic Germany, 251-6, 259
Cromwell, Oliver, 128
Cuno, Wilhelm (German Chancellor, 1922-3), 116, 118, 126
Curatorium for the Reconstruction of the German Economy, 37-8
Czechoslovakia, 244

Dahrendorf, Ralf, 175
DAP (German Workers' Party), 137
Dard, Emile, 122
David, Eduard, 52
Davis, Justice, 84
Dawes Plan, the, DNVP and, 17, 63, 67; Spengler's views on, 19, 21;

and political stability, 60, 64; passage of, 70 and fn.
DDP, German Democratic Party, enters 'Weimar Coalition', 30, 61; founding of, 32; membership, 33-34; programme in 1919, 36-41; and the peace settlement, 42-4; supported by industry, 38; electoral setbacks, 42; and Weimar constitution, 44-5; and Bavaria, 118; Streicher and, 141; and women, 186
Depression, the Great (1929-33), impact on Germany, 15, 22, 77, 91; and women's employment, 180, 184, 211
Der Arzt, 179
Deutsche Frauenwerk, das, 196-8, 203
Deutsche Volkswille, 135, 141
Deutsche Werkgemeinschaft des Abendländischen Bundes, 135, 137
Deutscher Akademikerinnenbund, 179, 194-5
Deutscher Beamtenbund, 34
Deutscher Schutz-und-Trutzbund, 134, 136
Deutscher Sozialist, 134-5, 137; *see also Deutsche Volkswille*
Deutscher Tag, in Nuremberg, 142, 152-6
Deutschlands Erneuerung, 167
Deutschnationaler Handlungsgehilfenverband, 134
Dicey, A. V. 80-1
Dickel, Dr Otto, 135, 143 fn.
Die Arztin, 179
Dietrich, Georg, 248
DNVP, German National People's Party (Nationalists), and Dawes Plan, 17, 63; and Young Plan, 18; and coalitions, 61-4, 70-3, 77; and agrarian interests, 66-7; and women, 186

Liberalism, German, 29; *see also* DDP, DVP
Liebknecht, Karl, 89
Lipp, Dr Franz, 107
Lipp, Dr Maria, 208
Locarno, treaty of 1925, 65
Lossow, General Otto von, 120, 126
Ludendorff, General Erich, 37, 113, 153
Lüders, Dr Marie-Elizabeth, 176, 186, 195
Ludwig Ferdinand, Prince, 153
Luppe, Dr Hermann, 31 (Mayor of Nuremberg), 129 fn., 141-2 and fn., 147 and fn., 148, 153
Luther, Dr Hans (German Chancellor 1925-6), 72-6, 91
Luxemburg, Rosa, 89

Machtübernahme, see NSDAP, attainment of power
Mann, Thomas, 251
Marx, Dr Wilhelm (German Chancellor, 1923-5 and 1926-8), 59, 68, 75
Meany, George, 245
Mein Kampf, see Hitler
Meissner, Dr Otto, 76
Morgenthau, Henry, Jr., 251, 255
Mühsam, Erich, 107
Müller, Hermann (German Chancellor, 1928-30), 55-6
Münchener Zeitung, 120 and fn.
Munich, home of NSDAP, 99-100, 111, 116-17, 130, 138; Soviet Republic in, 103, 105, 107, 118-19; political character of, 104, 108, 118; *see also* Hitler *Putsch*
Murphy, Robert, 124
Mussolini, Benito, 124

Napoleon III, 88
National Liberals, 30, 31, 37, 66

268

National Opposition, the, 18, 20, 21, 25, 27-8, 44, 65, 67
National Socialism, *see* NSDAP
Naumann, Freidrich, 30-1, 41
Neue Volks-Zeitung, 244, 252
Neumann, Sigmund, 55
New Beginning, the, 243, 245-6, 249, 251, 253
New York Herald Tribune, 252
Niebuhr, Reinhold, 246
Northcliffe, Lord, 20
Noske, Gustav, 43, 121
November Revolution, *see* Germany, Revolution in 1918-19
NS-Ärtzebund, 195
NSDAP, 21-3, rise of, 14; and Young Plan, 18; opposition to Weimar Republic, 28; attainment of power, 47-8, 54, 56, 185; in elections, 51; frictions within, 99; in Bavaria, 100, 107-13, 120; and Roman Catholics, 101; and Protestants, 129; programme of 1920, 109; in Nuremberg, 129-59; and foreign policy, 163, 171-4; and women, 177 fn., 182-213; and lessons drawn from November Revolution 1918, 215-39; defeat of, 254-5, 256
NS-Dozentenbund, 195
NS-Frauenschaft, 196, 199
NS-Frauenwarte, 203
NS-Lehrerbund, 195, 205
NS-Rechtswahrerbund, 195
NS-Studentenbund, 195
Nuremberg, 117; Streicher in, 129-159; political character of, 139; war crimes trials at, 132; Hitler at rally in, 173

Oberland, Freikorps, 154, 157
Ollenhauer, Erich, 249
Orgesch, 109
OSS (Office of Strategic Services), 257

INDEX

USPD, and Revolution 1918, 29, 48, 54, 105; reunited with SPD, 138

Vansittart, Sir Robert, 251-2
Vaterlandspartei, 104
Verein Deutscher Evangelischer Lehrerinnen, 179, 182
Verein katholischer Lehrerinnen, 179
Vernunftrepublikaner, 62
Versailles, Treaty of, and internal development of Weimar Republic, 13-28; *Schmachparagraph*, 17; revision of, 24; DDP and, 42-4; DNVP and, 63, bars protective tariffs, 66; mentioned, 235
Vogel, Hans, 249
Völkischer Beobachter, 127, 204
Vorbote, 229
Vorwärts, 23, 55, 244

Waldmann, Morris, 245
War guilt, 17, 105; *see also* Versailles, Germany, and Stab-in-the-back
Weber, Alfred, 31-2, 37
Weber, Dr Friedrich, 110, 155
Weber, Dr Helene, 177, 187
Weber, Max, 40
Weimar Rupublic, and Versailles, 13-28; Spengler's views on, 20; initial support for, 27; liberalism and the foundation of, 29-46; *see also* Germany

Wessel, Horst, 191
Westarp, Count Kuno von, DNVP leader, 63-4
Wikingbund, 155
Wilhelm II, German Emperor, 66, 218, 220-1
Wirth, Joseph (Reich Chancellor 1921-2), 123
Wirtschaftspartei, 177 fn.
Wiseman, Sir William, 245
Wittelsbach monarchy, the, 107, 113, 156
Wolff, Theodor, 32, 112
Woll, Matthew, 245
Women, status of, 175-213
Workmen's Circle, 246
World War, 1914-18, 85, 176, 217-219, 223, 236-7; 1939-45, 174, 206, 226, 236-7

Yalta, Conference at, 253
Young Plan, campaign against, 18; fulfilment of, 24; restrictions on Germany imposed by, 25

Zentrale Arbeitsgemeinschaft der industriellen und gewerblichen-Arbeitgeber-und Arbeitnehmerverbände, 36
Zimmermann, Ludwig, 13
Zuckmayer, Karl, 251

271